Essential Dutch grammar

Gerdi Quist and
Dennis Strik

For UK order enquiries: please contact Bookpoint Ltd,
130 Milton Park, Abingdon, Oxon OX14 4SB.
Telephone: +44 (0) 1235 827720. *Fax:* +44 (0) 1235 400454.
Lines are open 09.00–17.00, Monday to Saturday, with a 24-hour
message answering service. Details about our titles and how to
order are available at www.teachyourself.com

For USA order enquiries: please contact McGraw-Hill Customer
Services, PO Box 545, Blacklick, OH 43004-0545, USA.
Telephone: 1-800-722-4726. *Fax:* 1-614-755-5645.

For Canada order enquiries: please contact McGraw-Hill Ryerson
Ltd, 300 Water St, Whitby, Ontario L1N 9B6, Canada.
Telephone: 905 430 5000. *Fax:* 905 430 5020.

Long renowned as the authoritative source for self-guided learning –
with more than 50 million copies sold worldwide – the *Teach Yourself*
series includes over 500 titles in the fields of languages, crafts, hobbies,
business, computing and education.

British Library Cataloguing in Publication Data: a catalogue record
for this title is available from the British Library.

Library of Congress Catalog Card Number: on file.

First published in UK 2000 as *Teach Yourself Dutch Grammar*
by Hodder Education, part of Hachette UK, 338 Euston Road,
London NW1 3BH.

First published in US 2000 as *Teach Yourself Dutch Grammar* by
The McGraw-Hill Companies, Inc.

This edition published 2010.

The *Teach Yourself* name is a registered trade mark of
Hodder Headline.

Copyright © 2000, 2003, 2010 Gerdi Quist and Dennis Strik

Typeset by MPS Limited, A Macmillan Company.

Printed in Great Britain for Hodder Education, an Hachette UK
Company, 338 Euston Road, London NW1 3BH, by CPI Cox &
Wyman, Reading, Berkshire RG1 8EX.

The publisher has used its best endeavours to ensure that the URLs
for external websites referred to in this book are correct and active
at the time of going to press. However, the publisher and the author
have no responsibility for the websites and can make no guarantee
that a site will remain live or that the content will remain relevant,
decent or appropriate.

Hachette UK's policy is to use papers that are natural, renewable
and recyclable products and made from wood grown in sustainable
forests. The logging and manufacturing processes are expected to
conform to the environmental regulations of the country of origin.

Impression number   10 9 8 7 6 5 4 3 2 1

Year   2014 2013 2012 2011 2010

Acknowledgements

The authors would like to thank the following for their permission to use their copyrighted material in exercises in this book.

J. Bernlef (Section 18.7)
Herman Pieter de Boer (Section 7.1)
Joop Braakhekke and Tirion Uitgevers BV (Section 2.4)
Adriaan van Dis (Section 14.1)
Dutch Ministry of Environment (Section 5.1)
Ethnel Portnoy (Section 14.1)
Unicef (Section 18.7)

Credits

Contents

Meet the authors

Gerdi and Dennis are highly experienced language teachers and authors. Gerdi is a lecturer in Dutch at University College London (UCL), and conducts research into language teaching in general, and Dutch in particular, focusing on intercultural communication. Dennis worked as a lecturer in Dutch at UCL for ten years, before moving back to the Netherlands, where he continues to write language books, teaches Dutch and works as a professional translator.

Together Gerdi and Dennis have written a whole range of language course books for learners at all levels, from beginners to advanced learners at an academic level, both for self-study purposes and classroom environments. Amongst the titles Gerdi and Dennis have produced are *Get started in Dutch* and *Complete Dutch*, published by Hodder Education, aimed at beginners and students at intermediate level, and the Routledge Intensive Dutch Course, which is intended for academic learners.

Only got a minute?

Dutch has two definite articles (**de** and **het**) and one indefinite article (**een**). When adjectives directly precede a noun an **-e** is added to the adjective. No **-e** is added in front of an indefinitely used **het**-word.

The main verb takes up the second position in sentences. All other verbs go to the end. In sub-clauses all verbs are placed at the end. To find the stem of a verb (used with **ik**), you generally leave off the **-en** ending of the infinitive (**werken – werk**). For other singular forms you add a **-t**. In the plural the infinitive form is used.

The present perfect is formed with the verb **hebben** or **zijn** plus a past participle, which is placed at the end of the sentence. The past participle is formed by adding the prefix **ge-** to the stem of the verb plus a final **t** or **d**. Stems ending in **s, f, t, k, ch** or **p** get a **t**, all others a **d**.

The imperfect of regular verbs is formed by adding **te(n)** or **de(n)** to the stem of the verb. Stems ending in **s**, **f**, **t**, **k**, **ch** or **p** get **te(n)**, all others **de(n)**.

Modal verbs are combined with another verb, which is put at the end of the sentence in its full form.

Niet or **geen** are used to make a sentence negative. **Geen** is used in combination with indefinite nouns.

Sub-clauses are linked to main clauses by subordinating conjunctions. Examples are **dat** (*that*), **als** (*when/if*), **omdat** (*because*).

5 Only got five minutes?

Nouns, articles, demonstratives

Dutch has three articles: **de** and **het** (*the*) and **een** (*a/an*):

de man	*the man*
de vrouw	*the woman*
het kind	*the child*
een boek	*a book*

Nouns are generally made plural by adding one of the following endings to the noun: **-en, -s, -'s**:

boeken	*books*
telefoons	*telephones*
radio's	*radios*

Deze and **dit** are Dutch for *this*; **die** and **dat** are Dutch for *that*. **Deze** (*this*) and **die** (*that*) are used with **de–** words. **Dit** (*this*) and **dat** (*that*) are used with **het**-words.

Adjectives

When adjectives directly precede a noun an **-e** is added to the adjective. There is one exception: no **-e** is added in front of an indefinitely used **het**-word (i.e. used with the indefinite article **een** or no article at all): **Het interessante verhaal, een interessant verhaal.**

Subject and object pronouns

	Subject pronouns			Object pronouns		
singular	ik	('k)	*I*	mij	(me)	*me*
	jij	(je)	*you* (informal)	jou	(je)	*you* (inf.)
	u		*you* (formal)	u		*you* (form.)
	hij	(ie)	*he*	hem	('m)	*him*
	zij	(ze)	*she*	haar	(d'r)	*her*
	het	('t)	*it*	het	('t)	*it*
plural	wij	(we)	*we*	ons		*us*
	jullie		*you*	jullie		*you* (inf.)
	u		*you* (formal)	u		*you* (form.)
	zij	(ze)	*they*	ze		*them*

The unstressed forms are generally not used in writing. **Je** and **jij** are informal and used when speaking to people with whom you are on a first name basis. The pronoun **u** is the polite form of addressing people with whom you are not on a first name basis.

Possessive pronouns

	stressed	unstressed	
singular	mijn	(m'n)	*my*
	jouw	je	*your* (informal)
	uw	–	*your* (formal)
	zijn	(z'n)	*his*
	haar	(d'r)	*her*
plural	ons/onze	–	*our*
	jullie	je	*your* (informal)
	uw	–	*your* (formal)
	hun	–	*their*

Ons is used before **het**-words and **onze** before **de**-words.

Verbs

The finite verb is put in the second position in the sentence. All other verbs are placed at the end. In sub-clauses and relative clauses, all verbs are placed at the end of the clause.

For the first person singular (**ik**) in the present tense, you generally leave off the **-en** ending of verbs. This form is the stem of the verb. For all other singular persons you add a **-t**. In the plural the infinitive form is used.

When talking about a time period which started in the past and continues into the present the present tense is used together with **al** or **pas** or another adverb indicating time:

Ik woon al twee jaar in Deventer.   *I've lived in Deventer for two years.*

Talking about the past

Talking about the past is introduced, and often concluded, by using the perfect tense. Added information is given in the imperfect.

The present perfect is formed with the verb **hebben** or **zijn** plus a past participle, which is placed at the end of the sentence. The past participle of regular verbs is formed by adding the prefix **ge-** to the stem of the verb plus a final **t** or **d**. If the stem ends in **s, f, t, k, ch** or **p**, we add a **t**. In all other cases we add a **d**.

Mijn collega heeft die fout gemaakt.   *My colleague (has) made that mistake.*

The imperfect of regular verbs is formed by adding **te(n)** or **de(n)** to the stem of the verb. If the stem ends in **s, f, t, k, ch** or **p** you add **te(n)**. In all other cases you add **de(n)**.

Hij maakte een grote fout.   *He made a big mistake.*

Modal verbs

Modal verbs are normally combined with another verb, which is put at the end of the sentence in its full infinitive form:

We willen een huis kopen. *We want to buy a house.*

Separable verbs

Separable verbs are made up of a prefix and the main part of the verb: **uit** + **gaan** = **uitgaan**. When you use a separable verb, the main part of the verb takes its usual place and the prefix goes to the end of the sentence. If the separable verb is moved to the end of a clause, both parts are rejoined as one word.

Hij blijft vandaag thuis. *He is staying at home today*
Hij zegt dat hij vandaag *He says that he is staying at home*
thuisblijft. *today.*

Conditional

Conditional sentences are formed with the subordinating conjunction **als**:

Als je rode wijn hebt, wil ik *If you have red wine, then I'd like*
graag rode wijn. *red wine.*

Zou (singular) or **zouden** (plural) are also used:

Als ik een miljoen won, zou ik *If I won a million, I would buy*
een huis kopen. *a house.*

Zou and **zouden** are also used to ask polite questions or to give polite advice:

Zou je dat voor me willen doen?   *Would you mind doing that for me?*

The passive

In the present and imperfect tenses the passive is formed as follows: **worden** + past participle.

De was wordt voor me gedaan.   *The laundry is done for me.*
Vroeger werd Greetje op school   *Greetje used to be bullied*
  vaak gepest.   *frequently at school.*

In the perfect and past perfect tenses you form the passive according to the pattern: **zijn** + past participle.

De heroïne is in beslag genomen. *The heroin has been confiscated.*
De wasmachine was vaak   *The washing machine had been*
  gebruikt.   *used often.*

When talking about people in general you use a passive sentence with **er:**

Er werd veel gelachen.   *There was a lot of laughter.*
                                      (People laughed a lot.)

Negation

In making a sentence negative you normally use **niet** or **geen. Geen** is used in combination with indefinite nouns:

Isa drinkt niet.   *Isa doesn't drink.*
Chris drinkt geen bier.   *Chris doesn't drink beer.*

Er

Er can be used in combination with an indefinite subject:

Er is vanavond een mooie film op tv. *There is a beautiful film on tv this evening.*

Er can also be used to refer to something:

Ken je Amsterdam goed? *Do you know Amsterdam well?*
Nee, ik ben er maar een keer geweest. *No, I've only been there once.*

You also use **er** to refer to something in combination with a counting word:

Heb je een fiets? *Have you got a bike?*
Ja ik heb er een. *Yes, I've got one.*

Clauses and conjunctions

In a main clause finite verbs take the second position, and all other verbs the last. Co-ordinating conjunctions link main clauses. The most often used are **en** (*and*), **of** (*or*), **maar** (*but*), **want** (*because*), and **dus** (*so, thus*). In a sub-clause the verb(s) goes to the end of the clause. Sub-clauses are linked to main clauses by subordinating conjunctions. Examples are **dat** (*that*), **of** (*whether, if*), **als** (*when*), **als** (*if*), **omdat** (*because*), **hoewel** (*although*).

Ik weet dat je slim bent. *I know that you are smart.*

Relative clauses

A relative clause is introduced by **die** when referring to a **de** word, and by **dat** when referring to a **het**-word.

Het idee dat je hebt, is interessant. *The idea that you have is interesting.*

10 Only got ten minutes?

Spelling

Dutch spelling closely follows the way sounds are pronounced.
The vowel sounds **a, e, o, u** have a short variant and a long
variant. The short variants are spelled with one vowel in a closed
syllable (a syllable ending in a consonant). The long vowel sounds
are spelled with two vowels in a closed syllable and with one vowel
in an open syllable (ending in a vowel): **man** (*man*), **maan** (*moon*),
manen (*moons*). When making a word plural by adding **-en** to a
closed syllable, the final consonant is doubled to keep the syllable
closed: **man** (*man*), **mannen** (*men*).

Nouns, articles, demonstratives

Dutch has three articles: **de** and **het** (*the*) and **een** (*a/an*). **De man**
(*the man*), **de vrouw** (*the woman*), **het kind** (*the child*), **een boek**
(*a book*). Compound nouns, combining two or more nouns, are
written as one word: **het geld + de automaat = de geldautomaat**
(*the cashpoint*). Nouns are generally made plural by adding one of the
following endings to the noun: **-en, -s, -'s**: **boeken** (*books*), **telefoons**
(*telephones*), **radio's** (*radios*). Diminutives are formed by adding **-je** to
a noun and always get the article **het**: **het huisje** (*the little house*).

Deze and **dit** are Dutch for *this*; **die** and **dat** are Dutch for *that*.
Deze (*this*) and **die** (*that*) are used with **de**– words. **Dit** (*this*) and
dat (*that*) are used with **het**-words: **de jongen** (*the boy*), **deze
jongen** (*this boy*), **die jongen** (*that boy*); **het meisje** (*the girl*), **dit
meisje** (*this girl*), **dat meisje** (*that girl*).

Adjectives

When adjectives directly precede a noun an **-e** is added to the
adjective. There is one exception: no **-e** is added in front of an

indefinitely used **het**-word (i.e. with the indefinite article use **een** or no article at all): **het interessante verhaal** (*the interesting story*), **een interessant verhaal** (*an interesting story*). To make comparatives, you add **-er** to an adjective: **kleiner** (*smaller*). To make a superlative, you add **-st** to the adjective. When not preceding a noun, the superlative is used with **het: het mooist** (*the most beautiful*).

Subject and object pronouns

	Subject pronouns			Object pronouns		
singular	ik	('k)	*I*	mij	(me)	*me*
	jij	(je)	*you* (informal)	jou	(je)	*you* (inf.)
	u		*you* (formal)	u		*you* (form.)
	hij	(ie)	*he*	hem	('m)	*him*
	zij	(ze)	*she*	haar	(d'r)	*her*
	het	('t)	*it*	het	('t)	*it*
plural	wij	(we)	*we*	ons		*us*
	jullie		*you*	jullie		*you* (inf.)
	u		you (formal)	u		*you* (form.)
	zij	(ze)	*they*	ze		*them*

The unstressed forms are generally not used in writing. The pronouns **je** and **jij** are informal and used when speaking to people with whom you are on a first name basis. The pronoun **u** is the polite form of addressing people with whom you are not on a first name basis.

You use **het** to refer to **het**-words and **de** (or **die**) to refer to **de**-words. **Ze** is used to refer to plurals. When combined with a preposition the object pronoun cannot be used when referring to an object or thing. Instead you must use **er**. Compare the following sentences:

Kijk jij vanavond naar dat programma?
Will you watch that programme tonight?

Nee, ik ga er niet naar kijken.
No, I'm not going to watch it.

	stressed	unstressed	
singular	mijn	(m'n)	*my*
	jouw	je	your (informal)
	uw	–	*your* (formal)
	zijn	(z'n)	*his*
	haar	(d'r)	*her*
plural	ons/onze	–	*our*
	jullie	je	*your* (informal)
	uw	–	*your* (formal)
	hun	–	*their*

The stressed forms of the possessive pronouns are generally used in writing, and in speech to indicate contrast. The unstressed forms are more commonly used in speech. The unstressed forms in brackets are not generally used in writing. **Ons** is used before **het**-words and **onze** before **de**-words. To express *'s* in English, Dutch uses **van: het boek van David** (*David's book*). An **s** without apostrophe is also possible (**Davids boek**), but is less commonly used.

Verbs

Only the first verb in a sentence adapts its form to indicate tense. This verb is called the finite verb. The finite verb is put in second position in the sentence. All other verbs are put at the end of the sentence. In sub-clauses and relative clauses, all verbs, including the finite verb, are placed at the end of the clause. Questions often start with the finite verb.

To find the verb form for the first person singular (**ik**) in the present tense, you generally leave off the **-en** ending of verbs (**werk, loop, denk**). This form is the stem of the verb. For all other singular persons in the present tense, you add a **-t**. When a verb is used in front of **jij**, this **-t** is not added. In the plural the infinitive form (or whole verb) is used. The verbs **hebben** (*to have*) and **zijn** (*to be*) are irregular.

When talking about a time period which started in the past and continues into the present the present tense is used together with **al** or **pas** or another adverb indicating time:

Ik woon al twee jaar in Deventer.   *I've lived in Deventer for two years.*

Talking about the past

As a general rule, talking about the past is introduced, and often concluded, using the perfect tense. Added information is given in the imperfect. Habits and regular events in the past must be given in the imperfect tense.

The present perfect is formed with the verb **hebben** or **zijn** plus a past participle, which is placed at the end of the sentence:

Mijn collega heeft die fout gemaakt.   *My colleague (has) made that mistake.*

The past participle of regular verbs is formed by adding the prefix **ge-** to the stem of the verb plus final **t** or **d**. If the stem ends in **s, f, t, k, ch** or **p**, we add a **t**. In all other cases we add a **d**.

Most verbs use a form of the verb **hebben** in the perfect tense. However, a number of verbs that indicate a change of place or state use a form of **zijn**.

Verbs of motion such as **lopen** (*to walk*) and **fietsen** (*to cycle*) use **zijn** if the destination of the movement is mentioned. Otherwise **hebben** is used.

The imperfect of regular verbs is formed by adding **te(n)** or **de(n)** to the stem of the verb. In the singular **te** and **de** are used, and in the plural **ten** and **den**. If the stem ends in **s, f, t, k, ch** or **p** you add **te(n)**. In all other cases you add **de(n)**.

infinitive	stem	imperfect
werken (to work)	**werk**	**werkte(n)**

Modal verbs

The modal verbs are **zullen** (*shall/will*), **willen** (*want*), **kunnen** (*can, to be able to*), **mogen** (*may, to be allowed to*), **moeten** (*must, should, to have to*), **hoeven** (*to have to*). Their forms are irregular. Modal verbs are normally combined with another verb, which is put at the end of the sentence in its full infinitive form:

We willen een huis kopen.   *We want to buy a house.*

Separable verbs

Separable verbs are made up of a prefix and the main part of the verb, for instance **uit + gaan: uitgaan** (to go out). When you use a separable verb in a sentence the main part of the verb takes its usual place and the prefix goes to the end of the sentence.

We gaan vanavond samen uit.   *We're going out together tonight.*

When the word order in a sentence changes, for instance in sub-clauses, both parts of the separable verb are moved to the end of the sentence and are rejoined as one word.

Hij blijft vandaag thuis.   *He's staying at home today.*
Hij zegt dat hij vandaag   *He says that he's staying home*
  thuisblijft.   *today.*

Infinitive constructions

Some verbs are combined with an infinitive at the end of the sentence preceded by **te**. The most common of these verbs are: **zitten** (*to sit, to be sitting*), **liggen** (*to lie, to be lying*), **proberen** (*to try*), **hoeven** (*to have to*), **beginnen** (*to begin, to start*), **staan** (*to stand, to be standing*), **durven** (*to dare*).

Some verbs which can be combined with an infinitive do not have **te** before the infinitive. Apart from the modal verbs the most common of these are: **komen** (*to come*), **laten** (*to have something done, to let*), **gaan** (*to go*), **zien** (*to see*), **zijn** (*to be*):

| **Janneke is even koffie halen.** | *Janneke is getting a coffee.* |

Conditional

Conditional sentences are formed with the subordinating conjunction **als**:

| **Als je rode wijn hebt, wil ik** | *If you have red wine, I'd like* |
| **graag rode wijn.** | *red wine.* |

To indicate intention or things yet to happen, you can also use **zullen** + infinitive in the second part of the sentence:

| **Als je wilt, zal ik een biertje voor** | *If you want, I will get a beer* |
| **je halen.** | *for you.* |

Zou (singular) or **zouden** (plural) are used in conditional sentences too, in combination with the imperfect or past perfect:

Als ik een miljoen won, zou ik	*If I won a million, I would buy*
een huis kopen.	*a house.*
Als we een miljoen hadden	*If we had won a million, we would*
gewonnen, zouden we een huis	*have bought a house.*
hebben gekocht.	

Zou is also used to ask polite questions or to give polite advice:

| **Zou je dat voor me willen doen?** | *Would you mind doing that for me?* |

The passive

In the present and imperfect tenses the passive is formed as follows: **worden** + past participle.

De was wordt voor me gedaan.	*The laundry is done for me.*
Vroeger werd Greetje op school	*Greetje used to be bullied*
vaak gepest.	*frequently at school.*

In the perfect and past perfect tenses you form the passive according to the pattern: **zijn** + past participle:

De heroïne is in beslag genomen. *The heroin has been confiscated.*

De wasmachine was vaak gebruikt. *The washing machine had been used often.*

When talking about people in general you use a passive sentence with **er**:

Er werd veel gelachen. *People were laughing a lot.*

Negation

In making a sentence negative you normally use **geen** or **niet**. **Geen** (*not a*, *not any*) is used in combination with nouns which refer to something in general (indefinite nouns):

Chris drinkt geen bier. *Chris doesn't drink any beer.*

Niet, generally speaking, comes last in the sentence or clause (but before the words which take the very last position such as the past participle, the infinitive or prepositional phrases):

U beantwoordt mijn vraag niet. *You are not answering my question.*

Ik heb hem nog niet gezien. *I haven't seen him yet.*

Er

Er can be used as a subject or in combination with a subject. This happens in two situations:

1 In combination with an indefinite subject:

Er is vanavond een film op tv. *There is a film on tv tonight.*

2 As the subject in a passive sentence without a definite subject, describing human activities:

Er mag hier niet gerookt worden.   *Smoking is not allowed here.*

Er can also be used to refer to something else. In these cases, **er** often simply means there:

Ken je Amsterdam goed?   *Do you know Amsterdam well?*
Nee, ik ben er maar een keer   *No, I've only been there once.*
  geweest.

You also use **er** to refer to something in combination with a counting word such as a number.

Heb je een fiets?   *Have you got a bike?*
Ja ik heb er een.   *Yes, I've got one.*

Clauses and conjunctions

In a main clause the finite verb takes the second position, and all other verbs the last.

Co-ordinating conjunctions link main clauses. The most often used are **en** (*and*), **of** (*or*), **maar** (*but*), **want** (*because*), **dus** (*so, thus*). In a sub-clause the verb(s) goes to the end of the clause, and the sub-clause always starts with a subordinating conjunction:

Ik weet dat je slim bent.   *I know that you're smart.*

Sub-clauses are linked to main clauses by subordinating conjunctions. Examples are **dat** (*that*), **of** (*whether, if*), **als** (*when*), **als** (*if*), **omdat** (*because*), **hoewel** (*although*).

Relative clauses

A relative clause gives added information about a person or thing. A relative clause is often introduced by the pronoun **die** or **dat**.

Whether you use **die** or **dat** depends on the word you are referring to. **Die** is used for **de** words (including plural words), personal pronouns and names of people. **Dat** refers to **het** words.

Het idee dat je hebt, is interessant.

The idea (that) you have is interesting.

If you refer to something in combination with a preposition you use the following combinations:

preposition + **wie** if you refer to people

waar + preposition if you refer to things

Dat is de jongen over wie ik je heb verteld.

That is the boy about whom I told you.

Introduction

About this book

This *Essential Dutch grammar* is a reference and practice book in one. Explanations of various grammar points are followed by exercises designed to practise using the grammar points.

The contents pages give you an overview of the different points which are explained. In general, the sections are grouped by grammatical topic, e.g. all issues relating to verbs are grouped together, with the basic information and simpler points preceding more complex points.

The book is aimed at beginners – both beginners studying the Dutch language and beginners learning grammar – as well as more advanced learners of Dutch. In the earlier sections, all grammatical terminology is explained. In later sections we may use terminology without explaining what it is, but you can always refer to the glossary, or, better still, to the appropriate sections.

The exercises are designed to practise the specific points explained; they may deal with form or with function, or both. The language in the exercises of the earlier sections is kept fairly simple. In some of the later sections, we have assumed that you will have a slightly larger vocabulary. But even in these sections the language is straightforward, only the sentences might be longer.

Because grammar is a network of various rules and conventions of using language, you cannot, strictly speaking, study a point in isolation from others. In reality, of course, this is the only way we can learn about a foreign grammar, but it is worthwhile to keep in mind that many points have a bearing upon one another.

You will find many cross-references throughout the book, which will undoubtedly prove a useful aid in getting to grips with the greater picture.

This book can be used in various ways: as a self-study to learn about the Dutch language, in conjunction with a language course, or simply as a reference book to look up various points if and when the need arises.

1

Sentence composition

1.1 What's the use of grammar?

Please read this introduction before you start using the book.

Why learn grammar?

Learning grammar has long been associated with learning boring rules which do nothing to help you perform practical tasks and survive in a foreign country. But, as a matter of fact, learning grammar does help you do everyday things in a foreign language.

Learning grammar is not just about learning to speak and write correctly. It is also about understanding what the patterns and structures of the language are – patterns and structures which you can apply to lots of other words, so that you will be able to say infinitely more than if you only learn lists of ready-made phrases. Learning grammar helps you to learn effectively and efficiently.

Grammar and meaning

But, perhaps most important of all, learning grammar helps you to get under the surface of the language. It helps you to understand how language works and how grammar can effect the meaning of what people say. Learning grammar is just as much about *meaning* and *communication* as it is about understanding language patterns in a more abstract way.

For instance, when you come to learn a difficult structure such as the passive, you can learn its various forms, but it helps you more if you also learn about what the passive actually is, what it does, and why and when people use it.

Use and style

Throughout the book, we have tried to give you not only a clear and concise explanation of the rules and forms of the various grammatical points, but wherever possible we have also tried to give you a closer look at the meaning and use of a particular grammatical category. We have also included information and exercises on stylistic issues, as this will further help you understand how the language works and how a knowledge of grammar can contribute to the way you express yourself.

1.2 Double Dutch?

A changing language

Contrary to popular perception, Dutch is by no means a small language within Europe. Over 20 million people speak it, both in the Netherlands and in Flanders (the northern part of Belgium).

As with all living languages, Dutch reflects the history and the values of the country and its people and, even more importantly perhaps for foreign learners, the language continues to change as a result of historical, social and cultural changes.

One example of this is the absorption over the centuries of foreign words from many different languages into Dutch, as a result of Dutch trade and contacts with other countries and cultures. In more recent years, the influence of English in particular has been very strong, due in part to globalization, but also due to the desire of the Dutch to have an international orientation, and the continuation of a strong trading tradition.

Holland has had a reputation of being open and tolerant towards other cultures. While this image may be somewhat stereotypical, the openness has been an economic necessity; Dutch society is still fascinated with other cultures and many Dutch people are proud of their ability to speak foreign languages and are only too eager to prove it.

Different languages

There is not one single Dutch language – different social groups, different professions, people of different ages or people living in different parts of the country speak Dutch in their own slightly different way.

In this book we discuss only the 'ground rules' of the language which are shared by everybody. When a particular rule is not used by all speakers, this will be indicated if relevant to foreign learners.

Finally, Dutch grammar is quite straightforward; the rules are much more regular than those of English, and not as complicated as those of, say German (despite what many Dutch speakers say).

Good luck and happy learning!

1.3 What's in a sentence?

Sentences are made up of various elements; the most important are subject, verb and object.

1.3.1 Subject

Virtually all sentences have a subject. Subjects make things happen – it's the person, object or idea which performs the action in a sentence. Note that this action – indicated by the verb – needn't be a particularly active thing; it can also be something like *sleeping* or *thinking*. The subject, like the object, can be made up of more than one word. Examples of subjects could be:

ik	*I*
mijn buurman	*my neighbour*
de economie in de derde wereld	*the economy in the third world*

1.3.2 Verb

The verb is a word which tells you what someone or something is doing. As indicated, this needn't be anything active. Most sentences have at least one verb, but can – and frequently do in Dutch – have more than one. For more on verbs, see Sections 5.1–10.5. Examples of verbs:

parkeren	*to park*
zien	*to see*
denken	*to think*

1.3.3 Object

The object is the person, thing or idea which is at the receiving end of the action in the sentence. Not all sentences have objects.

There are two types of objects:
▶ Direct objects undergo the action of the sentence directly.
▶ Indirect objects 'receive' the direct object.

> **Ik geef de rozen aan mijn moeder.**
> direct object = *de rozen* (you're actually handling them)
> indirect object = *mijn moeder* (she receives the roses)

NB In practice, the difference between direct and indirect objects won't be an issue in this book.

1.3.4 Other categories

In addition to subject, verb and object you will find many other word categories in sentences, such as articles, nouns, pronouns, adjectives, adverbs, prepositions, conjunctions etc. These are all described in the glossary and under individual headings throughout the book.

Exercise 1A
Put the right sentence with the correct illustration.

a Harry kust Annie.
b Frederick geeft het cadeau aan zijn vriendin.
c Ik lees de krant.
d De baby eet de banaan.
e Jackie draagt de koffer.
f De popster signeert foto's.

Exercise 1B
Write the sentences from Exercise 1A in the box, breaking them down into subject, verb and object.

Subject	Verb	Object
a Harry	kust	Annie
b		
c		
d		
e		
f		

1.4 Spelling

This section gives you the main spelling rules of Dutch.

1.4.1 Vowels

Dutch spelling is very straightforward, and tries to follow the way sounds are pronounced as closely as possible. The main rule concerns the spelling of the vowel sounds **a, e, o, u**. Of these vowel sounds there is both a short variant and a long variant. The short and long vowel sounds are spelled according to strict rules. First some examples:

	a	**e**	**o**	**u**
short	man *man*	hek *fence/gate*	bos *forest*	bus *bus*
long	maan	heer *gentleman*	boom *tree*	buur
	moon			*neighbour*

▶ **Short vowel sounds** are always spelled with **one vowel** (see the examples) **in a closed syllable**, i.e. a syllable ending in a consonant.
▶ **Long vowel sounds** can be spelled in two ways;

1 with **two vowels in a closed syllable**, i.e. a syllable ending in a consonant (as in the examples).
2 with **one vowel in an open syllable**, i.e. a syllable ending in a vowel, as in the following examples:
manen (*moons*), **heren** (*gentlemen*), **bomen** (*trees*), **buren** (*neighbours*).

1.4.2 Changing vowels: a/aa

To make words plural in Dutch, you often add -en, which usually creates an extra syllable. If you add -en to, for instance, **maan**, you create a second syllable -nen. This means that the first syllable **maa-** is now an open syllable, and so the long a-sound should be spelled with only one a (see above): **manen**. The spelling of the vowel sound changes but the sound stays the same.

1.4.3 Changing consonants: n/nn

To make a word like **man**, with a short vowel sound, plural you also add -en and create a second syllable -nen. However, the first syllable **ma-** is now open, and only long vowel sounds can occur in open syllables. A short vowel sound can only occur in a closed vowel, so the first syllable has to end in a consonant. There's an easy solution to this: simply double the consonant in the middle: **mannen**. Now there are two closed syllables, **man-** and -nen.

Exercise 1C
Make these nouns plural by adding -en.

a	naam	*name*	**g**	boot	*boat*
b	taal	*language*	**h**	minuut	*minute*
c	been	*leg*	**i**	oog	*eye*
d	sigaret	*cigarette*	**j**	koor	*choir*
e	school	*school*	**k**	boom	*tree*
f	fles	*bottle*	**l**	muur	*wall*

Exercise 1D
Form the plural of these verbs (e.g. the form for *wij*).

ik draag	*I wear/carry*	**wij dragen**	*we wear/carry*
a ik maak	*I make*	**f** ik was	*I wash*
b ik ken	*I know*	**g** ik rook	*I smoke*
c ik vertel	*I tell (a story)*	**h** ik raak	*I hit (a target)*
d ik droog	*I dry*	**i** ik keek	*I looked*
e ik bezit	*I possess*	**j** ik praat	*I talk*

Exercise 1E

Of the following verbs, give the form that goes with *hij* and *zij*.

wassen to wash hij/zij *wa*st

a	lopen	*to walk*
b	bevallen	*to give birth* (only for **zij**!)
c	hopen	*to hope*
d	verdwalen	*to get lost*
e	koken	*to cook/boil*
f	overstappen	*to change (e.g. trains)* **NB overstappen** is a separable verb.
g	sturen	*to send*
h	ervaren	*to experience*
i	overwinnen	*to conquer*
j	horen	*to hear*
k	slapen	*to sleep*
l	tellen	*to count*

1.5 Spelling: consonants

This section gives you the most important spelling rules governing consonants.

1.5.1 Double trouble

There is a very simple Dutch spelling rule which says that a word cannot end in two consonants if they are the same. This may seem strange if you know English and, for instance, German, but you'll agree that it's an easy rule to remember.

I want should therefore be **ik wil** and *a ball* is always **een bal**! Look at the pictures opposite for some more examples.

1.5.2 z/s *and* v/f

The sounds **b, d, v, z** are not as important in the Dutch sound system as they are in English. In fact, at the end of words, **b, d, v, z** are pronounced as **p, t, f** and **s** (which lots of Dutch speakers also do in English giving them such a recognizable accent).

Moreover, **v** and **z** are usually also written as **f** and **s** at the end of words. This is why the singular of **brieven** (*letters*) is **brief** (*letter*), and the singular of **huizen** (*houses*) is **huis** (*house*).

een bel

een voetbal

hel

Insight

Dutch grammar is quite straightforward and relatively easy to learn for speakers of English. The reason for this is that Dutch and English are closely related; both are part of the Germanic family of languages. On the whole, written Dutch is pretty phonetic, i.e. you write what you hear. This also means that all the letters you see written on the page are usually pronounced: you say what you write.

Exercise 1F
Give the stem of the following verbs (the form to go with *ik*).

   spellen *to spell* (ik) spel

   a kussen   *to kiss*
   b verhuizen   *to move house*
   c voetballen   *to play football/soccer*
   d blazen   *to blow*
   e hakken   *to hack/cut*
   f bellen   *to call/ring*
   g tennissen   *to play tennis*
   h geven   *to give*
   i likken   *to lick*
   j streven   *to strive*

Exercise 1G
Make the following words plural by adding *-en*.

   a fles   *bottle*
   b vaas   *vase*
   c neef   *nephew/cousin*
   d brief   *letter*
   e huis   *house*
   f dief   *thief*
   g bus   *bus*

Exercise 1H
Form the plural of these verbs (i.e. the form to go with *wij*).

   a ik kies   *I choose*
   b ik leef   *I live*
   c ik was   *I wash*
   d ik beef   *I tremble*
   e ik geef   *I give*
   f ik raas   *I rage*

Things to remember

▶ *Subjects* make things happen – it's the person, object or idea which performs the action in a sentence.

▶ The *verb* is a word which tells you what someone or something is doing.

▶ The *object* is the person, thing or idea which is at the receiving end of the action in the sentence.

▶ Short vowel sounds are always spelled with one vowel in a closed syllable, i.e. a syllable ending in a consonant.

▶ Long vowel sounds are spelled with two vowels in a closed syllable or with one vowel in an open syllable, i.e. a syllable ending in a vowel.

2

Nouns and adjectives

2.1 Nouns and articles

Articles are the words for **the** and **a(n)**, which are used with a noun. Nouns are the words we use to name objects, ideas, places and people.

2.1.1 Articles

There are three articles in Dutch: **de, het** and **een**. **De** and **het** both mean *the*, and **een** means *a* or *an*. **De** and **het** are the definite articles, and **een** is the indefinite article.

2.1.2 Nouns

Examples of nouns are **huis** (*house*), **koffie** (*coffee*) and **baan** (*job*). Nouns can be countable or uncountable. Countable nouns are things that can be counted, like **huis** or **baan**. Uncountable nouns are things that cannot be counted, like **koffie**. For how to make nouns plural, see Section 2.8.

2.1.3 Use: indefinite

When a noun is used without an article or with the indefinite article **een**, we call the noun 'indefinite'. **Een** can only be used before single countable nouns.

People generally use nouns indefinitely when they believe others may not know what they are talking about, e.g.:

Ik heb gisteren een film gezien.   *I saw a film yesterday.*

or if they want to make a general statement, e.g.:

Een tuin is veel werk.   *A garden's a lot of work.*
Appels zijn erg goed voor je.   *Apples are very good for you.*

2.1.4 Use: definite

All nouns can be used with a definite article, i.e. **de** or **het**. Nouns which are combined with **de** are called common nouns, and nouns combined with **het** are called neuter nouns. Some examples: **de man** (*the man*), **de vrouw** (*the woman*), **het kind** (*the child*), **de vergadering** (*the meeting*), **het kantoor** (*the office*). There are no easy rules to tell you whether a word takes **de** or **het**; you simply have to remember for each word. There are roughly twice as many words with **de** as with **het**.

De is used as the definite article for all plural nouns. For example:

| **singular** | **de conclusie** (*conclusion*) | **het rapport** (*report*) |
| **plural** | **de conclusies** (*conclusions*) | **de rapporten** (*reports*) |

People generally use definite nouns when they expect their listeners to know what they are talking about:

De vergadering duurde lang.   *The meeting lasted a long time.*

or if they wish to talk about the noun in the abstract, as a phenomenon:

Het wiel bestond nog niet.   *The wheel didn't exist yet.*

Exercise 2A
Underline the nouns in the following text.

Ik heb veel werk, dus ik werk van 's ochtends vroeg tot 's avonds laat. Gelukkig heb ik een computer, dat is erg handig voor de administratie. Ik heb een collega. Zij werkt ook hard. We gaan vaak samen lunchen. We kopen meestal een broodje en een kopje koffie. Als het mooi weer is, eten en drinken we onze lunch in het park. Als ik geen honger heb, geef ik mijn broodje aan de eendjes. De koffie drink ik altijd zelf.

Exercise 2B
Which of the following nouns are countable, and which are not?

a potlood
b water
c zout
d telefoon
e oog
f droom
g hoop
h ding
i suiker
j vuil
k drop
l jaar

Exercise 2C
Fill in *de*, *het*, *een* or nothing. (Good dictionaries indicate whether a word is a *de* word or a *het* word – see Sections 19.2–19.3.)

a Wil je _____ glas wijn?
b Wanneer gaat _____ winkel open?
c _____ huis is erg groot.
d Harm vindt _____ wijn erg lekker, maar ik niet.
e Drink je _____ koffie met suiker?
f Zij heeft _____ mooie ring.
g Ik hou van _____ klassieke films.
h Heb je _____ nieuwe horloge van Simon gezien?
i De directeur heeft nu _____ tijd voor u.
j Ik heb trek in _____ thee.

2.1.5 Compound nouns

Nouns are often combined to make up new words – compound nouns. When this happens in Dutch, the new noun is written as one word:

het geld *(money)* **+ de automaat** *(machine)* **= de geldautomaat**
de wijn *(wine)* **+ het glas** *(glass)* **= het wijnglas**

Note that the compound noun takes its definite article from the last part of the word (in the first example, **de** from **de automaat,** and in the second, **het** from **het glas**).

Sometimes the two nouns are linked by -s-, -e- or -en-:

de stad *(city)* **+ het park** *(park)* **= het stadspark**
de erwt *(pea)* **+ de soep** *(soup)* **= de erwtensoep**

Compound nouns are also discussed in Section 2.9.

2.1.6 Gender

To indicate that people, jobs or animals are female, a suffix is often added to Dutch nouns to make them feminine.

	masculine	*feminine*
-e	**Chinees** *Chinese man*	**Chinese** *Chinese woman*
-es	**zanger** *singer*	**zangeres**
-in	**leeuw** *lion*	**leeuwin** *lioness*
-ster	**schrijver** *writer*	**schrijfster**

These feminine nouns are always **de**-words.

2.1.7 Making nouns of adjectives and past participles

The suffix -e is also used to make nouns of adjectives and past participles. By adding an -e to the adjective **blind** *(blind)* you can make the noun **de blinde** *(the blind person)*. By adding an -e to the past participle **overleden** (*deceased*) you make **de overledene** (*the deceased*). Some examples:

duur	*(expensive)*	**de dure**	*(the expensive one)*
geopend	*(opened)*	**de geopende**	*(the one that's been opened)*

These new nouns usually take **de** or **het** depending on what noun you are referring to. When used in an abstract sense, however, it's always **het**.

Het grappige was...	*The funny thing was...*

When these nouns refer to more than one person or thing, you add **-n**:

de overledene	*(one deceased person)*
de overledenen	*(more than one deceased)*

Exercise 2D
Combine the following nouns to make up new words. Indicate whether the new word is used with *het* or *de*.

e.g. de pen / de houder   de penhouder

   a de bus / de halte (*the stop*)
   b de koffie / de filter
   c de televisie / de gids (*the guide*)
   d de studie / het boek
   e de discussie / de leider
   f het hoofd (*head*) / het kantoor (*office*)
   g het toilet / het papier

Exercise 2E
Complete the sentences by making the adjectives in brackets into nouns.

e.g. Welke wil je hebben, de witte of (groen)?
       Welke wil je hebben, de witte of de groene.

a Welke wijn vind je lekkerder, (rood) of (wit)?
b Tom is (groot) en Willem is (klein).
c Het witte behang vind ik mooi, want (druk, *busy/loud*) is me te veel. (behang = *wallpaper*)
d Het huis is heel groot, maar (mooi) is dat het helemaal niet duur is.
e Ina en ik hebben drie poezen, een (zwart), een (bruin) en een (kaal, *bald*).

Exercise 2F
Complete the sentences by making the past participles in brackets into nouns.

e.g. Krijg je nog iets van (overleden).
Krijg je nog iets van de overledene?

a Hebben ze (gewond, *injured*) naar het ziekenhuis gebracht?
b Als (gevangen, *caught/imprisoned*) heb je niet veel privacy.
c Alle (genomineerd) voor een Oscar zijn heel nerveus.

2.2 Demonstratives

Deze and *dit* are Dutch for this; *die* and *dat* are Dutch for that. As a group they are known as demonstratives.

2.2.1 Form

Which demonstrative is used depends on the noun they are used with. **Deze** (*this*) and **die** (*that*) are used with **de**-words. **Dit** (*this*) and **dat** (*that*) are used with **het**-words:

de jongen	*the boy*	**deze jongen**	*this boy*	**die jongen**
				that boy
het meisje	*the girl*	**dit meisje**	*this girl*	**dat meisje**
				that girl

Since all plural words are **de**-words (see Section 2.1), **deze** and **die** are always used for plurals.

de kast	*cupboard*	**deze kasten**	*these cupboards*
het boek	*the book*	**die boeken**	*those books*

2.2.2 Use

The demonstratives can be used in front of a noun, just as they are in English:

Wil je naar deze film of naar die film?
Do you want to go to this film or to that film?
Ik vind dit boek beter dan dat boek.
I think this book's better than that book.

When it is clear what you are talking about, **deze**, **die**, **dit** and **dat** can also be used on their own. In English you often translate *this* or *that one* in these cases.

Gaat deze trein naar Parijs?	**Nee, deze gaat naar Antwerpen.**
Is this train going to Paris?	*No, this one is going to Antwerp.*
Vind je de schoenen mooi?	**Nee, ik vind deze niet mooi.**
Do you like the shoes?	*No, I don't like these.*

2.2.3 Dit is/Dat is

Dit and **dat**, as well as **het**, can also be used with the verb **zijn** (*to be*) to introduce people or things, both singular and plural. Note that **deze** and **die** are never used in these constructions:

Dit is de auto.	*This is the car.*	**Dit zijn de cijfers.**	*These are the figures.*
Dat is de baas.	*That's the boss.*	**Dat zijn de foto's.**	*Those are the photos.*
Het is de post.	*It's the post.*	**Het zijn studenten.**	*They are students.*

Exercise 2G
Fill in *deze*, *die*, *dit* or *dat* (usually two options are possible).

a Welke pen is van jou, _____ of _____ ?
b Kom jij ook naar _____ vergadering vanmiddag?
c Ik vind _____ soort muziek irritant.
d _____ is de kamer van Martijn.
e Heb je _____ mooie nieuwe musical al gezien?
f Ik heb _____ dieet nog nooit geprobeerd.
g _____ grote auto is van ons, _____ kleine is van de buren.
h Hij wil _____ vakantie zelf organiseren.
i Ik vind _____ lasagna niet lekker.
j Waarom ga je steeds dansen met _____ jongen?
k _____ vakantiehuisje op Vlieland is erg duur.

2.3 Adjectives

An adjective is a word which describes characteristics of objects, people and ideas. Examples: *red, big, hairy, strong, clever*.

2.3.1 Form

Sometimes an **-e** is added to the adjective. The rule for this is:

▶ If the adjective comes after the noun: no **-e**.

Het stadhuis is modern.   *The townhall is modern.*

▶ If the adjective comes before the noun: add an **-e**.

De dramatische gebeurtenis.   *The dramatic event.*

2.3.2 Exceptions

▶ No **-e** is added to the adjective in front of an indefinite **het**-word (i.e. used with the article **een** or no article at all – see Section 2.1).

| **Het interessante verhaal.** | *The interesting story.* |
| **Een interessant verhaal.** | *An interesting story.* |

▶ Adjectives which end in -en never get an extra -e.

| **De dronken student** | *The drunken student.* |

2.3.3 Spelling

You may have to change the spelling of the adjective if you add
an -e. Follow the spelling rules in Sections 1.4 and 1.5:

| **De oven is heet. / De hete oven.** | *The hot oven.* |
| **Dat boek is stom. / Het stomme boek.** | *The stupid book.* |

2.3.4 Use

Adjectives are used to describe nouns, and can give extra information
about appearance, quality, mood, physicality, etc. You can use as
many adjectives together as you like. The rule for adding an -e
(or not) applies to all of them:

| **Dit is mijn grote, sterke broer.** | *This is my big, strong brother.* |
| **Ik woon in een mooi, groot huis.** | *I live in a beautiful, big house.* |

2.3.5 Adverbial use

Sometimes adjectives can be preceded by words such as **erg** (*very*),
heel (*very*), **verschrikkelijk** (*terrible*), **bijzonder** (*remarkable*), which
look like adjectives but are used in an adverbial sense. In such cases
these words do not describe the noun but the adjective describing
the noun. These adverbs do not get an extra -e in the written
language. Compare:

| **Een verschrikkelijke man.** | *A terrible man.* |
| **Een verschrikkelijk aardige man.** | *A terribly nice man.* |

In the spoken language, however, the -e is often added.

Exercise 2H
Complete the following sentences using the words between brackets, adding an -e only if needed.

a Zij is __, __, __ en __ (mooi, slank, rijk, sexy)
b Hij is __, __, __ en __ (aantrekkelijk, arm, verliefd, artistiek)
c De ijsberg is __, __ en __ (groot, gevaarlijk, dodelijk)

Exercise 2I
Change the following sentences by putting the adjective before the noun. Change the spelling as needed.

Het boek is stom. *Het stomme boek.*

a De roos is rood.
b De bijbel is dik.
c De vader is boos.
d De keuken is vies.

Exercise 2J
Correct the job advertisement below, by adding an -e where needed. Change the spelling where necessary.

> Gevraagd:
> Een enthousiast_ en ervaren_ medewerker
> voor onze snel_ groeiend_ afdeling.
> Wij bieden een bijzonder_ hoog_ salaris en
> een erg_ prettig_ werkomgeving.

2.4 More information on adjectives

Adjectives are frequently derived from other words, such as verbs or nouns.

2.4.1 From verbs

Adjectives are often derived from verbs. These often take the form
of the present participle (infinitive + **d**) or past participle of the
verb (see Section 7.2). The rules for adding and -e remain the same.
Some examples:

koken	**een gekookt eitje**	*a boiled egg*
vervuilen	**het vervuilde milieu**	*the polluted environment*
(af)branden	**het afgebrande huis**	*the burned out house*
stelen	**een gestolen fiets**	*a stolen bike*
vernielen	**het vernielde parkbankje**	*the vandalized park bench*
lachen	**de lachende meisjes**	*the laughing girls*
(hard)werken	**de hardwerkende leerling**	*the hardworking pupil*

2.4.2 A new ending

Sometimes adjectives are derived from verbs by giving the verb a
new ending (think of English *-ible/able*). There are no rules for this
and the form of these adjectives has to be learned as you go along.

Some examples:

-baar	**eten → eetbaar**	**Deze patat is niet eetbaar.**
	to eat → edible	*These chips are not edible.*
-lijk	**geloven → ongelofelijk**	**Het was een ongelofelijke ervaring.**
	to believe → unbelievable	*It was an unbelievable experience.*
-loos	**werken → werkloos**	**Ik ben werkloos.**
	to work → out of work	*I am unemployed.*

NB There are more examples in Section 12.1.

2.4.3 Adjectives can also be derived from nouns. These can also take a variety of endings similar to the ones above:

zinloos geweld *senseless violence.*

Exercise 2K
Write out the noun that goes with the following adjectives.

e.g. gedachteloos → de gedachte

a mannelijk
b schandalig
c redelijk
d ongelukkig
e zinvol

Exercise 2L
Complete the following table. The first example is given.

Adjective	Noun	Verb
a fantastisch	de fantasie	fantaseren
b schriftelijk		
c gelovig		
d hoopvol		
e werkloos		
f brandbaar		

Insight

It can seem confusing when to use an **-e** ending for adjectives when used in front of nouns or not. However, the **-e** is added in most cases. The only case in which the **-e** is not added is when the adjective precedes a **het**-words which is used indefinitely, i.e. with the indefinite pronoun **een** (**een mooi boek** *a beautiful book*) or without any article at all (**leuke film** *nice film*). The **e**-ending makes a big difference in Dutch, so when speaking, make sure you pronounce the **-e** (which adds another syllable to the word) very clearly.

2.5 Adjectives: something nice...

This section looks at more special uses of adjectives.

2.5.1 Something nice

Adjectives used after **iets** (*something*), **niets** (*nothing*), **wat** (*something*), **veel** (*much*) and **weinig** (*little*) get an extra -s:

iets lekkers	*something nice (to eat)*
niets speciaals	*nothing special*
wat wits	*something white*
Er is vanavond weinig interessants op de televisie.	*There isn't much of interest on television tonight.*

2.5.2 The big one and the small one

You can make Dutch adjectives into nouns simply by adding an -e. Normally these nouns are **de** words.

groot	*big*	**de grote**	*the big one*
klein	*small*	**de kleine**	*the small one*
oud	*old*	**de oude**	*the old one*
arm	*poor*	**de arme**	*the poor one/person*
Wilt u de grote of de kleine?		*Would you like the big one or the small one?*	

If you're making an abstract noun (you're not referring to something physical) then it's a **het** word:

grappig	*funny*	**het grappige**	*the funny thing*
Het grappige was dat...		*The funny thing was that...*	

2.5.3 Quantity

You can make adjectives of quantity such as **sommige** (*some*) into nouns by adding -en: **sommigen** (*some people*). These nouns always refer to people.

veel	*many*	**velen**	*many people*
weinig	*few*	**weinigen**	*few people*
alle	*all*	**allen**	*all people/ everyone*
verschillende	*different/various*	**verschillenden**	*various people*
beide	*both*	**beiden**	*both people*
Velen hebben dit boek al.	*Many people already have this book.*		

Exercise 2M
Change the adjective in bold into an independent noun. Write out the whole sentence.

e.g. Ik heb een blauwe pen, maar ik wil liever een **zwarte** pen.
Ik heb een blauwe pen, maar ik wil liever een zwarte.

a Ik wil een kleine auto, maar mijn man wil een **grote** auto.
b Wilt u de gele bloemen? Nee de **rode** bloemen graag.
c Hans heeft een leuke docent, maar ik heb een **saaie** docent.
d Wie heeft het gedaan? Die grote jongen of die **kleine** jongen?

Exercise 2N
Something...? Use the words in brackets to finish these sentences following the example.

e.g. Wat wil je zien op video, iets (grappig) of iets (spannend)?
Wat wil je zien op video, iets grappigs of iets spannends?

a Waar heb je trek in, iets (zout) of iets (zoet)?
b Er was veel (mooi) te zien in het museum.
c Ze hadden iets (speciaal) voor me georganiseerd op mijn verjaardag.
d Het maakt me niet uit wat we doen, zolang het maar niets (actief) is.

2.6 Comparative and superlative

Comparatives are words such as bigger and better; superlatives are words such as biggest and best.

2.6.1 Use

Comparatives are patterns of language used to compare objects, people or ideas which are not equal, e.g. *I am older and wiser than you.* Superlatives are used to express that an object, person or idea surpasses everything else, e.g. *I am the greatest.*

2.6.2 Form

adjective (basic form)	comparative (add **-er**)	superlative (add **-st**)
vreemd *strange*	vreemd**er** *stranger*	vreemd**st** *strangest*
mooi *beautiful*	mooi**er** *more beautiful*	mooi**st** *most beautiful*

The spelling rules apply as normal (Sections 1.4 and 1.5). Note these examples:

lief *nice*	**liever** *nicer*	**liefst** *nicest*
zat *drunk*	**zatter** *more drunk*	**zatst** *most drunk*
vies *dirty*	**viezer** *dirtier*	**viest** *dirtiest*

When not followed by a noun, the superlative is used with **het**: **Mijn zoon is het snelst(e).** *My son is the fastest.* The -e at the end of the superlative is optional.

In front of a noun the basic rules for adding an -e apply to both comparative and superlative. They adopt the article that goes with the noun:

mijn jongere broer	*my younger brother*

2.6.3 Irregular forms

If the adjective ends in an -r, you must insert a -d- in the comparative. This doesn't apply to the superlative.

duur expensive   **duurder** more expensive   **duurst** most expensive

A small number of adjectives do not follow the regular pattern in making comparatives and superlatives. The most important are:

goed good   **beter** better   **best** best
veel much, many   **meer** more   **meest** most
weinig little, few   **minder** less, fewer   **minst** least, fewest

2.6.4 More/Most

Dutch equivalents of the English forms *more* and *most* also exist, but are used much less frequently.

De meest dynamische man   *The most dynamic man*
 die ik ken.   *I know.*

Exercise 20
Complete the chart.

adjective	comparative	superlative
warm		
aardig		
vervelend		
hard		
zacht		

Exercise 2P
Do the same, but adjust the spelling where necessary.

adjective	comparative	superlative
zuur		
creatief		
representatief		
gemeen		
boos		
dik		
idioot		

Exercise 2Q

Write whole sentences comparing these people, using the adjectives given. Write as many different sentences as you can.

zwaar
gespierd
jong
oud
vrolijk
depressief

Henry   Erik

2.7 More on comparisons

This section deals with direct comparisons (X is bigger/smaller than Y) and comparing like with like (X is as big as Y).

2.7.1 Direct comparisons: positive

You can use the word **dan** (*than*) to compare two (groups of) objects, ideas or people directly:

Ik ben slimmer dan mijn zus   *I am smarter than my sister.*

NB Even though strictly speaking only the word **dan** is grammatically correct, language use has changed in recent years and the word **als** is now also widely used. Example:

Amsterdam is groter als   *Amsterdam is bigger than*
  Rotterdam.   *Rotterdam.*

2.7.2 Direct comparisons: negative

If the comparison is negative, e.g. *X is not as old, strong, dirty as Y*, then you can use the following phrases:

Cider is minder duur dan   *Cider is less expensive than*
  champagne.   *champagne.*
Cider is niet zo duur als   *Cider is not as expensive as*
  champagne.   *champagne.*

2.7.3 Comparing like with like

To do this you can use the following patterns: **even ... als** and **net zo ... als**:

Ik ben even belangrijk als jij.   *I am as important as you.*
Ik verdien net zo veel als jij.   *I earn as much as you.*

You can also use **een even... als** and **net zo'n... als**:

Cruijf was een even goede speler als Van Basten.   *Cruijf was as good a player as Van Basten.*

Dynasty was net zo'n slechte serie als Dallas.   *Dynasty was just as bad a series as Dallas.*

NB Zo'n = zo + een.

2.7.4 Other patterns of comparing

▶ **hoe..., hoe...**: **Hoe** langer ik erover nadenk, **hoe** bozer ik word. *The more I think about it, the angrier I get.*

▶ **steeds...**: We worden **steeds** ouder. *We're getting older and older (or increasingly older).*

Exercise 2R
Positive: use the information provided to make positive comparisons.

e.g. ons huis – jullie huis (groot)
Ons huis is groter dan jullie huis.

a zijn fiets – haar fiets (duur)
b mijn hoofdgerecht (*main course*) – mijn voorgerecht (*starter*) (lekker)
c deze foto's van mij – die foto's van jou (mooi)
d mijn voetbalteam – jouw voetbalteam (goed)
e de carrière van Madonna – de carrière van mijn tante Truus (succesvol)

Exercise 2S
Negative: use the information provided to make negative comparisons.

e.g. deze film van Spielberg – zijn vorige film (spannend)
deze film van Spielberg is niet zo spannend als zijn vorige film
deze film van Spielberg is minder spannend dan zijn vorige film

a Amsterdam en Brussel – Londen (groot)
b de verfilming van het boek – het boek zelf (interessant)
c in Nederland wonen mensen – in de Verenigde State (weinig)
d de meeste van mijn collega's – de mensen op jouw werk (vriendelijk)
e de rest van mijn familie – mijn zus en ik (artistiek)

Exercise 2T
Give your own opinion – make sentences using the information provided.

e.g. Queen – goede band – de Rolling Stones
Queen is net zo'n goede band als de Rolling Stones.

a cricket – interessant – American football
b honden – lief – katten
c een Mercedes – comfortabele auto – een Rolls Royce
d pagers – handig – mobieltjes
e New York – dynamische stad – Londen
f een elektronische agenda – praktisch – een filofax

2.8 Plural nouns

The vast majority of nouns in Dutch are made plural in a predictable way, but you need to know which of the three plural forms to use: **-en**, **-s** or **-'s**.

2.8.1 -en

In Dutch you make nouns plural in the majority of cases simply by adding **-en**:

fiets	**fiets**en	*bicycles*
antwoord	**antwoord**en	*answers*

Note that the spelling of the plural form may change. See the spelling rules in Sections 1.4 and 1.5.

muis	muizen	*mice*
droom	dromen	*dreams*
duif	duiven	*doves/pigeons*
kop	koppen	*mugs/heads*

2.8.2 -s

The form -s after a noun also exists and is mainly used after words which end in the letter -el, -em, -en, -er, -je:

parel	parels	*pearls*
jongen	jongens	*boys*
computer	computers	*computers*
muisje	muisjes	*(little) mice*

2.8.3 -'s

The form 's is used after the vowels -a, -i, -o, -u, -y:

collega	collega's	*colleagues*
euro	euro's	*euros*
baby	baby's	*babies*

2.8.4 Irregular forms

There are a few irregular forms which are quite unpredictable:

stad	steden	*cities*
bedrag	bedragen	*amounts*
kind	kinderen	*children*
ei	eieren	*eggs*

2.8.5 Other plural forms

Other plural forms are:

▶ The suffix -heid changes into -heden:

| mogelijkheid | mogelijkheden | *possibilities* |

▶ The Latin suffix **-us** changes into **-i**:

politicus   **politic**i   *politicians*

Exercise 2U
Make the following nouns plural. Change the spelling where necessary.

e.g. brood   broden

a	rol	**h**	straat
b	auto	**i**	ezel
c	kalender	**j**	map
d	manchet	**k**	agenda
e	brief	**l**	kaas
f	kaart	**m**	medicus
g	krant	**n**	schoonheid

Exercise 2V
Make the following plural nouns singular. Change the spelling where necessary.

e.g. potloden   potlood

a	kisten	**h**	tralies
b	zonnevlekken	**i**	hekken
c	ruggen	**j**	muren
d	idioten	**k**	gevangenissen
e	partijen	**l**	eieren
f	Libanezen	**m**	verantwoordelijkheden
g	verliezen	**n**	politici

Exercise 2W
Put the nouns in brackets into the plural. Change the spelling where necessary.

Om 3 uur gisterenmiddag is de Rabobank in Haarlem overvallen door drie gewapende (dief). Er waren op dat moment tien (klant) aanwezig in het bankkantoor. De (overvaller) eisten alle (bankbiljet) en (munt) uit de kluis. In eerste instantie weigerden de (bankbediende) het geld te overhandigen. Daarop trokken de (boef) hun (pistool) en vuurden drie (kogel) door het raam. (Kind) en (baby) begonnen te huilen. Twee van de aanwezige (bankrekeninghouder) waren getrainde (lijfwacht) en overmeesterden de (crimineel). Enkele ogenblikken later arriveerde de politie.

dief *thief*	**overvaller** *attacker, raider*
klant *customer*	**munt** *coin*
bankbiljet *bank note*	**boef** *robber*
bankbediende *bank assistant*	**lijfwacht** *bodyguard*
kogel *bullet*	**bankrekeninghouder** *account holder*

2.9 Compound nouns

Compound nouns are made up of two or more words of which at least one should be a noun. They are written as one word.

2.9.1 Form

Compound nouns are formed by joining two words together. The new word takes the article from the last part of the word:

de bus + het station	= het busstation	the bus station
de telefoon + de gids	= de telefoongids	the telephone directory
het huis + de kamer	= de huiskamer	the living room/ lounge

2.9.2 Adding -s, -e or -en

You sometimes need to add an -s, an -e, or -en between the two nouns.

The rules for this are rather complex and initially you are better off learning the forms as you encounter them. As a rule of thumb you add an -s if you can hear one in the pronunciation. You cannot hear the difference between an -e and an -en, but normally you add -en if the first word has an -en plural form:

schoonheidsbehandeling	*beauty treatment*
liefdesverdriet	*love sickness*
schoenenzaak	*shoeshop* (plural of *schoen* is *schoenen*)
pannenkoek	*pancake* (plural of *pan* is *pannen*)

2.9.3 Adding the stem of a verb before the noun

You can also form a compound word by adding the stem of a verb before the noun:

timmeren	**+ de man**	**= de timmerman**	*carpenter* **(timmeren =** *to hammer***)**
werken	**+ de kamer**	**= de werkkamer**	*workroom*
lezen	**+ de tekst**	**= de leestekst**	*reading text*

2.9.4 Adding other kinds of word

Occasionally you can make a compound noun by adding another kind of word before the noun:

achter	**+ de deur**	**= de achterdeur**	*the backdoor*
linker	**+ de kant**	**= de linkerkant**	*the left side*
bij	**+ de rol**	**= de bijrol**	*the supporting role*

2.9.5 Adjectives or verbs

Compound words can also be made from adjectives or verbs:

donker	**+ rood**	**= donkerrood**	*dark red*
spier	**+ wit**	**= spierwit**	*whiter than white*

Exercise 2X
Write these compound nouns out with the correct article.

e.g. de waren + het huis = het warenhuis (*department store*)
het lichaam + s + de verandering de lichaamsverandering
(*bodily change*)

a de computer + het bedrijf
b de melk + de chocola
c de baby + het gehuil
d het afval + de bak
e het asfalt + de weg
f de tabak + s + de winkel
g het tarief + s + de verhoging
h het verkeer + s + de deskundige
i de president + s + de kandidaat
j het konijn + en + het hok

2.10 Diminutives

Diminutives are words which generally indicate the smallness of
something. In Dutch they end in **-je**.

2.10.1 Basic form

The basic ending for diminutives is **-je**:

huis	**huisje**	*little house*
kind	**kindje**	*little child*
grap	**grapje**	*(little) joke*
schaap	**schaapje**	*(little) sheep (NB not a lamb)*

Note that the spelling rules apply when the plural is used,
e.g. **schapen schaapjes**.

2.10.2 Other endings

For reasons of pronunciation, different endings have developed.
The rules for these are quite complex, but here are some guidelines:

▶ **-tje** after a long vowel and **-l, -r, -n** and after **-el, -en, -er**:

traan *(tear)*	**traantje**	**kerel** *(bloke)*	**kereltje**
schuur *(shed)*	**schuurtje**	**computer**	**computertje**

▶ **-pje** after a long vowel and **-m**:

boom *(tree)*	**boompje**	**kraam** *(stall)*	**kraampje**

▶ **-etje** after a short vowel and **-l, -m, -n, -r, -ng**:

bonbon *(praline)*	**bonbonnetje**	**kom** *(bowl)*	**kommetje**
pil *(pill)*	**pilletje**	**ding** *(thing)*	**dingetje**

▶ **-kje** in some cases after **-ng**:

koning *(king)*	**koninkje**	**beloning** *(reward)*	**beloninkje**

2.10.3 Use

Diminutives are used frequently in Dutch. They can indicate that something is small, but they also often refer to attitude:

▶ to show that you think something is not important:

Dat was een leuk verhaaltje. *That was a nice story.*

▶ as a term of endearment:

Dag kereltje. *Hello, my sweet little boy.*

▶ to show a positive attitude

In het zonnetje met een biertje. *Enjoying the sunshine with a (nice glass of) beer.*

▶ to show a negative attitude or even contempt:

Vreemd zaakje.   *Weird business, that.*
Wat een akelig ventje.   *What a horrible little man.*

NB All diminutives take the article **het**.

Exercise 2Y
Make the following nouns 'smaller' and change the article if needed.

e.g. de pen   het pennetje

a	het brood	**h**	de stroom
b	de label	**i**	de ring
c	het papier	**j**	de woning
d	het boek	**k**	de tafel
e	de wolk	**l**	het idee
f	de snor	**m**	de tong
g	de telefoon	**n**	de bloem

Exercise 2Z
Change the nouns in brackets into diminutives and indicate which of the following functions it fulfils:

  i to make smaller
  ii to show lack of importance
  iii to indicate a positive attitude
  iv as a term of endearment
  v a negative attitude

NB Sometimes there is more than one function.

e.g. Kijk eens naar dat (auto). Kijk eens naar dat autootje
     Function: i to make smaller, v a negative attitude.

  a Dag, (lieverd). Tot vanmiddag.
  b Ik moet mijn (artikel) nog afschrijven.

c Die (studenten) denken altijd dat ze het beter weten.
d Lekker (wijn).
e In mei leggen alle (vogels) een ei.
f Jaap ziet er grappig uit met zijn nieuwe (bril).

Things to remember

▶ There are three articles in Dutch: **de, het** (both meaning *the*) and **een** (*a/an*).

▶ Compound nouns (made up of two or more nouns) are written as one word and take the article of the last noun in the new compound noun.

▶ **Deze** and **dit** are Dutch for *this*; **die** and **dat** are Dutch for *that*.

▶ **Deze** and **die** are used with **de**-words. **Dit** and **dat** are used with **het**-words.

▶ An **-e** is added to adjectives when they precede a noun, except when the noun is an indefinite **het**-word.

▶ Comparatives are formed by adding **-er** to adjectives; superlatives by adding **-st**.

▶ For positive direct comparisons, use **dan: Ik ben slimmer dan mijn zus.** *I am smarter than my sister.*

▶ For negative direct comparisons, use **minder ... dan ...** *less ... than ...*, or **niet zo ... als ...** *not as ... as ...* .

▶ Most Dutch nouns are made plural by adding **-en, -s** or **-'s**.

▶ Diminutives end in **-je** in Dutch.

3

Numbers

3.1 Numbers: one, two, three

Numbers like one, two, three, 25, 99, etc. are called 'cardinal numbers'.

3.1.1 Numbers 0–30

Here are the cardinal numbers in Dutch up to 30.

0 nul				
1 een, één	6 zes	11 elf	16 zestien	21 eenentwintig
2 twee	7 zeven	12 twaalf	17 zeventien	22 tweeëntwintig
3 drie	8 acht	13 dertien	18 achttien	23 drieëntwintig
4 vier	9 negen	14 veertien	19 negentien	24 vierentwintig
5 vijf	10 tien	15 vijftien	20 twintig	25 vijfentwintig
26 zesentwintig		27 zevenentwintig, etc.		30 dertig

▶ The number one is written with two accents éé if it can be confused with the article een (a/an).
▶ In Dutch all numbers are written as one word up to the word **duizend**. **Duizend** is followed by a space, so 12.250 is **twaalfduizend tweehonderdvijftig**.
▶ A **trema** (e.g. ë) is used to indicate the start of a new syllable, so that you know that 22 sounds like 'twee-en-twintig'.
▶ The numbers 11–14 are irregular.

3.1.2 Numbers 31–1.000.000.000

Here are some more cardinal numbers.

31 eenendertig	111 honderdelf
32 tweeëndertig	125 honderdvijfentwintig
40 veertig	200 tweehonderd
50 vijftig	267 tweehonderdzevenenzestig
60 zestig	300 driehonderd
70 zeventig	350 driehonderdvijftig
80 tachtig	400 vierhonderd
90 negentig	1000 duizend
100 honderd	100.000 honderdduizend (een ton)
101 honderdeen	1000.000 een miljoen
102 honderdtwee	1000.000.000 een miljard

▶ The numbers 40 and 80 are irregular.
▶ Numbers over 1000 are usually pronounced in units of 100:
  1250 = **twaalfhonderdvijftig**. When talking about years
  before 2000, you can also leave out the **honderd**: 1968 =
  negentienachtenzestig, but 2003 = **tweeduizend drie**.

Exercise 3A
Write out these sums in full as you would say them.

> + plus   – min   × keer   ÷ gedeeld door   = is

a $2 + 6 = ?$
b $46 - 13 = ?$
c $99 + 23 = ?$
d $7 \times 8 = ?$

e $42 \div 7 = ?$
f $72 \div 8 = ?$
g $12 \times 5 = ?$
h $88 - 12 = ?$

Exercise 3B
You are checking the contents of the kitchen in the hotel where
you're working. Write the list in full.

a _____ kopjes   (101)
b _____ ontbijtbordjes   (75)

c	_____ grote borden	(82)
d	_____ kommen	(96)
e	_____ messen	(365)
f	_____ vorken	(238)
g	_____ lepels	(418)

Exercise 3C

The graph shows how much an average three-bedroom house costs per region or city. Write out in full the average price for each town or area.

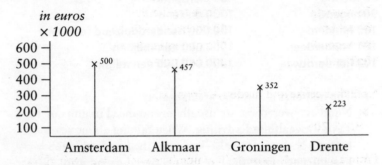

in euros
× 1000

Exercise 3D

How much is this? Write out in numbers.

a drie ton
b acht miljard
c zesenvijftig miljoen
d negenduizend achthonderdachtenzestig
e zevenentwintighonderdvijfentwintig

3.2 Numbers: first, second, third

Numbers like **eerste** (first), **tweede** (second), **derde** (third), **vijfentwintigste** (twenty-fifth) are called 'ordinal numbers'.

3.2.1 Ordinal numbers

Ordinal numbers in Dutch are formed by adding **-de** or **-ste** to the cardinal numbers. When you write these in numbers you add **-e**:

1e eerste	**11e elfde**
2e tweede	**12e twaalfde**
3e derde	**13e dertiende**
4e vierde	**14e veertiende**
5e vijfde	**15e vijftiende**
6e zesde	**16e zestiende**
7e zevende	**17e zeventiende**
8e achtste	**18e achttiende**
9e negende	**19e negentiende**
10e tiende	**20e twintigste**

Note that **eerste** and **derde** are irregular.

3.2.2 20+

From 20 onwards most ordinal numbers end in **-ste**. Only those ending with a number under 19 (apart from 1 or 8) end in **-de**:

21e	**eenentwintigste**
26e	**zesentwintigste**
33e	**drieëndertigste**
57e	**zevenenvijftigste**
100e	**honderdste**
103e	**honderd(en)derde**
117e	**honderd(en)zeventiende**
136e	**honderd(en)zesendertigste**
548e	**vijfhonderd(en)achtenveertigste**
1000e	**duizendste**
1000.000e	**miljoenste**

3.2.3 Dates

You can use ordinal numbers in Dutch to indicate dates, but mainly when you are using the number without indicating the month. When you do mention the month, you normally use the cardinal number. Compare:

Ik ben op twaalf januari jarig. *My birthday is on the twelfth of January.*

Joop komt op de vijftiende. *Joop is coming on the fifteenth.*

Exercise 3E
Write these numbers out in Dutch.

e.g. *4th* **vierde**

a   2nd
b   5th
c   12th
d   13th
e   219th
f   89th
g   53rd

Exercise 3F
Write these numbers out as you would say them in Dutch.

a   De (1st) baby die dit jaar is geboren.
b   Hij heeft de (3rd) prijs gewonnen.
c   Karel de Grote is in de (8th) eeuw geboren.
d   De (millionth) bezoeker van de tentoonstelling kreeg een vrijkaartje.
e   Ik zeg het nu voor de (152th) keer.
f   Het is morgen zijn (22nd) verjaardag.
g   Pas op voor de (53th) traptrede.

Exercise 3G
Write out these dates in Dutch.

a   Vandaag is het de (15th).
b   Remi is geboren op de (23rd).
c   Kim is jarig op de (17th) van de maand.
d   Ik moet dit afhebben op de (31st).

Exercise 3H
Ordinal or not? Write the numbers between brackets out as an
ordinal or cardinal number as appropriate.

  a Klaas is jarig op (11) december.
  b Mijn ouders komen op de (14).
  c De nieuwe brug wordt (15) augustus geopend.
  d De koningin is jarig op (31) januari.
  e Maar haar verjaardag wordt op (30) april gevierd.
  f De scholen in het noorden beginnen weer op de (6).

3.3 Numbers: 1/2, 7°, 15%

In daily activities you will come across the use of numbers in
mathematical terms, such as fractions, decimals and percentages.
This generally corresponds with the English use of numbers, apart
from the use of points and commas.

3.3.1 Commas, points

▶ In Dutch decimals you use commas instead of decimal points.
In speaking you say the comma out loud:

  2,3 twee komma drie   *2.3 two point three.*

NB The expression **nul komma nul** means *nothing at all.*

▶ Decimal points are used in Dutch instead of commas to
indicate multiples of thousands:

  6.900.000   *6,900,000*

3.3.2 Fractions

Here are some examples:
1/2 **een half / halve**
1/4 **een vierde / een kwart**

3/4 drie vierde / drie kwart
1/3 een derde
2/3 twee derde
5/8 vijf achtste

But note the following:

▶ 1½ = **anderhalf.**
▶ If ½ is used as an adjective, and if you need to add an -e
   (see Section 2.3), then **half** changes into **halve.**

3.3.3 Percentages, degrees

3% **drie procent.**

Because temperatures are always measured in centigrade you don't
have to add the letter C: 27° **zevenentwintig graden.**

If the temperature is close to zero you can add the phrase **boven nul:**

2° **twee graden boven nul** (*above zero*).

If the temperature is below zero, you can say:

−2° **twee graden onder nul** or **min twee.**

Exercise 3I
Write these fractions as you would say them. If there are two
possibilities write them both down.

e.g. 0,25   nul komma vijfentwintig

   a 0,13
   b 6,22
   c 32,05
   d 0,0
   e 3/4
   f 5/6
   g 2/3

Exercise 3J
Change these English numbers as you would write them in Dutch.

e.g. 6.3   6,3

a 1,900   **e** 0.4
b 200,000   **f** 1.13
c 3,825   **g** 8.17
d 2,670,000

Exercise 3K
What's the temperature? Write sentences about the temperatures in the chart. If there is more than one possibility, write both options.

Amsterdam	5°
Londen	9°
Athene	19°
Bonn	1°
Moskou	−8°

Exercise 3L
Where are they going to? Use the graph to write sentences in Dutch about the holiday destinations of the Dutch last year.

NB If the subject of the sentence is a percentage you use the singular form of the verb, unlike in English.

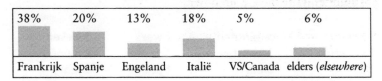

38%	20%	13%	18%	5%	6%
Frankrijk	Spanje	Engeland	Italië	VS/Canada	elders (*elsewhere*)

e.g. Vorig jaar ging achtendertig procent van de Nederlanders naar Frankrijk.

3.4 Weights, measurements, time

3.4.1 Weights

1 gram
1 ons (100 gram)
1 pond (1/2 kilo, 500 gram)
1 kilo (twee pond, 1000 gram)
2 liter

You don't normally use the plural forms of these weights.

You don't use the word *of* in Dutch:

| **twee pond kaas** | *two pounds of cheese* |
| **twee liter melk** | *two litres of milk* |

3.4.2 Measures

1 mm	**een millimeter**
9 cm	**negen centimeter**
5 m	**vijf meter**
3 m²	**drie vierkante meter**
100 km	**100 kilometer**

You don't normally use the plural forms of these measurements.

3.4.3 Time

1 minuut	5 minuten	1 week	3 weken
1 kwartier	3 kwartier	1 maand	2 maanden
1 uur	6 uur	1 jaar	5 jaar
een half uur			

You don't normally use the plural forms of **kwartier, uur** and **jaar**.

3.4.4 Expressions of time

There are various expressions related to time *e.g.* zoveelste, hoeveelste, laatste. There is no direct equivalent of the words zoveelste and hoeveelste in English.

De hoeveelste is het vandaag?	*What is the date today?*
Ik doe dit nu voor de zoveelste keer.	*I am doing this for the umpteenth time.*

3.4.5 Approximations

een maand of twee	*a month or two.*
een minuut of vijf	*a minute or five*
Hij loopt tegen de 50.	*He is close to 50.*
Het is rond de 20 euro.	*It's about 20 euros.*
Het is ongeveer 15 euro.	*It's about 15 euros.*

Exercise 3M
How much do the following weigh? Write sentences in Dutch. Give alternative ways of saying it, if appropriate.

e.g. Het potje pindakaas weegt 250 gram.
Het potje pindakaas weegt een half pond.

de bananen	de kaneel	de drop	het stuk kaas
300 g	35 g	100 g	750 g

Exercise 3N
Ask for the following in Dutch.

e.g. *30 g of curry powder* (**kerriepoeder**)
Dertig gram kerriepoeder

a *200 grams of ham* (ham)
b *500 grams of sugar* (suiker)
c *1 1/2 kilos of cheese* (kaas)
d *250 grams of biscuits* (koekjes)
e *3 litres of milk* (melk)

Exercise 3O
Answer the following questions in Dutch using the information
between brackets. Sometimes there is more than one option.

Note the use of the Dutch preposition **over** where in English *in*
is used.

e.g. **Wanneer ben je klaar?** (in about three quarters of an hour)
Over een kwartier of drie.

a Wanneer kom je? (*in about 5 minutes*)
b Wanneer heb je dat af? (*in about 2 hours*)
c Wanneer heb je vakantie? (*in about 3 weeks*)
d Wanneer moet je je werkstuk inleveren? (*in about 2 months*)
e Hoe oud is zij? (*she is close to 40*)
f Hoeveel kost die lamp? (*it is about 35 euros*)

Exercise 3P
Write these measures out as you would say them.

e.g. 3 mm   drie millimeter

a 1 m
b 1 m²
c 50 km
d 1 l
e 7 cm

Things to remember

▶ A trema (e.g. ë) is used to indicate the start of a new syllable.

▶ Ordinal numbes in Dutch are formed by adding **-de** or **-ste** to the cardinal numbers.

▶ In Dutch decimals you use commas instead of decimal points (2,3).

▶ Decimal points are used in Dutch instead of commas to indicate multiples of thousand (50.000).

▶ You don't normally use the plural forms of weights and measures (**2 liter melk** 2 *litres of milk*).

4

Pronouns

4.1 Personal pronouns

Personal pronouns are words like *I*, *you*, *they*; *me*, *it*, *us*, etc.

4.1.1 Function

▶ **Subject pronouns** are used as the subject of the sentence, which means that the person(s) to whom the subject pronoun refers is/are performing the action: **ik voetbal, hij voetbalt**. The verb changes its form depending on the subject pronoun used.

▶ **Object pronouns** function as the object in the sentence, which means that the person(s) to whom the object pronoun refers is/are not performing the action which is expressed in the verb: **ik hou van hem, maar hij houdt niet van mij.**

4.1.2 Form

	Subject pronouns			Object pronouns		
singular	**ik**	**('k)**	*I*	**mij**	**(me)**	*me*
	jij	**(je)**	*you (inform.)*	**jou**	**(je)**	*you (inf.)*
	u	**–**	*you (form.)*	**u**	**–**	*you (form.)*
	hij	**(ie)**	*he*	**hem**	**('m)**	*him*

	Subject pronouns			Object pronouns		
	zij	(ze)	she	haar	(d'r)	her
	het	('t)	it	het	('t)	it
plural	wij	(we)	we	ons	–	us
	jullie	–	you (inform.)	jullie	–	you (inf.)
	u	–	you (form.)	u	–	you (form.)
	zij	(ze)	they	hen/hun* (ze)		them

The pronouns given in brackets are the unstressed versions. Not all pronouns have an unstressed version.

*In everyday Dutch **hen** and **hun** are interchangeable.

4.1.3 Use

In speech you can use both stressed and unstressed forms, although people use the unstressed version more frequently. In writing, you mainly use the stressed form, although the forms **je, ze, we** and **me** are also frequently used. You *must* use the full form when:

▶ you want to stress the pronoun or emphasize a contrast:

Ik ga niet naar Amsterdam,   *I am not going to Amsterdam,*
  hij gaat.   *he is.*

▶ the pronoun is used on its own, i.e. without a verb:

Jij hebt het gedaan. Wie, ik?   *You have done it. Who, me?*
  Ja, jij.   *Yes, you.*

Exercise 4A
Fill in the correct full and stressed subject pronoun. (The English is given in brackets.)

a __ ben tandarts. Wat voor werk doe __?   (I, you)
b __ gaan vanavond naar het Nationaal Ballet.   (we)

c	__ gaan zeker niet mee?	(you plural)
d	__ komt elke dag laat thuis.	(he)
e	__ zitten altijd te roddelen (to gossip).	(they)
f	__ is verliefd op Jan.	(she)
g	Wilt __ nog een kopje koffie?	(you formal)
h	__ is nog vroeg.	(it)

Exercise 4B

Fill in the correct subject pronoun, using the stressed and full form only when needed.

a	Gaat __ op vakantie dit jaar?	(you formal)
b	Nee, __ blijven lekker thuis.	(we)
c	Kunnen __ vanavond eten klaar maken?	(you plural)
d	Begrijp __ wat dat betekent? __ begrijp het niet.	(you, I)
e	__ heeft alweer haar huiswerk niet gemaakt.	(she)
f	__ hebben nog niet betaald.	(they)
g	__ moet niet zo boos worden.	(you)

Exercise 4C

Fill in the correct object pronoun, using the stressed form only when needed.

a	Kom je met __ mee?	(us)
b	Kan jij die brief aan __ geven? Aan wie? Aan __?	(them, them)
c	Hoe vaak schrijf je __?	(him)
d	Geef __ maar een wit wijntje.	(me)
e	Ik bel __ morgen op.	(you formal)
f	Geloof je __? Nee, ik geloof __.	(him, her)
g	Je houdt niet meer van __.	(me)
h	Ik geef __ nog een kans.	(you plural)
i	Ga zitten. Ik zet koffie voor __.	(you)

Insight

The difference between the stressed and unstressed forms of pronouns in Dutch may be difficult to understand since English doesn't have these different forms. However, although English doesn't have different written forms for stressed and unstressed pronouns, when speaking, you can clearly hear the difference. Listen to the way you change your pronounciation of the pronoun *she* when reading aloud the following phrases. 1. *She is going out.* 2. *He is staying at home, but she is going out.* In the second sentence, you will hear your voice go up and become louder on the pronoun *she*, in order to give the word more stress. In Dutch this is done by using the stressed form of the pronoun, **zij**. 1. **Ze gaat uit** *She's going out.* 2. **Hij blijft thuis, maar zij gaat uit.** *He is staying at home, but she is going out.*

4.1.4 Addressing people

▶ **Informal:** The pronouns **je** and **jij** are informal and used when speaking to people with whom you are on a first name basis, e.g. children, young people, relatives, friends, acquaintances, colleagues.

▶ **Formal:** The pronoun **u** is the polite form of addressing people with whom you are not on a first name basis, e.g. people you don't know, such as shop assistants (unless very young) and people to whom you wish to show respect or social distance, such as your boss.

4.1.5 Referring to things (singular)

In English when you refer to an object or an idea you use the pronoun it. In Dutch you use either **het** or **hij**. Which one you use depends on the gender of the noun you are referring to:

	subject pronoun	object pronoun
a **het**-word	het	het
a **de**-word	hij	hem

Wat vind je van het boek?	*What do you think about the book?*
Het is spannend.	*It is exciting.*
Waar is de tv gids?	*Where is the tv guide?*
Hij ligt daar.	*It is there.*

Heb je het boek gelezen?	*Have you read the book?*
Ja, ik heb het gelezen.	*Yes, I have read it.*
Heb je de trein gehaald?	*Did you (manage to) catch the train?*
Nee, ik heb hem gemist.	*No, I missed it.*

4.1.6 Referring to things (plural)

In Dutch you use the pronoun **ze** to refer to things or ideas both as a subject and as an object pronoun (in English *they* and *them*, respectively).

Ze zijn niet lekker.	*They are not nice.*
(de chocolaatjes)	*(the chocolates)*
Heb je ze verstuurd?	*Did you send them?*
(de brieven)	*(the letters)*

4.1.7 Die

The demonstrative pronoun **die** is frequently used as an alternative to refer to **de**-words instead of **hij** (singular) and **ze** (plural).

Staat de koffie klaar?	*Is the coffee ready?*
Ja, die staat klaar.	*Yes, it is ready.*
Heb je de brieven vestuurd?	*Did you send the letters?*
Ja, die heb ik verstuurd.	*Yes, I've sent them.*

Exercise 4D
Fill in the appropriate subject pronoun *je/jij* or *u*.

a Jan, kom __ morgen ook? (to a friend or acquaintance)
b Weet __ misschien hoe laat het is? (to an adult you see in the street)
c Kun __ dit even voor me doen? (to a colleague)
d Kunt __ me helpen? (a child to an adult)
e Heeft __ deze een maat groter? (to a shop assistant)

Exercise 4E
Fill in the appropriate subject or object pronoun *hij, hem, het* or *ze*.

a Hoe duur zijn de appels? __ zijn 2 euro per kilo.

b Ben je blij met de nieuwe computer? Nee, __ werkt niet goed.

c Wanneer zijn de foto's klaar? __ zijn morgen al klaar.

d Hoe laat vertrekt de trein? __ vertrekt om negen uur precies.

e De wasmachine werkt niet goed. Is __ alweer kapot?

f Waar is het lijstje met adressen? __ zit in je agenda.

g Heb je de artikels gelezen? Ja, ik heb __ gisteren gelezen.

h Zet jij de afvalbak buiten? Ja, ik zal __ straks buiten zetten.

Exercise 4F
Fill in the pronoun, using *die* where appropriate.

a Waar staat de Martinitoren? __ staat in Groningen.

b Heb je de wijn geproefd? Ja, __ heb ik geproefd.

c Is het museum's zondags open? Nee, __ is 's zondags gesloten.

d Passen de schoenen je nog? Ja, __ passen me nog.

e Waarom koop je de broek niet? __ is te duur.

f Wil je het bandje nog een keer keer horen? Ja, ik wil __ nog een horen?

g Heb je Rembrandts zelfportretten niet gezien. Nee, __ heb ik nog al gezien?

4.2 Possession

Possessive pronouns indicate ownership and work the same way in Dutch as in English, *my*, *your*, *his*, etc.

4.2.1 Form

The possessive pronouns in Dutch look like this:

	Stressed		*Unstressed*
singular	mijn	(m'n)	*my*
	jouw	je	*your* (informal)
	uw	–	*your* (formal)
	zijn	(z'n)	*his*
	haar	(d'r)	*her*
plural	ons/onze	–	*our*
	jullie	je	*your* (informal)
	uw	–	*your* (formal)
	hun	–	*their*

4.2.2 Use

The stressed forms of the possessive pronouns are generally used in writing, and in speech to indicate contrast, for example:

Het is niet jouw CD maar   *It isn't your CD but her CD.*
haar CD.

The unstressed forms are more commonly used in speech. The unstressed forms in brackets are usually considered too informal to use in writing.

Ons is used before **het**-words and **onze** is used before **de**-words:

Dit is ons huis en onze auto.   *This is our house and our car.*

4.2.3 Other forms

Comparable to the English 's, you can also use a simple -s in Dutch. You don't use an apostrophe in Dutch, except where the additional s would alter pronunciation (see Sections 1.4 and 1.5)

Dit is Johns hond.	*This is John's dog.*
Het zijn Marina's kinderen.	*They are Marina's children.*

However, it is much more common in Dutch to express possession with the word **van**:

Is dit boek van David?	*Is this David's book?*
Dat is een vriendin van ons.	*That's a friend of ours.*

English *mine*, *yours*, etc. is usually: **die/dat + van +** object pronoun (for object pronouns, see Section 4.1). **Die** is used to refer to **de**-words, and **dat** to **het**-words.

Is dit mijn boek of dat van jou?	*Is this my book or yours?*
Zijn auto is rood, die van	*His car is red, hers is*
haar is zwart.	*black.*

Exercise 4G
Fill in the correct possessive pronoun.

a	*your*	Ik denk dat dit ___ boek is.
b	*his*	Heb je gezien dat Harry ___ haar heeft geverfd?
c	*our*	Dit is ___ eigen huis.
d	*her*	Hoe laat gaat Linda 's ochtends naar ___ werk?
e	*your* (plural)	Geef ___ jassen maar, ik hang ze wel op.
f	*their*	Theo en Marion kunnen ___ sleutels niet meer vinden.
g	*my*	Weet je waar ___ paspoort is?
h	*our*	Ik heb geen idee waar we ___ auto hebben geparkeerd.
i	*his*	De buurman wandelt elke ochtend en avond met ___ hond.

Exercise 4H
Follow the instructions.

e.g. Ask if this is Ans' car.
Is dit de auto van Ans? or: Is deze auto van Ans?

a Ask if this is David's diary (de agenda).
b Answer that it is Erwin's diary.
c Ask whether we're going in Esther's car.
d Answer that we are going in Esther's car.
e Say that you're driving your parents' car.
f Say that your brother's computer cost 1500 euros.
g Ask whether Josje's father is coming too.
h Answer that only Josje's mother is coming.

Exercise 4I
Complete these sentences in Dutch using *die/dat* + *van* + object pronoun.

a Mijn mobieltje ligt hier, waar is (*yours* – singular/informal)?
b Gaan we met jouw auto of (*mine*)?
c De buren willen onze fax gebruiken want (*theirs*) doet het niet.
d Mijn bril was 150 euro, maar Marloes zegt dat (*hers*) goedkoper was.
e Welk horloge vind je mooier, (*his*) or (*mine*)?

Things to remember

▶ Subject pronouns are used as the subject of the sentence.

▶ Object pronouns function as the object in the sentence.

▶ In speech, people mostly use the unstressed versions of pronouns.

▶ In writing, you mainly use the stressed forms of pronouns.

▶ The pronouns **je** and **jij** are informal and used when speaking to people with whom you are on a first name basis.

▶ The pronoun **u** is the polite form of addressing people with whom you are not on a first name basis.

▶ In Dutch you use **het** to refer back to **het**-words and **hij** to refer back to **de**-words.

▶ Possession is most commonly expressed in Dutch with **van**: **Het boek van David** *David's book.*

5

Verbs (1) – introduction and present tense

5.1 Basic information on verbs

This unit takes a look at verbs in general: how you can recognize them, where you can find them and what they do.

5.1.1 What's a verb?

Verbs are 'do'-words and often describe an action or activity: **rennen**, *to run*, **schrijven**, *to write*, **denken**, *to think*.

Some verbs don't describe an action or activity as such, but are combined with other verbs for different purposes. Examples are auxiliaries and modal verbs (see Sections 5.1–5.2 and 6.1–6.2).

5.1.2 What do verbs look like?

The basic form of the verb is called the *infinitive*. This form of the verb is usually easy to recognize in Dutch since most infinitives end in -en (in English the infinitive is the form of the verb preceded by the word 'to'). Here are some examples:

werken	*to work*
slapen	*to sleep*
winnen	*to win*

However, verbs also change their form. Most of the forms a verb can take are based on the stem of the verb. The stem can be found by taking -en from the infinitive. Remember that the spelling rules apply (see Sections 1.4 and 1.5), so vowels may be doubled or consonants taken away. For example:

infinitive	werken	kijken	slapen	winnen
	to work	*to look*	*to sleep*	*to win*
stem	werk	kijk	slaap	win

Different endings can be added to the stem of the verb in different circumstances. In the present tense, -t or -en can be added to the stem (see Section 5.2), and in the imperfect -te(n) or -de(n) (see Section 7.6), and for the past participle you add **ge-** to the beginning and a **t** or a **d** to the end (see Section 7.2).

5.1.3 Which form?

As you have seen, verbs can take different forms. Which form you need depends on the tense and subject of the sentence (who or what you're talking about). For **ik** in the present tense, for instance, you simply need the stem of the verb, but for **jij**, **hij** and **zij** you add a -t, and in the imperfect you add either -te or -de for all of these. The rules for the various verb forms are explained under each tense individually.

There are also irregular verbs which don't follow these rules (**gaan**, to go, for instance, or **zijn**, *to be*) and have unusual looking forms (**ging**, *went*, for instance, or **bent**, *are*). For more irregular verbs, see Section 19.5.

Exercise 5A
Underline the verbs in the following two texts. The second text is quite a difficult one on purpose – it'll be good practice to work on a text which you don't understand completely.

1 Nederland en België
   Er wonen in Nederland ongeveer 15 miljoen mensen. België, ten zuiden van Nederland, heeft zo'n 10 miljoen inwoners.

Aan het begin van de negentiende eeuw hoorden zowel het noorden (nu Nederland) als het zuiden (nu België) bij het Koninkrijk der Nederlanden, dat na de val van Napoleon was gevormd. In 1830 scheidde het zuiden zich af en werd de staat België gevormd. In het noorden van België, Vlaanderen, woont iets meer dan de helft van alle Belgen en spreekt men Nederlands.

2 Het Klimaat

Klimaatverandering kan voor het leven op aarde verstrekkende gevolgen hebben. Zo leidde een daling van de temperatuur met enkele graden tijdens de ijstijden ertoe dat grote gebieden voor bepaalde planten en diersoorten totaal onleefbaar werden – waardoor bijvoorbeeld de mammoet gedoemd was uit te sterven. De klimaatverandering tijdens de ijstijden had natuurlijke oorzaken, waarbij veranderingen in de baan van de aarde rond de zon een belangrijke rol speelden. Nu is het de mens die het klimaat op aarde verandert.

Source: Klimaatverandering, Dutch Ministry of VROM
(Housing, Planning and the Environment) brochure

Exercise 5B

Once you've checked your answers to Exercise 5A, have another look at both texts, and try to establish which verb goes with which subject (and whether this subject is singular or plural). Don't worry if you find this exercise difficult. You might want to try it again at a later stage in your studies.

5.1.4 Main function

One of the main functions of a verb, apart from describing an action, is to give an indication of tense – to indicate whether you are talking about the past, present or future. Usually only the first verb in a sentence adapts its form to indicate tense; this verb is called the finite verb. For the other verbs you don't indicate tense; you either use the whole verb (the infinitive) or a past participle.

Marie wilde het niet nu bespreken.   *Marie didn't want to discuss it now.*

5.1.5 Combination verbs

Some verbs can be combined with other verbs with different effect:

▶ Modal verbs like **willen** (*to want*), **moeten** (*must/have to*) and **kunnen** (*can/be able*) add meaning to a sentence to indicate that you want to do something, or you have to do something, for instance. Modal verbs are discussed in Sections 6.1 and 6.2:

Jantien wil een huis kopen.	*Jantien wants to buy a house.*
Hij moet de huur betalen.	*He has to pay the rent.*

▶ The verbs **hebben** (*to have*) and **zijn** (*to be*) can be used as auxiliary verbs together with other verbs to form the perfect tenses.

Jan-Peter heeft een huis gekocht.	*Jan-Peter has bought a house.*
De buren zijn in Egypte geweest.	*The neighbours have been to Egypt.*

5.1.6 Where can I find them?

Practically all sentences contain a verb. The finite verb in a Dutch sentence is put in second position (the second 'item' in the sentence) and all the other verbs are put at the end of the sentence. Note that you'll find a verb at the very beginning of some questions, and that word order changes in sub-clauses (see Section 15.1–15.6).

Ik *voetbal* **elke dag.**	*I play football every day.*
Ik *moet* **elke dag** *werken.*	*I have to work every day.*
Ga **jij morgen naar het feest?**	*Are you going to the party tomorrow?*

The first position can be taken by a group of words:

John en Ans *zijn* **er nog niet.**	*John and Ans aren't there yet.*

And verb(s) in the final position can be followed, for instance, by word groups starting with a preposition (see Section 17.3).

We *gaan* **morgen met Jonas** *zwemmen* **in het nieuwe zwembad.**	*We're going swimming with Jonas tomorrow in the new swimming pool.*

Exercise 5C

In the following sentences, indicate which is/are the finite verb(s).

a Ik ben nog nooit in Rome geweest.
b Mogen wij de rekening hebben?
c Wanneer viert Remco zijn verjaardag?
d Ik weet niet hoe hij heet.
e Marijke had nooit gedacht dat ze die baan zou krijgen.
f Moet ik elke avond de afwas doen?
g Die brief is verstuurd op de vierentwintigste.
h Zonder make-up zul je mij niet op straat zien lopen!
i Ik heb die oude LP's weggegooid omdat je toch geen platenspeler meer hebt.
j Ondanks deze slechte resultaten moeten we toch positief aan de toekomst werken.

Exercise 5D

Indicate whether the underlined verbs are in second or in final position and explain why they are in this position, choosing from the following options:

1 It's a past participle in final position.
2 It's an infinitive in final position.
3 It's the finite verb moved to the end of a sub-clause.
4 It's the finite verb in a main clause.

a Deze poster <u>heb</u> ik van een vriend gekregen.
b Waar heb ik de afstandsbediening van de TV <u>gelegd</u>?
c Peter zei dat hij deze week vrij <u>had</u>.
d Al mijn collega's op mijn afdeling zijn gisteravond uit eten <u>geweest</u>.

e Jeannette wil eigenlijk liever een kleurenprinter <u>kopen</u>.
f Als ik mijn bonus <u>krijg</u>, ga ik direct een nieuwe stereo kopen.
g Wil je eerst iets drinken of <u>zullen</u> we meteen aan tafel gaan?
h Zulke taal <u>wil</u> ik nooit meer horen!

Insight

One of the most important rules of Dutch grammar is that the finite verb is usually put in second position in the sentence. Try to make adhering to this rule a priority when forming sentences, and you're halfway there. Note that any other verbs besides the finite verb are all moved to the end of the sentence, and that there are a few exceptions to the general rule: In questions without a question word, the sentence starts with the finite verb: **Ga je vroeg naar huis?** *Are you going home early?* And in subclauses all verbs, including the finite verb, are moved to the end of the clause: **Omdat ik te hard heb gelopen, ...** *Because I walked too fast, ...* (Note that this subclause takes up the first position of a longer sentence, which has to have its finite verb in second position right after the subclause: **Omdat ik te hard heb gelopen, ben ik nu moe.** *Because I walked too fast, now I'm tired.*)

5.2 Present tense

This section gives the basic rules for forming the present tense for regular verbs.

5.2.1 General

As in English, the endings of verbs change depending on the subject. With *regular verbs*, the rules for this are simple and easy to learn, but you must understand the concepts of *infinitive* and *stem*.

5.2.2 Infinitive

The infinitive is the full form of the verb and in Dutch generally ends in -**en**: **geven** (*to give*), **drinken** (*to drink*), **typen** (*to type*) etc.

5.2.3 Stem

The stem is generally formed by taking off the **-en** of the infinitive.

infinitive   *stem*
werken *to work*   **werk**

Don't forget to apply the spelling rules when forming the stem:

spelen *to play*	→	**speel**
stoppen *to stop*	→	**stop**
schrijven *to write*	→	**schrijf**
genezen *to cure*	→	**genees**

5.2.4 Form

The present tense is formed by adding **-t** or **-en** to the stem:

subject	*verb*	*inversion*
ik	**werk**	
jij/je	**werkt**	**werk jij?**
u	**werkt**	
hij/zij/het	**werkt**	
wij/we	**werken**	
jullie	**werken**	
zij	**werken**	

5.2.5 Inversion

Inversion means reversing the place of the verb and the subject. This happens for instance when asking a question:

Woont Lex in Utrecht?   *Does Lex live in Utrecht?*

It is important to remember that in the present tense you drop the **-t** at the end of the verb when **je** or **jij** come after the verb. This happens only with **je** and **jij** and applies to all verbs:

Jij drinkt veel.   *You are drinking a lot.*
Drink jij wijn?   *Do you drink wine?*

Exercise 5E
Find the stem of the verbs below.

a	helpen	**e**	tuinieren
b	wandelen	**f**	ontbijten
c	fietsen	**g**	vergaderen
d	schilderen	**h**	roddelen

Exercise 5F
As above, but note that you need to apply the spelling rules.

a	nemen	**g**	zwemmen
b	lopen	**h**	stappen
c	koken	**i**	lezen
d	maken	**j**	reizen
e	studeren	**k**	geloven
f	slapen	**l**	blijven

Exercise 5G
Fill in the correct form of the verb between brackets.

a Ik ___ altijd lekker. (slapen)
b Jannie ___ nu samen met Bas. (wonen)
c Wim ___ morgen een dagje thuis. (blijven)
d Ineke ___ met roken (stoppen)
e Het ___ minstens 10 graden. (vriezen)
f Jullie ___ zeker ook? (komen)
g Ik ___ altijd in de keuken. (ontbijten)

Exercise 5H
Fill in the correct form of the verb in brackets, taking note of inversion.

a Ik help Karin vandaag met haar huiswerk. ___ jij haar morgen? (helpen)
b Geert verdient veel geld. ___ jij net zo veel? (verdienen)

c Goed, Hans neemt een wijntje. En jij? ___ jij een biertje? (nemen)
d Jij ___ weinig fouten in je Nederlands. (maken)
e ___ je je andere talen net zo goed? (spreken)
f Jij ___ veel, hè? (lezen)
g Ik ga zo weg. ___ jij nog even? (blijven)
h Jij ___ hem toch niet, hè? (geloven)

5.2.6 Irregular forms

Some verbs in Dutch do not follow the regular pattern set out in
the previous section. There are no clear rules about how these
irregular verbs change their form, so you have to learn them by
heart. The most common and important ones are **hebben,** *to have*
and **zijn,** *to be.*

	hebben	*zijn*
ik	heb	ben
jij	hebt	bent
u	heeft/hebt*	bent
hij/zij/het	heeft	is
wij	hebben	zijn
jullie	hebben	zijn
u	heeft/hebt	bent
zij	hebben	zijn

*__Heeft__ is the formal version to go with **u**. Increasingly the form **hebt** is used. This applies
to both singular and plural forms of **u**.

5.2.7 Komen, doen, gaan

These verbs are also irregular:

	komen (to come)	*doen (to do)*	*gaan (to go)*
ik	kom	doe	ga
jij/je	komt	doet	gaat
u	komt	doet	gaat

	komen (to come)	doen (to do)	gaan (to go)
hij/zij/het	komt	doet	gaat
wij	komen	doen	gaan
jullie	komen	doen	gaan
u	komt	doet	gaat
zij	komen	doen	gaan

5.2.8 Modal verbs

Some modal verbs also have irregular forms. See Section 6.1 for the full list.

Exercise 5I
Wat hebben ze? *What have they got?* **Fill in the correct form of the verb *hebben*.**

  a Jaapje ___ de waterpokken.
  b Sieme ___ een computer.
  c Ik ___ een vriendje.
  d ___ jij een auto?
  e Wij ___ een feestje vanavond.
  f Zijn ouders ___ veel geld.
  g Jij ___ een naaimachine, hè?

> de waterpokken *chicken pox*   naaimachine *sewing machine*

Exercise 5J
Wat zijn ze? *What are they?* **Fill in the correct form of the verb *zijn*.**

  a Marieke ___ blij.
  b Jij ___ mooi slank.
  c Wij ___ goede vrienden.
  d Het ___ een goed idee.
  e Ik ___ bij Louise thuis.
  f Jullie ___ erg vervelend.
  g ___ jij tevreden?

Exercise 5K
Complete each sentence with an appropriate verb from the box.

gaat	komen	doet
doe	komt	kom
ga	doen	gaan

a Robert ___ de huishouding.
b Petra ___ vanmiddag naar haar werk.
c Ik ___ de boodschappen.
d Jij ___ toch ook, hè?
e Nee, maar Sandra en Hugo ___ wel.
f Jullie ___ veel dingen in de vakantie, zeg.
g Ik ___ morgen even langs.
h Wij ___ dit jaar naar de Pyreneeën.
i Leuk hoor. Ik ___ naar Peru.

5.3 Present tense – use

5.3.1 Here and now

As you would expect, the Dutch use the present tense to talk about the here and now:

Ik schrijf een brief.   *I am writing a letter.*

5.3.2 Future

People very frequently use the present tense in Dutch to talk about the future:

Ik werk morgen in Haarlem.   *I am working in Haarlem tomorrow.*

The effect is more snappy than using the future tense with the verb **zullen**.

5.3.3 Past

Occasionally, as in English, the present tense is used when talking about past events. This is used particularly to liven up an account:

Ze grijpen hem en sleuren hem　*They grab him and drag him*
van zijn fiets.　*from his bike.*

5.3.4 Past and present

An important difference with English is that you use the present tense in Dutch when you talk about a certain time period which started in the past and continues in the present. In English you use the perfect tense in those situations.

Ik woon hier al tien jaar.　*I have been living here for ten*
　years already.
Ik werk hier pas 3 weken.　*I have been working here for only*
　three weeks.

If you mention *the time period* specifically, you must use **al** or **pas** or another adverb indicating time, such as **sinds,** or **nu:**

Ik kom nu twee jaar op deze　*I have been coming to this*
camping.　*campsite for two years now.*
Ik ben al 3 weken ziek.　*I have been ill for three weeks.*

Note that **al** and **pas** are not neutral and in this context indicate the attitude of the speaker:

al = the speaker thinks it has been a long time.
pas = the speaker thinks it has been a short time.

5.3.5 Now!

To indicate that something is happening now, you can use:

▶ **zijn... aan het** + infinitive.
▶ **zitten/liggen/staan... te** + infinitive.

With **zitten/liggen/staan** (*to sit/lie/stand*) you add information about the position of the person/animal performing the action.

NB You can also use these structures in the past tense.

De kinderen zijn lekker aan het spelen.	*The children are playing nicely.*
Renee zat een boek te lezen.	*Renee was reading a book.*

Exercise 5L

For each of the following sentences say why the present tense is used: a) talking about the here and now; b) talking about the future; c) livening up an account of the past; or d) talking about the past and the present.

a De bankovervallers grijpen het geld en rennen weg.
b Ik ben er morgen om half 10.
c We werken al 8 jaar samen.
d Louise slaapt slecht sinds ze in verwachting is.
e We komen echt wel op tijd.

> bankovervaller *bankrobber*   in verwachting zijn *to be pregnant*

Exercise 5M

Answer the following questions in Dutch using the information in brackets. Use *al* or *pas* as appropriate.

a Hoe lang werkt u hier al?   (drie jaar, *you think it is a long time*)
b Sinds wanneer woont u in België?   (zes maanden)
c Hoe lang studeert u hier al?   (een jaar, *you think it's a short time*)
d Hoe lang bent u getrouwd?   (een half jaar, *you think it is a short time*)
e Hoe lang heeft u die hoofdpijn nu?   (twee weken, *you think it is a long time*)

Exercise 5N
Translate the following, using *al*, *pas* and *sinds* as appropriate.

  a I have been living here for only five months.
  b Harry has been living here for ten years already.
  c I have been studying here for only one year.
  d Harry has been studying here for six years already.
  e Harry has been smoking for eight years already.
  f I have been smoking only since last week. (vorige week)

Exercise 5O
What are they doing? Use the information to describe these people's activities.

e.g. Jeroen – met zijn autootjes spelen
       Jeroen is met zijn autootjes aan het spelen.
       Jeroen zit met zijn autootjes te spelen.

  a Maaike – een jurk naaien (*to sew a dress*)
  b Connie – druk praten (*busy talking*)
  c Richard – in de schuur werken (*working in the shed*)
  d Harm – een boek lezen (*reading a book*)

_____

Things to remember

  ▶ The basic form of the verb is called the infinitive. Most infinitives in Dutch end in -**en**.

  ▶ Most verbs forms are based on the stem of the verb: usually the infinitive of the verb without the -**en** ending.

  ▶ Usually only the first verb in a sentence adapts its form to indicate tense – this verb is called the finite verb.

  ▶ In the present tense of regular verbs, -**t** or -**en** can be added to the stem of the verb.

▶ The finite verb is put in second position in the sentence, and all other verbs are put at the end of the sentence.

▶ Inversion means reversing the order of the verb and it's subject; this happens for instance when asking a question.

▶ In the present tense you drop the -t ending of verbs when the verb is directly followed by the pronouns **je** or **jij**.

▶ The present tense of verbs is frequently used to talk about the future.

▶ The present tense is used to talk about a time period which started in the past and continues into the present, by using **al** or **pas** or another adverb indicating time.

6

Verbs (2) – modal verbs and talking about the future

6.1 Modal verbs

Modal verbs are verbs such as **may, must, want, can,** etc.

6.1.1 What?

Modal verbs are used to express various things such as saying what you can, wish, may, must or should do.

The Dutch modal verbs are **zullen** (*shall/will*), **willen** (*want*), **kunnen** (*can, to be able to*), **mogen** (*may, to be allowed to*), **moeten** (*must, should, have to*), **hoeven** (*have to*).

6.1.2 Form

The forms of the modal verbs are irregular. Further below you will find tables with all forms.

6.1.3 Structure

Modal verbs are normally combined with another verb, which is put at the end of the sentence in its full infinitive form:

Wij *zullen* **echt** *betalen.*	*We really will pay.*
Ik *moet* **eerst dit** *opruimen.*	*I've got to tidy this up first.*
Bert *kan* **mooie verhalen** *vertellen.*	*Bert can tell beautiful stories.*

Note the following points:

- ▶ Verbs used in combination with the modal verb **hoeven** are preceded by **te: Hij hoeft geen boete te betalen.** *He doesn't have to pay a fine.*
- ▶ The infinitives of **hebben** and **gaan** are often left off the end of the sentence:

Ik wil een glaasje wijn (hebben).	*I would like a glass of wine.*
Ik moet naar mijn werk (gaan).	*I have to go to work.*

6.1.4 Independent use

Modal verbs can also be used on their own:

Dat kan.	*That's possible.*
Dat hoeft niet.	*That's not necessary.*

6.1.5 Perfect and past perfect tenses

When a modal verb is used with another verb in the (past) perfect tense, the modal does not become a past participle, but an infinitive. It always combines with **hebben:**

Ik *heb* **het niet** *kunnen doen.*	*I haven't been able to do it.*
Ik *had* **je** *willen schrijven.*	*I (had) wanted to write to you.*

The modal verbs do have a past participle (e.g. **gemoeten, gewild;**
see Section 6.1), but these are only used when the modal verb is
used independently:

Ik heb het nooit gewild.   *I have never wanted it.*
Dat had niet gehoeven.   *That wasn't necessary.*

NB Do these exercises with the information from both sections on
modal verbs (6.1 and 6.2).

Exercise 6A
Fill in the correct form of the modal verb.
e.g. willen ik _____ naar de bioscoop vanavond.
    Ik wil naar de bioscoop vanavond.

a kunnen   Peter _____ goed zwemmen.
b moeten   We _____ het rapport voor volgende week
          afmaken.
c zullen   Ik _____ de rekening betalen.
d willen   Coen en ik _____ liever thuisblijven.
e mogen   Je _____ niet te lang televisie kijken.
f hoeven   'Margot, je _____ vandaag niet te koken. Ik doe
          het!'
g moeten   Hij _____ het boek lezen voor zijn examen.
h kunnen   _____ jij goed tekenen?
i willen   De kinderen _____ naar het strand als het mooi
          weer is.
j zullen   Ik _____ een mooi souvenir voor je meenemen uit
          Indonesië.
k hoeven   Mijn broertje _____ nooit van mijn moeder af te
          wassen.
l mogen   Het spijt me, maar je _____ hier niet roken.

Exercise 6B
In which of the following sentences can the final verb be left out?

a Mijn vader wil zelf de vakantie organiseren.
b Ik wil een nieuwe computer hebben.

c Lieverd, mag ik vanavond naar het café gaan?
d Wil je wijn of bier hebben?
e Je moet de videorecorder programmeren.
f Zullen we deze zomer naar Marokko op vakantie gaan?

Exercise 6C

Put the following sentences into the perfect tense.
e.g. Ik mag mijn eigen verjaardagscadeau uitkiezen.

Ik heb mijn eigen verjaardagscadeau mogen uitkiezen.

a Hij moet een grote geldboete betalen.
b Ze kunnen dat huis goedkoop kopen.
c Ze willen het zelf.
d Karin hoeft het natuurlijk niet te doen.

6.1.6 Present tense - forms

Here is the full list of the various forms of the modal verbs in the present tense.

	zullen	**willen**	**kunnen**	**mogen**	**moeten**	**hoeven**
ik	zal	wil	kan	mag	moet	hoef
jij	zal/ zult*	wil/ wilt*	kan/ kunt*	mag	moet	hoeft
u	zal/ zult	wil/ wilt	kan/ kunt	mag	moet	hoeft
hij/zij/ het	zal	wil	kan	mag	moet	hoeft
wij	zullen	willen	kunnen	mogen	moeten	hoeven
jullie	zullen	willen	kunnen	mogen	moeten	hoeven
u	zal/ zult	wil/ wilt	kan/ kunt	mag	moet	hoeft
zij	zullen	willen	kunnen	mogen	moeten	hoeven

6.1.7 Imperfect - forms

See Sections 7.1 and 7.6 for the formation and use of the imperfect tense.

	zullen	willen	kunnen	mogen	moeten	hoeven
ik	zou	wilde/ wou*	kon	mocht	moest	hoefde
jij	zou	wilde/ wou	kon	mocht	moest	hoefde
u	zou	wilde/ wou	kon	mocht	moest	hoefde
hij/ zij/ het	zou	wilde/ wou	kon	mocht	moest	hoefde
wij	zouden	wilden/ wouden*	konden	mochten	moesten	hoefden
jullie	zouden	wilden/ wouden	konden	mochten	moesten	hoefden
u	zou	wilde/ wou	kon	mocht	moest	hoefde
zij	zouden	wilden/ wouden	konden	mochten	moesten	hoefden

6.1.8 Perfect

See Sections 7.1–7.4 for the formation and use of the perfect tense.

	zullen	willen	kunnen	mogen	moeten	hoeven
	–**	gewild	gekund	gemogen	gemoeten	gehoeven

*The forms zult, wilt, kunt and wilde(n) are more formal.

** The verb zullen does not have a past participle.

6.2 Modal verbs – use

6.2.1 Zullen is used for various functions which all relate to the future:

▶ to talk about the future (see Section 6.3):

We zullen straks naar huis gaan.   *We will go home in a minute.*

▶ to make a suggestion:

Zullen we even koffie drinken?   *Shall we have a coffee?*

▶ to make a prediction or state an expectation:

Ik zal wel weer laatst komen.   *I expect I will be last again.*

▶ To make a promise:

We zullen je morgen bellen.   *We will phone you tomorrow.*

For information on the use of **zou/zouden,** the past tense forms of **zullen,** see Section 10.1 on the conditional tense.

6.2.2 Willen is mainly used to express a wish:

Ik wil de kamer opnieuw behangen.   *I want to redecorate the room.*

It can also be used without another verb:

Wil je een pilsje?   *Do you want a beer?*

6.2.3 Kunnen is used in various functions:

▶ to express ability:

| **Mijn dochter kan goed schrijven.** | *My daughter can write very well.* |

▶ to express possibility:

| **Ik kan morgenmiddag komen.** | *I can come tomorrow afternoon.* |

▶ to make a polite request:

| **Kunt u mij morgen opbellen?** | *Could you phone me tomorrow, please?* |

Note that here the present tense of **kunnen** is used where in English the past tense *could* is used.

6.2.4 Mogen is used to express (lack of) permission:

| **U mag hier niet fotograferen.** | *You are not allowed to take pictures here.* |

6.2.5 Moeten is used to express a rule or necessity:

| **U moet alle vragen beantwoorden.** | *You have to answer all questions.* |

6.2.6 Hoeven is frequently used as the negative for **moeten** to express that something is not necessary:

| **Moet je nog veel doen?** | *Do you still have a lot to do?* |
| **Nee, ik hoef niet veel meer te doen.** | *No, I don't have much more to do.* |

Exercise 6D
Fill in the correct form of a modal verb. Sometimes there's more than one possibility.

e.g. Hij _____ wel moe zijn, als hij thuiskomt.
Hij zal wel moe zijn, als hij thuiskomt.

a Ik _____ je morgen pas betalen. Is dat OK?

b Waarom _____ je zo graag naar het concert van die stomme popgroep?

c De auto is kapot, dus Kees _____ met de trein naar zijn werk.

d _____ je me het zout even geven?

e We _____ in de bibliotheek niet te hard praten.

f Joop en Marleen _____ verhuizen, maar ze weten niet waarnaartoe.

g Wanneer _____ we een avondje gaan stappen?

h Jullie _____ niet zo hard schreeuwen!

i Is er iemand met wie je over dit probleem _____ praten?

j Die muziek is zo mooi, daar _____ ik uren naar luisteren.

k _____ we de buren ook uitnodigen op het feest, of is dat geen goed idee?

l _____ u bier of heeft u liever iets fris?

> bibliotheek *library*   fris *a cold drink*   kapot *broken down*
> stappen *to go out for a drink (or two)*

Exercise 6E
Fill in the correct form of a modal verb. Sometimes there's more than one possibility.

a Onze auto is kapot, dus ik _____ gisteren op de fiets naar mijn werk.

b We zijn naar Mauritius op vakantie geweest. Jan _____ naar Thailand, maar daar had ik geen zin in.

c _____ ik u iets vragen?

d Mijn oma was helemaal niet streng. We _____ bij haar in huis altijd met alles spelen, zelfs haar antieke meubels!

e Ik _____ vroeger goed schaatsen, maar dat is jaren geleden.

f Wat _____ jij vroeger worden?

g Ik vraag me af of we deze hele oefening _____ doen.

h De trein uit Den Haag _____ bij aankomst een vertraging hebben van 10 minuten.

> schaatsen *ice skating*   streng *strict*
> vertraging *delay*

Exercise 6F
It's a rainy day and you're bored. You call a friend and make some suggestions for what the two of you might do. Make sentences with zullen.

e.g. schoonmaken (mijn huis)
Zullen we mijn huis schoonmaken?

a huren (een video)
b squashen
c winkelen (in het nieuwe winkelcentrum)
d gaan (naar de bioscoop)
e koffie drinken (in de stad)

Exercise 6G
You have lots of ideas about what you'd like to do on your weekend off, but there are lots of chores you should do instead. Make sentences following the example.

e.g. uitslapen (*to sleep in*) / de was doen (*do the laundry*)
Ik wil eigenlijk uitslapen, maar ik moet de was doen.
I really want to sleep in, but I have to do the laundry.

a televisie kijken / de woonkamer stofzuigen (to vacuum clean the living room)
b naar het strand gaan / de afwas doen (to do the dishes)
c iets met vrienden drinken / bij mijn ouders op visite gaan (visit my parents)
d op mijn nieuwe computer internetten / de wc schilderen (paint the toilet)
e naar muziek luisteren / mijn huiswerk doen

Exercise 6H
Use the information to make a list of questions to ask people to find out what they're good at.

e.g. zwemmen (jij)
Kun jij goed zwemmen?

a brieven schrijven (hij)
b luisteren (je)
c zwemmen en snorkelen (ze, *plural*)
d Engels praten (u)
e professionele presentaties geven (ze, *singular*)

6.3 Talking about the future

This section outlines the different ways you can talk about
the future.

6.3.1 Present tense

The present tense is used frequently in Dutch to talk about the
future. (For formation of the present tense, see Sections 5.2–5.3.)

Ik speel morgen om 10 uur   *I'm playing tennis at 10 tomorrow.*
tennis.
We zijn er volgende week   *We won't be here next week.*
niet.

6.3.2 Gaan

Another common way of talking about the future is by using
gaan + infinitive:

Esther *gaat* **dinsdag** *winkelen.* *Esther is going shopping on Tuesday.*
Wanneer *gaan* **jullie** *verhuizen?* *When are you moving (house)?*

6.3.3 Zullen

Zullen is not used as frequently as the present tense or **gaan** to talk
about the future. The main function of **zullen** when talking about
the future is to make a promise or give a guarantee.

Hij *zal* **u direct** *terugbellen.* *He will call you back immediately.*
We *zullen* **het** *proberen.* *We will try.*

See Section 6.2.1 for other uses of **zullen**.

Exercise 6I
Translate diary entries for the coming week into full sentences
(use the present tense).

e.g. Woensdag – voetballen met Marco.
  Op woensdag voetbal ik met Marco.

MAANDAG	DONDERDAG
vergaderen over het project	koffie drinken met Amy
DINSDAG	VRIJDAG
lunchen met Willem	boodschappen doen
WOENSDAG	ZATERDAG
voetballen met Marco	eten bij Jolanda
	ZONDAG
	opa en oma bezoeken

Exercise 6J

Wat ga je doen? You're going on holiday. Use the information below to tell your friends what you plan on doing while you're away.

e.g. met de auto naar Zuid-Frankrijk
We gaan/willen met de auto naar Zuid-Frankrijk.

a Eerst een paar dagen ontspannen op het strand.
b Daarna een paar dagen de Provence bekijken.
c De tweede week naar de Pyreneeën.
d Wandelen in de bergen.

Exercise 6K

Promises – give an adequate promise using *zullen* and the verb between brackets.

e.g. Je moet beter je best doen. (proberen)
Ik zal het proberen.

a Dus je komt me van het vliegveld ophalen? (niet vergeten)
b Kunt u dit voor me wegleggen? (doen)
c De voorstelling begint om half 8, dus ik zie je om 7 uur.
(er op tijd zijn)
d Het is belangrijk dat je een goed cijfer haalt. (mijn best doen)

Insight

Perhaps the trickiest modal in Dutch for speakers of English is **willen,** which is easily confused with English *will*, but does in fact mean *to want*. English *will* is expressed in Dutch by simply using the present tense, **gaan + infinitive** or the verb **zullen** (see above).

Note that **moeten** means *must* or *have to*, and that *should* is **zou/zouden + moeten + infinitive** in Dutch (see Section 10.2).

Things to remember

▶ The Dutch modal verbs are **zullen** (*shall/will*), **willen** (*want*), **kunnen** (*can, to be able to*), **mogen** (*may, to be allowed to*), **moeten** (*must, should, have to*), **hoeven** (*have to*).

▶ Modal verbs are combined with another verb, which is placed at the end of the sentence in its full infinitive form.

▶ The infinitives of **hebben** and **gaan** are often left off the end of the sentence.

▶ Verbs used in combination with the modal verb **hoeven** are preceded by **te**.

▶ When a modal verb is used with another verb in the (past) perfect tense, the modal does not become a past participle but an infinitive.

▶ The most commonly used ways of talking about the future are using the present tense, or the verb **gaan** plus an infinitive.

7

Verbs (3) – perfect and imperfect

7.1 Use of the perfect and imperfect

It is not always easy to choose between the present perfect and the imperfect in Dutch. This unit deals with the main differences between these tenses.

7.1.1 General

As a general rule, talking about the past is introduced, and often concluded, using the perfect tense. Added information is given in the imperfect:

Ik *ben* gisteren *thuisgebleven*. Ik *voelde* me niet zo lekker. Ik *had* koorts en *was* misselijk. 's Avonds *voelde* ik me beter en *ben* ik naar de bioscoop *gegaan*.

I stayed at home yesterday. I didn't feel very well. I had a fever and felt sick. In the evening I felt better and went to the cinema.

It may be helpful to think of the imperfect as a pair of binoculars that is used to look at things in close-up.

7.1.2 Dramatic effect

The perfect tense is used to transport the listener to the past. The imperfect tense brings this past alive, as in a story:

Ik heb **in Peru wel eens in een bergmeer** gezwommen. **Ik** sprong **erin. Het water** was **ijskoud. Ik** hapte **naar adem. Daarna** heb **ik het nooit meer** gedaan.

I once swam in a mountain lake in Peru. I jumped in. The water was ice cold. I gasped for breath. After that, I never did it again.

7.1.3 Habits/regular events

Habits and regular events in the past must be given in the imperfect tense, which may mean that, when using this tense, you start with a description.

Mijn vader was een succesvol zakenman. Hij investeerde in aandelen. Mijn moeder werkte altijd. Wij zagen ze bijna nooit.

My father was a successful business man. He invested in shares. My mother always worked. We hardly ever saw them.

7.1.4 Involvement

Sometimes either the perfect or the imperfect tense is grammatically correct. The difference is one of involvement. With the perfect tense your main concern is to give factual information. The imperfect tense creates a feeling of greater involvement with the past and brings the event to life, emphasizing the personal aspect of what is being said. **We hebben in Amsterdam gewoond** (in the perfect), for instance, is a purely factual statement. **We woonden in Amsterdam,** that is the imperfect, conjures up a picture of the scene as if you were there.

Exercise 7A
You are a policeman and relate the following event about your work to a friend. Put the verbs in brackets into the correct tense (perfect or imperfect) and form. See also Sections 7.2–7.6.

Ik (zien) gisteren iets raars. We (rijden) over de autoweg, de A15, en we (aanhouden) een vrachtauto omdat hij te langzaam (rijden). Het (blijken) dat de chauffeur tijdens het rijden met een gasstel op zijn schoot water (koken). Hij (moeten) dus langzaam rijden om op het water te letten. We (geven) hem een boete van 240 euro.

> iets raars *something strange*   aanhouden *to pull over*
> gasstel *(camping) gas stove*   schoot *lap*
> letten op *to keep an eye on*   boete *fine*

Exercise 7B
Reconstruct the following newspaper article by putting the verbs in brackets in the correct tense (perfect or imperfect) and form. See Section 7.3.

Een woordvoerder (bekendmaken) gisteren dat het veilinghuis Christie's in Londen de oorlogscollectie van de familie Rothschild (veilen). De collectie (bestaan) uit 250 kostbare schilderijen van beroemde schilders. In 1938 (in beslag nemen) de nazi's de collectie. Na de oorlog (dwingen) de Oostenrijkse regering de joodse familie om de collectie aan musea te geven. De Oostenrijkse minister van Onderwijs en Cultuur (vertellen) de musea enkele maanden geleden de collectie aan de familie Rothschild terug te geven. Deskundigen (schatten) de opbrengst van de veiling op 63 miljoen euro.

> veilinghuis *auction house*   oorlog *war*   kostbaar *valuable*
> in beslag nemen *to confiscate*   deskundigen *experts*
> schatten *to estimate*   opbrengst *proceeds*

Exercise 7C
The following text is an adapted excerpt from a short story. The main character has been talking about a favourite holiday destination from his childhood. Complete his account by filling in the correct form and tense (perfect or imperfect) of the verbs in brackets.

In 1996 (besluiten) ik terug te gaan. Woensdag 24 augustus (arriveren) ik op het station van N. De laatste keer dat ik daar (aankomen), was in 1953. De banken in de trein (zijn) toen van hout. Het raam (doen) je open met een leren band. De reizigers (aanbieden) elkaar pepermuntjes. In 1953 (zien) het perron er ook anders uit, er (liggen) bakstenen. Nu (stappen) ik op grijze tegels, tegenover een nieuw zelfbedieningsrestaurant. Op een bankje (zitten) een soldaat in een pornoblaadje te kijken.

> bakstenen *bricks*   tegels *paving slabs*   soldaat *soldier*

7.2 The present perfect

The perfect (or present perfect) is the tense most frequently used when talking about events in the past.

7.2.1 Use

The perfect is used to describe events in the past which have now finished. (See also use of the perfect and imperfect, Section 7.1.)

7.2.2 Form

The present perfect is formed with an auxiliary, i.e. a form of the verbs **hebben** or **zijn,** and a past participle. The auxiliary takes the second position in the sentence and the past participle comes at the very end. The form of hebben or **zijn** depends on the subject (**hij heeft** but **wij hebben**) and is always in the present tense (hence the present perfect). The past participle never changes:

Mijn collega heeft die fout gemaakt.   *My colleague made that mistake.*

7.2.3 The past participle of regular verbs is formed by taking the stem of the verb and adding the prefix **ge-** and a final **t** or **d: ge +** stem + **t/d**. To decide whether to add a **t** or a **d**, you must look at the last letter of the stem. If the stem ends in **s, f, t, k, ch** or **p** (you may find it helpful to think of them as soft ketchup) we add a **t**. (but see 7.2.4 below) In all other cases we add a **d**. (Note that a Dutch word cannot end in double **t** or **d**.)

infinitive	stem	past participle
stoppen to stop	**stop**	**gestopt**
wonen to live	**woon**	**gewoond**

7.2.4 Spelling

Verbs whose stem ends in an **s** or **f**, but which have a **z** or **v** in their infinitive form, end their past participle in a **d**:

reizen to travel	**reis**	**gereisd**
durven to dare	**durf**	**gedurfd**

7.2.5 Fixed prefixes

To past participles of verbs with a fixed prefix **be-, er-, ge-, her-, ont-** or **ver-**, you don't add **ge-**:

vertellen to tell	**vertel**	**verteld**

7.2.6 Separable verbs

If the verb is separable, **ge** is placed between the prefix and the verb:

opbellen to call	**bel op**	**opgebeld**

The past participles of irregular verbs are not formed according to the rules outlined here, and have to be learned individually (see Section 19.5).

Exercise 7D
Complete the following sentences by filling in the past participle of the verb in brackets.

During a wet summer (*natte zomer*) the Dutch tourist office issued the following statements...

a Volgens het VVV hebben buitenlanders nog niet over het weer in Nederland (klagen).
b Het VVV heeft van toeristen nog geen rampverhalen (horen).
c De meeste hotels zijn (volboeken).
d Het aantal boekingen is met 10% (groeien).

> VVV *the Dutch tourist office*   rampverhalen *disaster stories*

Exercise 7E
Use the following phrases to make a list of things that you have done. Use a form of the verb *hebben* unless stated otherwise. Make sure you use the perfect.

a 's ochtends mijn huis schoonmaken
b met een vriend aan de telefoon praten
c het avondeten koken
d een brief versturen
e naar mijn favoriete CD luisteren
f mijn moeder bellen
g met roken stoppen (use zijn)
h de videorecorder programmeren

Exercise 7F
Put the following sentences into the perfect. Use a form of the verb *hebben* unless indicated otherwise. Some sentences are questions.

a Jef installeert zelf zijn nieuwe computer.
b We verhuizen naar een andere stad. (use zijn)
c Jullie protesteren tegen het buitenlandse beleid van de regering?
d Wie maakt dat project af?
e Maartje regelt haar bankzaken erg goed.
f Ik vertel het hem nooit.
g De minister zegt het tijdens haar reis door China.
h Leonardo di Caprio reist met zijn moeder naar Venetië. (use zijn)

7.3 The present perfect – hebben or zijn

This section outlines when to use the auxiliaries **hebben** or **zijn** in the perfect.

7.3.1 Main rule

Most verbs use a form of the verb **hebben** in the perfect tense. However, a number of verbs that indicate a change of place or state use a form of **zijn**:

hebben	**Ik heb gisteren te veel gedronken.**	*I had too much to drink yesterday.*
zijn	**De omzet is in 2010 gestegen.**	*Turnover increased in 2010.*

In the second sentence you use **zijn** because **stijgen** (to *increase* or *go up*) indicates a change.

7.3.2 Zijn

The following list gives some of the most frequently used verbs that are combined with **zijn**. Note that the main rule in terms of indicating a change does not always apply in an obvious way and that some verbs in fact indicate the opposite of a change. It's best simply to learn these verbs individually (see also Section 19.5).

beginnen	*to begin*
blijven	*to stay*
komen	*to come*
stoppen	*to stop*
worden	*to become*
gaan	*to go*
zijn	*to be*

7.3.3 Verbs of motion

Verbs of motion, such as **lopen** (*to walk*), **rijden** (*to drive/ride*) and **fietsen** (*to cycle*), sometimes use **zijn** and sometimes **hebben**. If the destination is mentioned towards which the movement takes (or took) place, a form of the verb **zijn** is used. In all other cases you use **hebben**. Examples:

Harmen is naar huis gelopen.	*Harmen walked home.*
Heb je hard gelopen?	*Did you walk fast?*

We zijn naar de stad gefietst.	*We cycled to town.*
Adeline heeft een uur gefietst.	*Adeline cycled for an hour.*

Exercise 7G
Fill in the correct form of the verb *hebben* or *zijn*.

e.g. Ik _____ te veel gegeten.
   Ik heb te veel gegeten.

a Annemieke _____ een nieuwe keuken gekocht.
b Vanmorgen _____ we naar de markt gegaan.
c We _____ de hele week hard gewerkt.
d Zijn vriendin _____ het feest georganiseerd.
e Mijn collega's _____ samen uit eten geweest.
f Wanneer _____ zij met roken gestopt? (plural)
g Onze vakantie _____ veel geld gekost.
h Ronald _____ gisteravond laat naar huis gegaan.

Exercise 7H
Fill in the correct form of the verb *hebben* or *zijn*.

a Ik _____ vanochtend vroeg met Jos naar het strand gefietst.
b We _____ heerlijk in zee gezwommen.
c Daarna _____ we ook in de duinen gewandeld.
d 's Middags _____ we naar een restaurant gewandeld om iets te eten.
e Later _____ we terug naar het strand gegaan.

f We _____ ook nog een eind langs het strand gejogd, heerlijk!

g We _____ 's middags laat niet direct terug naar huis gegaan, maar we _____ nog iets in de stad gedronken.

Exercise 7I

Travelling: you've just landed at Schiphol airport for a weekend in Amsterdam. On arrival you are asked to answer a few questions for market research. Use the information in brackets.

a Waarvandaan bent u naar Nederland gekomen? (give your home town)

b Hoe laat bent u vanochtend van huis gegaan? (8.15)

c Van welk vliegveld bent u naar Schiphol gevlogen? (name the airport nearest your home)

d Waar heeft u uw vlucht geboekt? (via the internet)

e Hoe lang heeft de vlucht geduurd? (2.5 hours)

f Heeft u accommodatie gereserveerd? (yes, you've reserved a hotel room for five nights)

7.4 The present perfect – past participles

7.4.1 Hebben/zijn

A small group of frequently used verbs do not form their past participle according to the rules given in Section 7.2. The two most important of these are **hebben** and **zijn**:

Ik heb een verjaardagskaart *gehad.*	*I have had a birthday card.*
Ina is nog nooit in Shanghai *geweest.*	*Ina's never been to Shanghai.*

7.4.2 Common verbs

Here is a list of some of the most commonly used verbs with irregular past participles in the perfect (for more verbs see Section 19.5).

infinitive	past participle	infinitive	past participle
beginnen start	**begonnen**	**blijven** to stay	**gebleven**
brengen take/ bring	**gebracht**	**doen** to do	**gedaan**
gaan to go	**gegaan**	**geven** to give	**gegeven**
komen to come	**gekomen**	**kopen** to buy	**gekocht**

7.4.3 Patterns

There are several groups of verbs which change their vowel in the perfect (and imperfect: see Section 7.6) according to a pattern. These are called strong verbs. Examples are:

infinitive	past participle
drinken to drink	**gedronken**
vinden to find	**gevonden**
nemen to take	**genomen**
spreken to talk	**gesproken**
liggen to lie	**gelegen**
zitten to sit	**gezeten**

7.4.4 Modal verbs

If a modal verb is used in the perfect tense together with another verb, both verbs are put in the infinitive at the end of the sentence.

Compare:

Ik *heb* **een laptop** *gekocht.*	*I (have) bought a laptop.*
Ik *heb* **een laptop** *willen kopen.*	*I (have) wanted to buy a laptop.*

This is the same for some other verbs, like **laten** (*to have something done*):

ik *heb* **mijn haar** *laten knippen.*	*I (have) had my hair cut.*

Exercise 7J

Look at your diary entries for last week. Write them out into full sentences, describing everything you did last week.

e.g. maandag: 9.00 dokter
Maandag ben ik om negen uur bij de dokter geweest.

maandag	dinsdag	woensdag	donderdag	vrijdag	zaterdag	zondag
9.00 dokter			8.30 zwemmen	8.00 baas rapport geven		
		10.30 thee drinken bij Karin			's ochtends boodschappen doen	
	's middags schoenen kopen					
				19.00 uitgaan met Jan		20.00 eten bij mam/pap

7K Read the following questions and answer using the pattern given (and the modal *moeten*).

e.g. Je bent te laat opgestaan, hè?
You got up too late, didn't you?
Ja, ik had vroeger moeten opstaan. *Yes, I should've got up earlier.*

   a Je bent niet vroeg genoeg begonnen, hè?
   b Je bent niet zuinig genoeg geweest, hè?
   c Je hebt teveel gekocht, hè?
   d Je hebt niet goed geluisterd, hè?

Exercise 7L

Answer the following questions with *laten*, saying that you have had it done.

e.g. Is de auto al gewassen? *Has the car been washed yet?*
Ja, ik heb de auto laten wassen. *Yes, I had the car washed.*

a Is je computer al gerepareerd?
b Is je haar al geknipt?
c Is je videorecorder al gemaakt?
d Is je flat al schoongemaakt?

7.5 The past perfect

The past perfect tense is used to refer to events that happened in the past before something else.

7.5.1 Form

The past perfect tense is formed, like the present perfect, by an auxiliary and a past participle. With the past perfect the auxiliary is a past tense form of **hebben** (**had/hadden**) or **zijn** (**was/waren**).

Ik *had* **net** *gegeten* **toen...**	*I had just had dinner when...*
Ze *waren gestopt* **voordat...**	*They had stopped before...*

The past participle and the choice between **zijn** and **hebben** is the same as for the present perfect (see Sections 7.2–7.4).

7.5.2 Use

▶ The main use of the past perfect is the same as in English, to indicate that one event happened before another event in the past:

Margriet had haar man net een e-mail **gestuurd** toen hij belde.
Margriet had just sent her husband an e-mail when he called.

▶ The past perfect is also used to fantasize about a past that might have been:

Als ik dat had geweten dan **was** ik niet naar zijn feest **gegaan**.
If I had known that I wouldn't have gone to his party.

Note that the past perfect is used twice in the Dutch sentence (although a different structure with **zou** can be used as well. See Section 10.1).

7.5.3 Modals

Modals used with another verb in the past perfect work the same as in the present perfect (see Section 7.4). Both verbs are moved to the end of the sentence and are used in their infinitive form:

Hij had kunnen zeggen dat ...   *He could (also) have said that ...*
Jane had ook willen komen.   *Jane had wanted to come too.*

Exercise 7M
You're given two phrases – make them into one sentence, saying that one happened after the other (one of them has to be put in the past perfect).

e.g. Ik kwam net thuis. Mijn moeder belde.
Ik was net thuisgekomen toen mijn moeder belde.

a Andy sprak af bij Arjen te gaan eten. Gwen vroeg Andy te eten.
b Ik waste af. Mariëlle bood aan te helpen. (aanbieden is a separable verb)
c Jane verkocht haar huis. De huizenmarkt stortte in. (instorten is a separable verb)
d Ik zag de film nog niet. Mick vertelde me het einde.
e Het feest eindigde. Ik arriveerde eindelijk.
f Ik savede mijn bestanden nog niet. Mijn computer crashte.

Exercise 7N
It's the end of the year and you are musing about how things might have turned out if you had done things differently. Make *als* and *dan* phrases using the information given.

e.g. geld sparen – op vakantie gaan
Als ik geld had gespaard, dan was ik nu op vakantie gegaan.

a harder werken – promotie krijgen
b minder sporten – niet zo fit zijn
c de hele tijd thuis blijven – niet zoveel goede films zien
d een piercing nemen – een zilveren ring kunnen kopen
e beter luisteren naar mijn moeder – gelukkiger zijn
f een miljoen winnen – niet hier zijn

Exercise 7O
Put the following sentences in the right order. The first sentence is:
Net nadat jij had gebeld, belde Django.

a Mijn zus kwam bij mij nadat ze een avondje met een jongen was uitgeweest.
b Nadat ik haar binnen had gelaten, eindigde ik m'n gesprek met Django.
c Het eten was erg goed, maar nadat hij haar blouse had gebruikt als servet, wilde ze weg.
d Nog voor hij had opgehangen, kwam m'n zus langs.
e Zij hadden in een duur restaurant gegeten.

7.6 The imperfect

This tense is used to describe habits and regular events in the past, and to describe a series of events.

7.6.1 Use

The imperfect is used in two main situations:

▶ To describe things or events that took place regularly in the past.
▶ To describe events in the past after the listener's attention has already been moved to the past (see also use of the perfect and imperfect in Section 7.1).

7.6.2 Form

The imperfect of regular verbs is formed by adding **te(n)** or **de(n)** to the stem of the verb. In the singular **te** and **de** are used, whereas in the plural **ten** and **den** are used. To decide whether to add **te(n)** or **de(n)**, we must look at the last letter of the stem. If the stem ends in **s**, **f**, **t**, **k**, **ch** or **p** you add **te(n)**. In all other cases you add **de(n)**. (You may find it helpful to remember the letters **s**, **f**, **t**, **k**, **ch** and **p** as the words **soft ketchup**):

infinitive	stem	imperfect
werken to work	**werk**	**werkte(n)**
wonen to live	**woon**	**woonde(n)**

We woonden in Hillegom.	*We lived in Hillegom.*
Ik werkte in Hoorn.	*I worked in Hoorn.*

If the stem of the verb ends in a **t** or a **d**, this **t** or **d** will double in the imperfect:

praten to talk	**praat**	**praatte(n)**
redden to save	**red**	**redde(n)**

Verbs whose stem ends in an **s** or **f**, but which have a **z** or **v** in the infinitive form, make the imperfect with **de(n)**:

reizen to travel	**reis**	**reisde(n)**
leven to live	**leef**	**leefde(n)**

Separable verbs are used in the imperfect in the same way as in the present, i.e. with the prefix at the end of the sentence:

We *studeerden* **in 1997** *af.*   *We graduated in 1997.*

Exercise 7P
Cora tells a story about something that happened to her some time ago. Put her sentences into the imperfect.

a Mijn televisie werkt niet.
b Ik ontdek het 's ochtends vroeg.
c Ik bel een vriend, hij belooft 's middags langs te komen.
d Ik wacht de hele middag, en om half 6 belt hij op.
e Hij vertelt dat zijn auto niet goed start.
f Ik protesteer natuurlijk.
g Woedend gooi ik de telefoon op de haak, en bel een professionele monteur.

Exercise 7Q
Make up a fictitious past. Pretend you are someone else – very rich and famous, of course – and use the verbs below to make sentences in the imperfect, describing a particularly wonderful period from your past.

a wonen
b verdienen
c reizen
d regelen
e kennen
f uitnodigen
g spelen
h lachen

Exercise 7R
Finish the following descriptions by putting the verbs in brackets into the imperfect.

a Ik ben gisteren thuisgebleven. Ik (voelen) me niet lekker. Ik (bellen) mijn baas. Hij (wensen) me beterschap. Ik (beloven) de volgende dag weer te komen.

b Ik ben naar Canada op vakantie geweest. Ik (ontmoeten) daar een stel Nederlanders. Zij (reizen) door de hele wereld op de fiets. Ze (willen) elk land ter wereld bezoeken. Ze (proberen) in het *Guinness Book of Records* te komen.

7.6.3 Form

There is a relatively large group of irregular verbs which do not follow the rules for forming the imperfect as given in Section 7.6. The forms of the imperfect for these verbs simply have to be learned. Here is a list of the most commonly used verbs with irregular forms in the imperfect. The endings for plural forms are given in brackets. (For more verbs see Section 19.5.)

infinitive	imperfect	infinitive	imperfect
beginnen *to start*	begon(nen)	blijven *to stay*	bleef, bleven
brengen *to take/bring*	bracht(en)	doen *to do*	deed, deden
gaan *to go*	ging(en)	geven *to give*	gaf, gaven
hebben *to have*	had(den)	komen *to come*	kwam(en)
kopen *to buy*	kocht(en)	kunnen *to be able*	kon(den)
moeten *to have to*	moest(en)	mogen *to be allowed*	mocht(en)
willen *to want*	wilde(n)	zijn *to be*	was, waren

7.6.4 Patterns

There are several groups of verbs which change their vowel in the imperfect (and perfect: see Section 7.4) according to a pattern. These are known as strong verbs. Examples are:

infinitive	imperfect
drinken *to drink*	dronk(en)
vinden *to find*	vond(en)
nemen *to take*	nam(en)

infinitive	imperfect
spreken *to talk*	sprak(en)
liggen *to lie*	lag(en)
zitten *to sit*	zat(en)

Unfortunately, there are many groups and they can be hard to identify. You may therefore find it easier to learn each verb individually. You can find more strong verbs in Section 19.5.

Exercise 7S
Translate this picture story about a day in the working life of Donald into sentences in the imperfect. Use the information given in the present tense.

Donald komt om 7.30 uur op het kantoor.

Hij kijkt vrolijker dan normaal. Hij lacht opgewekt.

Hij vraagt zijn secretaresse niet om koffie. Hij maakt het zelf.

Hij roept om 9 uur iedereen bij elkaar.

Hij zegt dat hij iets belangrijks moet zeggen.
Hij geeft iedereen een extra bonus.

Hij vertelt iedereen dat het goed gaat.

Insight

It can be difficult to decide when to use the present perfect and when to use the imperfect. Start off by observing how native Dutch speakers use these tenses, by having a good look at the use of tenses in Dutch texts that you read, and by listening carefully to native speakers. As a rule of thumb, the present perfect is used if you are simply giving a list of more or less unrelated facts (I went here and there, I did this and then that, etc) and the imperfect is used to give more details about any of these facts (it was really busy, I was tired, I became angry...).

Ik ben bij m'n ouders geweest. Ik heb met m'n zus geluncht. Ik heb schoenen gekocht. Ik heb boodschappen gedaan. In de supermarkt was het druk. Er stond een lange rij. Ik was moe, ik werd boos... *I dropped by my parents'. I had lunch with my sister. I bought shoes. I did the (grocery) : shopping, It was busy in the supermarket. There was a long queue. I was tired. I became angry...*

Things to remember

▶ Talking about the past is introduced, and often concluded, using the perfect tense. Added information, which often brings the past 'alive', is given in the imperfect.

▶ For habits and regular events in the past, the imperfect tense is used.

▶ The present and past perfect are formed with the verbs, **hebben** or **zijn** in second position, plus a past participle at the end of the sentence.

▶ The past participle of regular verbs is formed by adding the prefix **ge-** to the stem of the verb and adding a final **-t** (when the stem ends in **s, f, t, k, ch** or **p**) or **d**.

▶ Most verbs use a form of **hebben** to make the present or past perfect tense. However, a number of verbs that indicate a change of place or state use a form of **zijn**.

▶ Verbs of motion take **zijn** in the present and past perfect if the destination towards which the motion takes place is mentioned; in all other cases they take **hebben**.

▶ The past participle of **hebben** is **gehad** and the past participle of **zijn** is **geweest**.

▶ The imperfect is formed by adding **-te(n)** or **-de(n)** to the stem of a verb. You add **-te(n)** if the stem ends in **s, f, t, k, ch,** or **p**.

Verbs (4) – separable and inseparable

8.1 Separable verbs

Separable verbs are verbs which are made up of two parts that can
sometimes be separated when used in a sentence.

8.1.1 What do separable verbs look like?

Separable verbs are made up of two parts: the prefix and the main
part of the verb. The prefix is usually an ordinary preposition,
for instance **uit** (*out*), and the main part of the verb is usually an
ordinary verb, like **gaan** (*to go*), for instance. Together these make
up the whole separable verb, in this instance **uitgaan**, *to go out*:

opbellen *to call up*	**thuisblijven** *to stay at home*	**opeten** *to eat up*
afmaken *to finish*	**aankomen** *to arrive*	**weggaan** *to go away*
uitgeven *to spend*	**meenemen** *to take along*	**aandoen** *to put on*

8.1.2 When and how to separate separable verbs

When you use a separable verb in a sentence the main part of the
verb takes its usual place and the prefix goes to the very end of the
sentence.

We *gaan* **vanavond samen** *uit.*	*We're going out together tonight.*
Hoeveel *geeft* **Bea per maand** *uit?*	*How much does Bea spend a month?*

8.1.3 When not to separate separable verbs

▶ When the word order in a sentence changes, for instance in sub-clauses (see Section 17.2), both parts of the separable verb are moved to the end of the sentence and are rejoined as one word.

Hij *blijft* **vandaag** *thuis.*	*He's staying at home today.*
Hij *zegt* **dat hij vandaag** *thuisblijft.*	*He says that he's staying home today.*

▶ Whenever there is more than one verb in the sentence and the separable verb is moved to the end of the sentence, you join the prefix and the main part of the verb into one word again.

Ik *maak* **mijn werk** *af.*	*I'm finishing my work.*
Ik moet mijn werk *afmaken.*	*I have to finish my work.*

8.1.4 Past participle

The past participle of separable verbs is made by putting the prefix in front of the past participle of the main verb:

Hij heeft al drie keer *opgebeld.*	*He's already called three times.*
Janet is om 12 uur *weggegaan.*	*Janet left at 12 o'clock.*

Exercise 8A
Put the prefixes of the separable verbs in bold in the correct place (the prefix is given at the start of each sentence).

e.g.	schoon	Wanneer **maak** je het huis? Wanneer maak je het huis schoon?
a	thuis	Wil je uit eten of **blijf** je liever?
b	uit	Ik had geen idee dat ik elke maand zoveel geld **gaf**.

c	op	Moet ik mijn moeder **bellen**, of doe jij het?
d	aan	Hoe laat **komt** de trein op het station?
e	mee	Als je het goed vindt, **neem** ik vanavond een vriend.
f	aan	Wat doe jij naar het feest? (**aandoen**, *to wear*)
g	op	Papa wil dat je alles **eet**!

Exercise 8B
Rewrite the following sentences following this pattern: *Ik vind dat...*

e.g. Ik ga te vaak uit.
Ik vind dat ik te vaak uitga.

a Jij geeft te veel geld uit.
b Zij doet altijd zulke rare kleren aan.
c Jullie maken je werk te laat af.
d Hij belt zijn vriendin niet vaak op.
e Het eten in dit restaurant valt erg tegen.

Exercise 8C
Rewrite the sentences according to the pattern, making them into more definite statements (leaving out the modal verb).

e.g. De bankmanager zegt dat hij zijn schuld moet afbetalen.
Hij betaalt zijn schuld af.

a De dokter zegt dat hij diep moet inademen.
b Ik hoop dat ik volgend jaar kan afstuderen.
c De leraar zegt dat hij zijn werk moet afmaken.
d Jet gelooft dat ze om 9 uur zal aankomen.
e Hij zegt dat hij het journaal op TV niet wil mislopen.
f Wanneer denk je dat je mijn CD kunt teruggeven?

> **Insight**
>
> Separable verbs may seem rather strange, but if you think of them in the same way as an English verb such as *put on*, then they won't seem so alien. *Put your coat on* is simply **Doe je jas aan** in Dutch, from the verb **aandoen**.

8.1.5 Splitting up separable verbs

In the previous section you saw that separable verbs are written as one word whenever a change in word order unites the prefix with the main part of the verb at the end of the sentence. However, sometimes the two parts of the separable verb are split up again.

▶ Infinitive constructions + **te**: If the separable verb is used in an infinitive construction with **te**, **te** is placed between the prefix and the main verb: **Jan probeert haar op te bellen.** *Jan's trying to call her up.*
▶ With another verb: If the separable verb is put at the end of a sentence or phrase together with another verb, you can split up the separable verb by placing the other verb in between both parts. This can be done with separable verbs both in the infinitive and as a past participle.

Els zegt dat ze niet *op* **wil** *bellen*.	*Els says she doesn't want to call.*
Ik denk dat het *goed* **is** *gekeurd*.	*I thinks that it's been approved.*

NB You don't have to split the verb: it's an option you have. It's usually considered slightly more informal to split the separable verb in such cases, and more formal to keep them together.

Denk je dat hij *af* **zal** *studeren*?	*Do you think that he'll graduate?*
Denk je dat hij zal *afstuderen*?	*Do you think that he'll graduate?*

8.1.6 Separable and inseparable

You can tell whether a verb is separable by listening to it; if the prefix is stressed it's separable, otherwise it isn't. Some verbs have a separable form (prefix stressed) and an inseparable form (prefix unstressed). For example:

voor**komen**	**Hoe vaak** komt **dat voor?**
to occur/happen	How often does that occur/happen?
voor**ko**men	**Een rotonde** voorkomt **ongevallen.**
to prevent	A roundabout prevents accidents.

For more information on inseparable verbs, see Section 8.2.

Ik sta om 7 uur op.

Exercise 8D
Answer the questions following the example (watch out for separable verbs – the syllable which is stressed is in bold).

e.g. Wat doe je, de vergadering **voor**bereiden of niet?
Ik bereid de vergadering voor.

a Wat doe je, de presentatie **bij**wonen of niet? (*to attend*)
b Wat doe je, onder**han**delen of niet? (*to negotiate*)
c Wat doen jullie, het werk **neer**leggen of niet? (*to lay/put down*)
d Wat doe je, het plan onder**steu**nen of niet? (*to support*)
e Wat doe je, eerst **uit**rusten of niet? (*to relax/rest*)
f Wat doen jullie, hem die baan **aan**bieden, of niet? (*to offer that job*)
g Wat doen we, het probleem be**spre**ken of niet? (*to discuss*)

Exercise 8E
Holidays: Marijke has booked a few days off to do the following things. Make sentences following the pattern.

e.g. een paar vrienden opbellen
Marijke neemt een paar dagen vrij om een paar vrienden op te bellen.

a het huis schoonmaken
b de garage opruimen
c haar belastingformulier invullen
d haar cursus astrologie voorbereiden
e lekker uitrusten

Exercise 8F
Make the following sentences slightly more informal by separating the separable verb as in the example.

e.g. Eileen denkt dat ze volgend jaar zal afstuderen.
Eileen denkt dat ze volgend jaar af zal studeren.

a De arbeiders in de fabriek weten nog niet of ze het werk zullen neerleggen.
b Je moet je tante vragen of ze het cadeau dit jaar niet kan opsturen.
c Ik heb geen idee waar je die informatie kan opzoeken.
d We zijn bijzonder blij dat we u deze baan mogen aanbieden.
e Weet jij of we die vergadering vanmiddag moeten bijwonen?

8.2 Inseparable verbs

Some verbs with prefixes cannot be separated. A special group of these inseparable verbs start with the prefixes **be-, ge-, her-, ont-, ver-, er-**.

8.2.1 Form

There are two different kinds of inseparable verbs:

▶ The prefix is a word in its own right, often a preposition, but cannot be separated from the verb part. You can tell a verb with a prefix is inseparable when the prefix is not stressed (cf. Separable verbs, Section 8.1), for instance, onderhandelen:

De minister onderhandelt met de vakbond.
The Secretary of State is negotiating with the union.

▶ Verbs starting with the prefixes **be, ver, her, ge, er** or **ont**.

8.2.2 Past participle

Verbs starting with **be, her, ver, ge, er** and **ont** do not form their past participle with **ge** (see also Section 7.2):

beloven *to promise*	→	**beloofd**
verliezen *to lose*	→	**verloren**
geloven *to believe*	→	**geloofd**

8.2.3 Meaning

The prefixes **be, her, ver** and **ont** can sometimes change the meaning of the verb, although this is not a hard and fast rule:

- ▶ **her-** often means doing something again and translates into re-: **herschrijven** (*to rewrite*), **herzien** (*to revise*), **herontdekken** (*to rediscover*).
- ▶ **ont-** often means undoing something and translates into un-, de-, dis-: **ontbossen** (*to deforest*), **ontcijferen** (*to decipher*), **ontdoen** (*to undo*)
- ▶ **ver-** often indicates a process of change: **verkleinen** (to make smaller), **vergroten** (*to enlarge*).

  In combination with a reflexive pronoun (e.g. **zich**) the prefix **ver** can also mean making a mistake: **zich verrekenen** (*to miscalculate*), **zich verkijken op** (*to misjudge*).

- ▶ **be-** often intensifies the meaning of a verb. Contrast:
  Ze kijkt naar me. *She is looking at me.*
  Ze bekijkt me. *She is looking me up and down.*

  Most verbs starting with **be-** are transitive. This means they can have a direct object. Often this means a preposition is not needed. Contrast:

  Ik antwoord op de brief. *I am answering the letter.*
  Ik beantwoord de brief. *I am answering the letter.*

There is no particular meaning associated with the prefixes **er-** nd **ge-**.

Exercise 8G
Form the past participle of the following verbs:

a Hij heeft ____ dat voor me te doen. (beloven)
b De docent heeft dat grammaticapunt al vier keer ____ (herhalen)
c Jan heeft eindelijk ____ dat hij die brief had geschreven. (erkennen)
d In Nederland wordt het gebruik van softdrugs niet officieel toegestaan, maar het wordt ____ (gedogen)
e Ik heb dat verhaal gisteren al aan je ____ (vertellen)

> **erkennen** to admit **toestaan** to permit **gedogen** to tolerate

Exercise 8H
Replace the underlined words with a verb starting with her-.

e.g. Je moet niet alles weggooien. Je kunt veel dingen <u>opnieuw gebruiken</u>.
Je kunt veel dingen hergebruiken.

a Het toneelstuk is niet goed. Hij gaat het <u>opnieuw schrijven</u>.
b De taken zijn niet goed verdeeld. We moeten ze <u>opnieuw verdelen</u>.
c We moeten het milieu sparen. We gaan meer dingen <u>opnieuw gebruiken</u>.
d Ik heb geen goede opleiding. Ik moet me <u>opnieuw</u> laten <u>scholen</u>.
e Het systeem werkt niet. We moeten het <u>opnieuw structureren</u>.

Exercise 8I
Choose the correct verb between brackets and change the form if necessary.

a Ik zal naar je voorstel ____ (kijken/bekijken)
b Ik zal je voorstel ____ (kijken/bekijken)
c Kun je op mijn vraag ____ alsjeblieft? (antwoorden/beantwoorden)
d Kun je mijn vraag ____ alsjeblieft? (antwoorden/beantwoorden)

e Ik _____ graag naar klassieke muziek. (luisteren/beluisteren)
f Ik moet die CD nog _____ (luisteren/beluisteren)

Exercise 8J
Replace the underlined words with a verb starting with _ver-_.

_e.g._ Ik voel me al veel beter. De pijn <u>wordt minder</u>.
De pijn vermindert.

a Het plan <u>wordt</u> steeds <u>anders</u>.
b Marie wil een operatie om haar borsten <u>kleiner</u> te laten <u>maken</u>.
c James wil zijn positie <u>beter maken</u>.
d De regisseur gaat <u>van</u> haar boek <u>een film maken</u>.
e De lampen zijn te fel. Ze <u>maken</u> me <u>blind</u>.

Things to remember

▶ Separable verbs are made up of two parts: a prefix and the main part of the verb.

▶ When a separable verb is used in a sentence, the main part of the verb takes up the usual (second) position in the sentence, and the prefix is placed at the very end.

▶ When word order changes, for instance, in sub-clauses, the two parts of the separable verb are both moved to the end of the sentence and are rejoined as one word.

▶ The past participle of separable verbs is made by putting the prefix in front of the past participle of the main verb.

▶ When separable verbs are written as one word at the end of a sentence, they may be split up by **te** (in infinitive constructions) or by another verb.

▶ You can tell whether a verb is separable by listening to it; if the prefix is stressed it's separable, otherwise it isn't.

9

Verbs (5) – reflexive, imperative, infinitive

9.1 Reflexive verbs

Reflexive verbs are verbs whose subject and object refer to the
same person/animal/idea. For example: *The cat is washing itself.*

9.1.1 Reflexive pronouns

Reflexive verbs are used with a reflexive pronoun. You can find the
reflexive pronouns in the table below. The verb **zich voelen** (to feel)
is used as an example. Note that quite a few reflexive verbs, like
zich voelen, are not reflexive in English.

	Reflexive pronoun		
Ik voel	**me**	niet goed.	*I don't feel well.*
Jij voelt	**je**	altijd goed.	*You always feel well.*
U voelt	**zich/u**	niet goed?	*You don't feel well?*
Hij/zij voelt	**zich**	prima.	*He/she feels fine.*
Wij voelen	**ons**	genomen.	*We feel fooled.*
Jullie voelen	**je**	belazerd.	*You feel taken for a ride.*
Zij voelen	**zich**	gebruikt.	*They feel used.*

For the polite form, both **zich** or **u** can be used. There is no difference in meaning.

9.1.2 Where to put the reflexive pronoun

▶ You put the reflexive pronoun directly after the first verb in the sentence:

Ik schaam me **dood.**	*I'm so embarrassed.*
Je moet je **niet met zijn zaken bemoeien.**	*You mustn't interfere in his affairs.*

▶ Whenever inversion occurs, which means that you move the verb in front of the subject, the reflexive pronoun doesn't move. The reflexive pronoun now follows the subject (for inversion see Section 10.3).

Billy verveelt zich thuis.	*Billy's bored at home.*
Waarom verveelt hij zich thuis?	*Why is he bored at home?*

▶ Be aware that you may end up with **je je**.

Vergis je je nooit?	*Are you never mistaken?*

Exercise 9A
Fill in the correct reflexive pronoun.

> **zich veroorloven** *to afford* **zich concentreren** *to concentrate*
> **zich aantrekken** *to take to heart* **zich vergissen** *to mistake*
> **zich zorgen maken** *to worry* **zich ergeren aan** *to be annoyed by*

a Wij kunnen _____ geen nieuwe auto veroorloven.
b Ik trek _____ niets aan van kritiek.
c Je maakt _____ altijd teveel zorgen.
d Helène vindt het moeilijk om _____ te concentreren.
e Ze hebben _____ in de datum vergist.
f Ergeren jullie _____ niet aan hoe hij eet?

Exercise 9B
Answer the questions.

e.g. Vermaak jij je op feestjes? *Do you enjoy yourself at parties?*
Ja, ik vermaak me op feestjes.
(or Nee, ik vermaak me niet op feestjes.)

a Maakt je beste vriend(in) zich zorgen over de toekomst?
Does your best friend worry about the future?
b Ergeren je buren zich aan lawaai?
Are your neighbours irritated by noise?
c Trek jij je iets aan van kritiek?
Do you take criticism to heart?
d Interesseert jouw vader of moeder/broer/zus/tante (etc.) zich voor moderne kunst?
Is your father or mother/brother/sister/aunt (etc.) interested in modern art?
e Kun jij je goed concentreren?
Can you concentrate well?
f Kan je baas zich goed uitdrukken in het Nederlands?
Can your boss express him/herself well in Dutch?
g Waar interesseer je je voor?
What are you interested in?

Exercise 9C
Finish the sentences with the verbs in brackets, following the example. (of doen jullie net alsof = *or are you pretending?*)

e.g. (zich concentreren, of doen jullie net alsof?)
Concentreren jullie je, of doen jullie net alsof?

a (zich inspannen *to make an effort*), of doen jullie net alsof?
b (zich bedrinken *to get drunk*), of doen jullie net alsof?
c (zich dood schrikken *to be frightened to death*), of doen jullie net alsof?

9.1.3 Part-time reflexive verbs

Not all reflexive verbs are always reflexive. Some verbs, like **zich wassen** (*to wash*) can be used as a reflexive verb or not: *you can* *wash yourself*, which is reflexive, or *you can wash your dog*, which isn't. If the subject (you) and the object (yourself) are the same you use a reflexive pronoun, if they aren't (you and the dog) you don't need a reflexive pronoun:

reflexive	**Ik was me elke maand!**	*I wash myself every month!*
	De poes wast zich constant.	*The cat washes itself constantly.*
non-reflexive	**Ik was de hond elke zondag.**	*I wash the dog every Sunday.*
	Ik was hem elke zondag.	*I wash him every Sunday.*

Here are some other verbs which can be used as a reflexive verb or not:

(zich) vervelen	*to be bored/to bore*
(zich) verdedigen	*to defend (oneself)*
(zich) verbazen	*to amaze (oneself)*
(zich) amuseren	*to amuse (oneself)*
(zich) herinneren	*to remember (or remind oneself)*

We amuseren ons

9.1.4 Zelf

If you use a part-time reflexive verb (see Section 9.1.3) and you are contrasting two things, you have to add **-zelf** to the reflexive pronoun to emphasize the contrast:

Ze verbaasde niet alleen het publiek, ze verbaasde ook *zichzelf.*
She didn't only amaze the public, she also amazed herself.
De poes waste eerst *zichzelf* **en daarna haar jongen.**
The cat first washed herself and then her young.

Exercise 9D

Reflexive or not? Indicate whether the verbs in bold are used reflexively or not. If they are used reflexively, fill in the appropriate reflexive pronoun in the right place.

a **Herinner** jij wat de directeur in de memo heeft gezegd?
b Hij **amuseerde** ons allemaal met zijn spannende verhalen.

c **Herinner** jij me eraan dat ik vanmiddag Tim moet bellen?
d Onze hond **verdedigde** goed tegen die honden van de buren.
e Het **verbaast** ons dat Carina en Joop nog steeds bij elkaar zijn.
f Je **verveelt** me met je flauwe grapjes!
g Er is niet veel te doen op m'n werk dus ik **verveel** de hele week al vreselijk.
h Wanneer heb je de hond voor het laatst **gewassen**?

Exercise 9E

Fill in the correct reflexive pronoun.

a Je ziet er beter uit, maar voel je ook beter?
b Dat is nou al de tweede keer dat je vergist in mijn naam.

c Irene zou wat minder met andermans zaken moeten bemoeien.

d Bedankt voor het oppassen, Oma. Hebben de kinderen goed gedragen de afgelopen twee dagen?

e Ik hoop dat iedereen heeft geamuseerd tijdens de vakantie.

f Hij verbaasde over dat hoge bod van de Amerikanen.

g Toen je opeens met dat masker voor me stond, schrok ik dood!

9.2 Imperative

The imperative is a verb form such as *go! come! sit down!* and is mainly used to give commands or instructions.

9.2.1 Stem

Most commonly, you form the imperative by using the stem of the verb (see Section 5.2) on its own:

kom hier   *come here*
ga zitten   *sit down*

NB The verb **zijn** takes the stem **wees** in the imperative:

wees voorzichtig   *be careful*

9.2.2 Separable verbs

With separable verbs the prefix is usually moved to the end:

Hou mijn jas even **vast.**   *Hold my coat, please.*

9.2.3 Polite form

When addressing someone in a formal situation you can use the pronoun **u**. In that case you will also use the verb form of **u**:

| **gaat u zitten** | *do sit down* |
| **begint u maar** | *do start* |

9.2.4 Infinitive

Dutch also frequently uses the infinitive when issuing commands. This is used particularly in impersonal situations such as written instructions (e.g. recipes), or in advertising. It is also frequently used on signs:

Het vlees in blokjes snijden.	*Cut the meat in dice.*
Niet parkeren	*No parking*
Nu kopen!	*Buy now!*

9.2.5 Use

The imperative is most commonly used to give orders or instructions:

| **Ruim je kamer op!** | *Tidy up your room!* |

But the imperative is also frequently used to solicit certain reactions or to give advice:

| **Bel haar op en zeg dat het je spijt.** | *Phone her, and say you're sorry.* |
| **Doe mee aan deze actie.** | *Take part in this campaign.* |

Commands can be made less harsh by using words such as **maar, even, eens, toch** (see Section 18.4):

| **Kom** *maar* **binnen.** | *Please, come in.* |
| **Doe het raam** *even* **open.** | *Please, open the window.* |

Exercise 9F
Fill in the correct form. Use the basic imperative form.

e.g. __ je jas __ (uittrekken) **Trek** je jas **uit.**

a __ de boodschappen niet! (vergeten)
b __ met dat gezeur __ (ophouden)
c __ de onderstaande bon __ (invullen)
d __ de paprika in stukjes (snijden)
e __ de tekst op bladzijde 26 en __ oefening 4 (lezen, maken)

Exercise 9G
Complete the following advertisements and slogans.

a __ uw huid met *Suntan*. (beschermen)
b __ van een heerlijk kopje koffie. (genieten)
c __ gratis de informatie lijn. (bellen)
d __ veilig of __ niet. (vrijen, vrijen)
e __ voor een hypotheek van de postbank. (kiezen)
f __ het eens van de andere kant. (bekijken)

Exercise 9H
Create signs by choosing from the verbs below. The first one is done for you.

> parkeren   storen   betalen   rijden   ontsteken   kloppen

a niet **storen**, alstublieft
b hier __
c lichten __
d langzaam __
e verboden te __
f a.u.b __ voor u binnen komt

Exercise 9I
The following instructions for a coffeemaker are written in the infinitive. Make them snappier by using the basic imperative form.

e.g. Het koffiezetapparaat met koud water vullen.
Vul het koffiezetapparaat met koud water.

a Vier schepjes koffie in het koffiefilter doen.
b Het deksel op de koffiepot doen.
c De koffiepot onder het filter plaatsen.
d Op het aan/uit knopje drukken.

9.3 Infinitive constructions

The infinitive is the full form of the verb and in Dutch normally
ends in **-en**. There are two groups of verbs which can be combined
with an infinitive.

9.3.1 Verbs with te + infinitive

When you use an infinitive at the end of the sentence, you need
to add **te** before the infinitive. The most common verbs which
combine with **te** + infinitive are:

zitten	*to sit, to be sitting*	**beloven**	*to promise*
liggen	*to lie, to be lying*	**proberen**	*to try*
hoeven	*(not) to have to*	**beginnen**	*to begin, to start*
staan	*to stand, to be standing*	**weigeren**	*to refuse*
durven	*to dare*	**vergeten**	*to forget*

Het kind probeert op de kast te klimmen.
The child is trying to climb on the cupboard.

NB In the perfect tense you don't form a past participle with the
verbs **zitten, liggen, staan, hoeven** and **durven**. You use an infinitive
form instead, and **te** becomes optional:

Ik heb nooit in het diepe durven (te) springen.
I've never dared to jump in the deep end.

9.3.2 Verbs without te

Some verbs which can be combined with an infinitive do not have te before the infinitive. Apart from the modal verbs (see Sections 6.1 and 6.2) the most common of these verbs are:

komen	*to come*	**laten**	*to have something done, to let*
gaan	*to go*	**zien**	*to see*
blijven	*to stay, to remain*	**horen**	*to hear*
zijn	*to be*		

Janneke is even koffie halen. *Janneke is getting a coffee.*
Waar laat jij je haar knippen? *Where do you have your hair cut?*

NB In the perfect tense you don't form a past participle with these verbs, but you use their infinitive form instead. You do, however, use the auxiliary (**hebben** or **zijn**) belonging to that verb. Note that zijn becomes **wezen**:

Freek is wezen voetballen. *Freek has been playing football.*
Petra is bij ons blijven slapen. *Petra stayed the night with us.*
Jan heeft zijn auto laten repareren. *Jan had his car repaired.*

Exercise 9J
Complete the sentences using the information given.

> **van een hoge brug springen**   *jump from a high bridge*
> **je altijd trouw zijn**   *always be faithful to you*
> **je erg aardig vinden**   *to really like you*
> **met de buurvrouw praten**   *talk with the (female) neighbour*
> **de krant lezen**   *read the newspaper*
> **naar muziek luisteren**   *listen to music*

a Karel zit _____
b Peter ligt _____
c Francien staat _____

d Ik begin ___
e Ik beloof ___
f Eddie weigert ___

Exercise 9K
Answer the following questions in the perfect tense making use of the information in brackets.

a Wat heb je gisteren gedaan?   (zitten lezen)
b Heb je vroeger vaak moeten   (niet vaak hoeven afwassen)
   afwassen?
c Wat heb je nooit durven   (nooit op het dak durven
   doen?   klimmen)
d Wat heb je hem beloofd?   (de boodschappen doen)
e Ben je iets vergeten?   (mijn moeder bellen)
f Wat ben je begonnen?   (Nederlands studeren)
g Wat heb je geprobeerd?   (de Matterhorn beklimmen)

Exercise 9L
Complete the sentences using the information given.

> huilen   eten   een eind fietsen   lekker voetballen
> zijn huis verbouwen

a Kom je morgen _____ ?
b Jan gaat _____
c Marcel laat _____
d Hoor ik de baby nu _____?
e Zie je de kinderen _____?

Exercise 9M
Answer the following question in the perfect tense making use of the information in brackets.

e.g. Ben je met de auto gekomen? Nee, (komen lopen)
     Nee, ik ben komen lopen.

a Heb je Jaap gezien? Ja, (voorbij zien fietsen)
b Heb je de kinderen gehoord? Ja, (horen zingen)
c Heb je de gordijnen zelf gemaakt? Nee, (laten maken)
d Heb je gezwommen? Nee, (gaan fietsen)

9.3.3 aan het + infinitive

This structure indicates that something is happening *now*. You use it with a form of the verb **zijn**.

De jongens zijn aan het voetballen.	*The boys are playing football.*

9.3.4 zitten/liggen/staan... te + infinitive

This structure also indicates that something is happening now, but adds information about the position of the subject. The verbs **zitten/liggen/staan** usually translate as *to be sitting/lying/standing* in English.

Helen ligt in de tuin te zonnen.	*Helen is sunbathing in the garden.*
Hij zit weer te werken.	*He's working again.*

Insight

The structures **aan het + infinitive** and **zitten/liggen/staan ... te + infinitive** are used a lot in Dutch to indicate that something is happening at the moment. You can say **Ik schrijf een brief** *I'm writing a letter*, but **Ik zit een brief te schrijven** inserts the statement with a sense of action and immediacy. Similarly, instead of **Isa praat met onze buurvrouw** *Isa is talking to our neighbour*, the alternative **Isa staat met onze buurvrouw te praten** conjures up a picture of Isa and the neighbour talking in a very immediate sense.

9.3.5 om + te + infinitive

You *must* use this construction:

▶ When you want to express a purpose, reason or function:

Ik fiets *om* **fit** *te blijven.*	*I am cycling (in order to) to stay fit.*
Lex gaat naar Engeland *om* **zijn vriendin** *op te zoeken.*	*Lex is going to England (in order) to visit his girlfriend.*

▶ After you have used **te** (when it means too) plus an adjective:

Je bent *te* **oud om mee te doen.**   *You're too old to take part.*
Het museum *is* **te groot om**   *The museum is too big to*
  helemaal te zien.   *(be able to) see all of it.*

Om is also often used with verbs which combine with **te** and an infinitive. However, the use of **om** is optional in these situations:

Ik zal proberen (om) je morgen   *I'll try to call you tomorrow.*
  te bellen.
Ik beloof (om) het niet meer te   *I promise not to do it anymore.*
  doen.

The word **om** is used more frequently in spoken than in written language.

NB Verbs which cannot take **om** are: **zitten, staan, liggen, hoeven,** and **durven.**

Pam zit op hem te wachten.   *Pam is waiting for him.*

9.3.6 More than one infinitive

If there is more than one infinitive at the end of a sentence, generally the verb which carries the most important information comes at the end:

Martin wil daar niet blijven   *Martin doesn't want to*
  werken.   *continue working there.*
Marijke zal dat feestje zelf   *Marijke will want to organize*
  willen organiseren.   *that party herself.*

Exercise 9N
Place the infinitives in the correct order.

e.g. Kees wil morgen __te__ (schilderen/beginnen)
Kees wil morgen beginnen te schilderen.

a Wim wil vandaag ___ te ___ (proberen/ werken)
b Rinus zal ons een zeldzame plant ___ (laten/ zien)
c Hanna zal nog een jaar in Maastricht ___ (wonen/blijven)
d Ik heb Kiri Te Kanawa in Nieuw-Zeeland ___ (optreden/ zien)
e Ik ben gisteren ___ (dansen/gaan)
f Michel zal Django ___ (komen/ophalen)
g Waar heb jij je auto ___? (laten/repareren)

Exercise 9O
Wat kun je ermee doen? *What do you use it for?* **Write sentences
to explain what you use the following objects for.**

e.g. een mes – Je kunt er brood mee snijden.
Ik gebruik een mes om er brood mee te snijden.
een glas – Je kunt er wijn uit drinken.
Ik gebruik een glas om er wijn uit te drinken.

a papier – Je kunt er een boodschappenlijstje op schrijven.
b schaar – Je kunt er je nagels mee knippen.
c punaise – Je kunt er een foto mee aan de muur prikken
d doos met een roze lintje – Je kunt er je liefdesbrieven in doen.

Exercise 9P
Waarom ga je hier naartoe? *Why are you going there?*

e.g. de kroeg – mijn vrienden ontmoeten
Ik ga naar de kroeg om mijn vrienden te ontmoeten.

a de kerk – naar het orgel luisteren.
b het strand – zonnebaden.
c het sportveld – mijn vriendje zien.
d de bibliotheek – slapen.

Exercise 9Q
In which sentences could you add *om*?

a Ik probeer een vliegende auto te ontwerpen.
b We zitten hier al lang te wachten.
c We staan hier al een tijdje te praten.
d Hij weigert gewoon te komen.
e Jullie hoeven die laatste tekst niet te lezen.
f Niet vergeten de vuilnisbak buiten te zetten!

Things to remember

▶ Reflexive verbs are verbs whose subject and object refer to the same person/animal/idea and are used with a reflexive pronoun.

▶ Quite a few Dutch reflexive verbs are not reflexive in English.

▶ The reflexive pronoun is placed directly after the first verb in the sentence.

▶ The imperative (a command or instruction) is formed using the stem of the verb. In formal situations **u** plus its appropriate verb form can be used.

▶ Many verbs can be combined with an infinitive. With a large number of these verbs, **te** has to be placed in front of the infinitive (for instance: **zitten** *to sit*, **liggen** *to lie*, **staan** *to stand*). With some verbs this is not necessary (for instance: the modal verbs and **komen** *to come*, **gaan** *to go*, **blijven** *to stay*).

▶ You can indicate that something is happening right now by using the structures **aan het** + infinitive, or **zitten/liggen/staan ... te** + infinitive.

▶ **Om + te** + infinitive expresses a purpose, reason or function.

▶ **Te** + adjective must be followed by **om + te** + infinitive.

10

Verbs (6) – conditional, *zou*, word order, passive

10.1 The conditional

If a condition is given for something to happen, you use one of the following structures in Dutch.

10.1.1 Conditional

In a conditional sentence, a condition has to be met before something else can happen. In English, this often involves an 'if' clause. In Dutch you use the subordinating conjunction **als** (see Sections 15.3 and 15.4):

Als je rode wijn hebt, wil ik graag rode wijn.
If you have red wine, I'd like red wine.

10.1.2 Different conditional structures

▶ **Present tense** This is the easiest way of making a conditional sentence; just use the present tense throughout.

Als ik een miljoen win, ga ik op vakantie.
If I win a million, I'm going on holiday.

(For word order, see Section 17.2.)

▶ **Zullen + infinitive** To indicate intention or things yet to happen, you can also use **zullen** + infinitive in the second part of the sentence:

Als je wilt, **zal** ik een biertje voor je **halen**.
If you want, I will get a beer for you.

▶ **Zou** (singular) or **zouden** (plural) are used in conditional sentences to:

1 Fantasize about a different present/future

als	+	imperfect,	zou(den)	+	infinitive
Als	ik een miljoen	won,	zou	ik een huis	kopen

Als ik een miljoen won, zou ik een huis kopen.
If I won a million, I would buy a house.

2 Fantasize about a different past

als	+	past perfect,	zou(den)	+	infinitive
Als	we een miljoen	hadden gewonnen	zouden	we een huis	hebben gekocht

Als we een miljoen hadden gewonnen, zouden we een huis hebben gekocht.
If we had won a million, we would have bought a house.

NB In both these cases, the structure with **zou(den)** can be replaced by copying the tense from the **als** phrase, i.e. either the imperfect or past perfect:

Als ik een miljoen had, kocht ik een huis.
If I had a million, I'd buy a house.

Exercise 10A

Time travel: use the information given to say who you'd like to meet or what you'd like to do if you could travel back in time (of course, you may add your own suggestions too). Start with the phrase: **Als ik terug in de tijd kon** (*if I could go back in time*).

e.g. Napoleon ontmoeten
Als ik terug in de tijd kon, zou ik Napoleon willen ontmoeten.

a Cleopatra opzoeken
b naar een concert van Mozart gaan
c Versailles in de tijd van Louis XIV bezoeken
d met Marilyn Monroe/James Dean trouwen
e bij Freud in behandeling gaan (behandeling, treatment)
f een goedkoop schilderij van Rembrandt kopen
g Jeanne d'Arc redden
h dinosauriërs willen zien

Exercise 10B

The right conditions: choose the right condition from the column on the left to logically complete one of the sentences on the right.

a	Als het gaat vriezen	**1**	kunnen we naar de bioscoop of zo.
b	Als ik promotie krijg	**2**	koop ik een nieuwe computer.
c	Als ik belasting terugkrijg	**3**	neem ik je mee uit eten.
d	Als mijn moeder belt	**4**	ga ik dit weekend schaatsen.
e	Als je zin hebt	**5**	ben ik er niet.

Exercise 10C

Wat zou je doen als... ? Use the information in brackets to say what you'd do if...

e.g. Wat zou je doen als je een miljoen won? (een butler in dienst nemen)
Als ik een miljoen won, zou ik een butler in dienst nemen.

a Wat zou je doen als je de Minister President was?
   (het onderwijs verbeteren)
b Wat zou je doen als je perfect Nederlands sprak?
   (in Nederland gaan wonen)
c Wat zou je doen als je meer vrije tijd had? (meer naar muziek
   luisteren)

10.2 Zou: more uses

Besides the conditional, *zou* has several other uses.

In Section 10.1 we outlined how you can use **zou(den)** in
conditional sentences. Here are some more uses of **zou(den)**:

10.2.1 Ask polite questions

To ask polite questions you can use the following structure. Note
that the modal verb is always an infinitive.

zou(den)	+	modal verb	infinitive
Zou	je dat voor me	willen	doen?

Zou je dat voor me willen doen? *Would you mind doing that for me?*
Zouden jullie het kunnen *Could you repair it, please?*
repareren?

10.2.2 Give polite advice

You can also use **zou(den)** to give a friendly, polite piece of advice.
Look at the structure in the example. The **als**-phrase is optional.

zou(den)	+	infinitive	als-phrase
Wij zouden	het niet	doen.	
Ik zou	die bank	kopen,	als ik jou was.

Wij zouden het niet doen.   *We wouldn't do it.*
Ik zou die bank kopen, als ik jou was.   *I'd buy that sofa, if I were you.*

To say that someone *should* do something, you can add **moeten**:

Je zou je huiswerk moeten doen.   *You should do your homework.*

10.2.3 Uncertainty/hearsay

To indicate that you are not sure about something or that you've only heard the information from others, you can also use **zou(den)**. You can combine **zou(den)** with any other tense, depending on whether you're talking about the past, present or future. Remember that the auxiliaries **hebben** and **zijn** and modal verbs always occur in their infinitive form after **zou(den)**.

Zou Harmen vanavond niet komen?   *Wasn't Harmen going to come tonight?*
Er zou een vliegtuig zijn neergestort.   *A plane is said to have crashed.*

As you can imagine, you come across this use of **zou(den)** a lot in newspapers and other media:

De tornado zou aan 200 mensen het leven hebben gekost.   *200 people are reported to have lost their lives in the tornado.*

Exercise 10D

Make these questions more polite by using a structure with *zou*.

e.g. Kan je dit even voor me vasthouden?
Zou je dit even voor me kunnen vasthouden?

a Wil je me even helpen met deze brief?
b Kun jij die booschap voor me aannemen?
c Wil je dit werk even voor me nakijken?
d Kun je deze brief vanmiddag voor me op de post doen?
e Kun je me dat boek even geven?
f Kun je me over een uurtje terugbellen?

Exercise 10E

Agony aunt: use the information in brackets to give polite advice to people who've written in with the following problems.

e.g. Mijn auto is kapot. (met de fiets naar je werk gaan)
Ik zou met de fiets naar mijn werk gaan, als ik jou was.

a Ik verslaap me altijd. (vroeger naar bed gaan)
b Ik voel me slap. (gezonder eten)
c Ik vind mijn werk saai. (een nieuwe baan zoeken)
d Ik heb ruzie met mijn vriend(in). (alles met hem/haar bespreken)
e Mijn telefoonrekening is te hoog. (minder vaak naar het buitenland bellen)
f Mijn CD-speler is kapot. (naar de radio luisteren)

> **slap** *weak* **zich verslapen** *to oversleep*

Exercise 10F

Unconfirmed reports: rephrase the following information by using a structure with *zou(den)*.

e.g. Men zegt dat hij erg ziek is.
Hij zou erg ziek zijn.

a Men zegt dat je op die cursus hard moet werken.
b Men zegt dat er een coup heeft plaatsgevonden.
c Men zegt dat er een bom is ontploft in een winkelcentrum.
d Men zegt dat alle kaartjes zijn uitverkocht.
e Men zegt dat er in Amerika een UFO is geland.
f Men zegt dat er een vliegtuig is neergestort.

> **ontploffen** *to explode* **uitverkocht** *sold out*

10.3 Verb word order

This section gives you a survey of where to place verbs in different types of Dutch sentences.

10.3.1 Statements

In Dutch statements, you normally put the verb in second position. This means that the verb is the second item in the sentence, and that it – not surprisingly – follows the first item, which can consist of one word or a group of words. Examples:

Ik *loop* **altijd een uur met mijn hond.**	*I always walk with my dog for an hour.*
Die lamp *kost* **niet veel.**	*That lamp doesn't cost much.*

10.3.2 Turned around: inversion

Usually you start a Dutch sentence with a <u>subject</u>, followed by the **verb**:

<u>Bas</u> *gaat* **elke dag naar het strand.** *Bas goes to the beach every day.*

If you want to start the sentence with another word or phrase, you have to let the verb follow it immediately in second position. This means that you're placing the verb in front of the <u>subject</u>. This is called inversion:

Morgen *gaat* **<u>Bas</u>** niet. *Tomorrow Bas isn't going.*

10.3.3 More than one verb

If there is more than one verb in a sentence, you put the finite verb in its normal place at the beginning of the sentence, and the other verb(s) at the end. Examples:

Ze *heeft* **10 dozen wijn** *gekocht*.	*She bought ten boxes of wine.*
Mijn Bob *wil* **nooit** *afwassen*.	*My Bob never wants to do the dishes.*

10.3.4 Questions

If a question starts with a question word, such as **waarom?** (*why?*), **waar?** (*where?*) or **wie?** (*who?*), the verb comes after the question word in second position. If you don't use a question word the verb is put at the beginning of the sentence. In both types of questions, inversion occurs, i.e. the verb is put in front of the subject. Examples:

Waarom *zit* **je in het donker?**   *Why are you sitting in the dark?*
Hebben **jullie de hond gezien?**   *Have you seen the dog?*

Exercise 10G
Has inversion (of subject and finite verb) taken place in the following sentences or not? If it has, indicate the verb and the subject which have been inverted.

e.g. Elke maandagochtend moeten we naar ons werk.
Inversion of the subject **we** and the finite verb **moeten**.

a Mijn broer en ik gaan vaak samen squashen.
b Welke tien boeken zou je meenemen naar een onbewoond eiland?
c Ina belde vanochtend nog voor je.
d Hoewel ze werkt, heeft ze toch veel tijd voor haar hobby's.
e Haat jij al die lange vergaderingen ook?
f Naast Ierland is Frankrijk ook een van onze favoriete landen voor vakanties.
g Ik vond die theaterproduktie van Romeo en Julia niet zo goed als de film.
h Verleden jaar zijn alle foto's van mijn vakantie mislukt.

Exercise 10H
Rewrite the following sentences, starting with the word(s) given in brackets.

e.g. Sam scheert zich 's ochtends nooit. (in het weekend)
In het weekend scheert Sam zich 's ochtends nooit.

a Henk houdt niet van Westerns. (meestal)
b Ik ben lid van een filmclub in de stad. (sinds kort)
c Mijn baas is op vakantie gegaan. (gisteren)

d Heb jij Carolien gezien? (wanneer)

e Ik vind mijn elektronische agenda erg handig. (over het algemeen)

f Ze is te laat omdat er een probleem is met de auto. (misschien)

g Jan-Peter en zijn vriendin hebben de kaartjes gereserveerd. (hopelijk)

h We hebben net allemaal nieuwe computers. (op kantoor)

10.3.5 Verbs to the end

In relative clauses (see Section 15.6) and sub-clauses (see Section 15.1) all the verbs are moved to the end of the clause in question.

De vakantie die ik *heb geboekt...*   *The holiday that I've booked...*
Als ze vandaag weer te laat *is...*   *If she's late again today...*

10.3.6 Complex sentences

Relative clauses or sub-clauses as described under A can also take up the first position in a sentence. Even though such constructions can look quite complicated, you just stick to normal word order in the main clause (the whole sentence). As usual, the verb of the main sentence still has to come in second position – in these cases directly after the clause. The following examples will make this clear [the relative clauses and sub-clause are placed in square brackets]:

[De man die daar loopt,] *is*   *The man who walks there is*
steenrijk.   *filthy rich.*
[Als je tijd hebt,] *bel* **me dan.**   *If you have the time, then call me.*

10.3.7 Elements placed after the final verb

Sometimes you come across a situation where the verb(s) which should be in final position is/are not actually the last thing in the sentence. This is not incorrect. Some things can actually be placed in final position, even after the verb(s). It happens quite a lot, particularly with prepositional phrases (phrases starting with a preposition) and in comparisons. See also Section 17.3. Some examples:

Ik heb kaartjes besteld *voor 22 juni.*   *I've booked tickets for 22nd of June.*
Jet heeft meer gegeten *dan Jeroen.*   *Jet's eaten more than Jeroen.*

10.3.8 Order amongst verbs

If you have two verbs at the end of a clause or sentence, either verb can come first. If there are two infinitives, the infinitive of the modal verb comes first.

Hij zegt dat hij drie boeken heeft gekocht/gekocht heeft.
Hij heeft beide auto's willen kopen.

If there are more than two verbs, a past participle can come first or last, and of the other verbs the finite verb comes first, and infinitives last, with the infinitive of modal verbs preceding others.

Je begrijpt dat je dit goed geleerd zal moeten hebben.
Je begrijpt dat je dit goed zal moeten hebben geleerd.
You understand that you'll have to have learned this well.

Exercise 10I

Combine the sentences using the word in brackets, following the example.

e.g. Hans belooft. Hij zal de kinderen om 3 uur ophalen. (dat)
Hans belooft dat hij de kinderen om 3 uur zal ophalen.

a David gaat naar huis. Hij heeft veel te veel gedronken. (omdat)
b Mijn moeder vraagt. Wij willen morgenavond komen eten. (of)
c Heb je die bank gekocht. Jij wilde hem zo graag hebben. (die)
d k zei. Ik was tot voor kort nog nooit in Afrika geweest. (dat)
e Ik heb die nieuwe film gezien. Hij heeft zoveel geld gekost. (die)
f Klaas zegt. Hij heeft geen zin om naar Peru op vakantie te
gaan. (dat)

Exercise 10J

Indicate which is the finite verb that belongs to the underlined subject.

e.g. Ik geloof niet dat <u>hij</u> zoveel geld verdiend kan hebben.
kan

a Marjan zegt dat <u>ze</u> een mobieltje van Jaap gekregen heeft.
b Ik geloof dat <u>ze</u> hun huis voor een zacht prijsje hebben kunnen
kopen.
c Wie zegt dat <u>ik</u> dat werk morgen niet klaar zal kunnen krijgen?
d Je moet zelf zeggen of <u>ik</u> je kan komen helpen.
e We hadden geen idee dat <u>onze rapporten</u> vandaag ingeleverd
hadden moeten worden.
f Ze zegt dat <u>ze</u> voor haar studie al deze boeken heeft moeten
lezen.

Exercise 10K

Underline the subject which goes with the underlined verb.

a Ik geloof niet dat ze vanavond <u>kan</u> komen.
b Hij heeft gehoord dat we die vakantie al vroeg <u>zullen</u> moeten
boeken.
c Denk je dat hij altijd al piloot <u>heeft</u> willen worden?

d Waarom denk jij dat Sandra het werk beter <u>zal</u> kunnen doen dan ik?

e Over wie <u>hebben</u> jullie nu weer zitten roddelen?

f Er staat dat je eerst de boter en dan de suiker erin <u>moet</u> doen.

10.4 The passive

In this section you will find general information about the passive, and how to form the present and imperfect tense.

10.4.1 What is it?

The passive form is the opposite of the active form. In active sentences the subject (i.e. the person or thing that the sentence is about) is *doing* the action. Conversely, in the passive form, the subject of the sentences is passive, i.e. *undergoing* the action. The person(s) or thing(s) responsible for the action is/are called the agent. The agent is either not mentioned at all in Dutch, or its role is indicated by **door** + agent. Compare:

Active: **Ik sla mijn kinderen.**   *I am smacking my children.*
The subject – **ik** – is doing the action.

Passive: **Mijn kinderen worden**   *My children are being smacked*
(door mij) geslagen.   *(by me).*
The object from the active sentence – **de kinderen** – has become the subject in this passive sentence.

10.4.2 Place of agent

In the sentence, the phrase **door** + agent can either come after the past participle or it can come after the finite verb (note that other possibilities also exist):

Op oudejaarsavond wordt *door veel mensen* **vuurwerk afgestoken.**
On New Year's Eve fireworks are being set off by many people.
Op oudejaarsavond wordt vuurwerk afgestoken *door veel mensen.*

10.4.3 Present and imperfect tenses

In these tenses the passive is formed by a form of the verb **worden** and a past participle:

present and imperfect = **worden** + past participle

Worden is the main verb and changes its form depending on the subject and the tense of the sentence.

Present tense

De was *wordt* **voor me gedaan.**	*The laundry is done for me.*
De klanten *worden geholpen.*	*The customers are being served.*

Imperfect

Vroeger *werd* **Greetje op school vaak** *gepest.*	*Greetje used to be bullied frequently at school.*
De auto's *werden* **allemaal** *gecontroleerd.*	*The cars were all checked.*

Exercise 10L
Write down in sentences where the following products are produced, grown, sold or traded.

e.g. Swatch horloges/ Zwitserland/ maken
Swatch horloges worden in Zwisterland gemaakt.

  a Ford auto's/ Engeland/ produceren.
  b Camembert/ Frankrijk/ maken
  c Tomaten/ het Westland/ kweken
  d Philips radio's/ over de hele wereld/ verkopen.
  e Aandelen/ de beurs/ verhandelen

Exercise 10M
Change the following sentences into the active form. Use the same tense as in the original sentence.

e.g. Anna werd vaak door haar grote broer geholpen.
Haar grote broer hielp Anna vaak.

a De reis wordt door Himalayan Treks georganiseerd.
b De vluchtelingen worden door het Rode Kruis opgevangen.
c De boot werd door een paar mannen op het strand getrokken.
d Het eten wordt vanavond door mijn kinderen klaargemaakt.
e De boeken worden door de studenten vaak te laat
teruggebracht.

Exercise 10N
**Answer the following questions using the passive and making use
of the information given in brackets. Use the underlined words as
the subject. Make sure you use the correct tense.**

e.g. Wie kopte <u>die bal</u> in het doel? (Maarten)
Die bal werd door Maarten in het doel gekopt.

a Wie leest <u>de Telegraaf</u>? (veel Nederlanders)
b Wie won vorig jaar <u>de P.C. Hooftprijs</u>? (Judith Herzberg)
c Wie helpt <u>Bernadette</u> met haar huiswerk? (haar moeder)
d Wie gaf <u>het startsignaal voor de marathon</u>?
(de burgemeester)
e Wie steunt <u>de beslissing van de regering</u>? (weinig mensen)

10.4.4 Perfect and past perfect tense

In the perfect and past perfect tenses you form the passive
according to the pattern: **zijn** + past participle. The verb **zijn** is the
main verb and changes its form depending on the subject of the
sentence.

Perfect tense

500 kilo heroine *is* **in beslag** *genomen*.	*500 kg of heroin have been confiscated.*
De gevangenen *zijn vrijgelaten*.	*The prisoners have been released.*

Past perfect

De wasmachine *was* **vaak** *gebruikt.*	*The washing machine had been used often.*
De flessen wijn *waren* **allemaal** *leeggedronken.*	*The bottles of wine had all been finished.*

10.4.5 Future and conditional

The passive can also be formed in the future and conditional tenses and in combination with a modal verb. In all these situations the passive is formed according to the following formula:

[a form of the verbs] **zullen/zouden/**modal + past participle + **worden** as infinitive

Het *zal* **morgen** *bekend worden gemaakt.*	*It will be announced tomorrow.*
Het *kan* **zeker** *gedaan worden.*	*It can certainly be done.*
De bewoners *moeten gewaarschuwd worden.*	*The inhabitants must be warned.*
Als ik veel geld had, *zou ik* **beleefder** *behandeld worden.*	*If I had lots of money, I would be treated more politely.*

For the order among these verbs, see Section 10.3.8.

10.4.6 Er

Often when it is not important to say who is performing the action – when talking about people in general in a certain situation, or if you don't know who is performing the action – you use a passive sentence with **er** in Dutch:

Er werd veel gelachen.	*People were laughing a lot.*
Er wordt op de deur geklopt.	*Someone's knocking at the door.*

Insight

The passive is often perceived as one of the more complex grammatical structures, not only in Dutch, but also in many other languages. This is partly due to the fact that the passive is a somewhat abstract notion. However, in Dutch the basic structure of the passive is not really all that difficult. The basic rules are, in short: for the present and imperfect use a form of the verb **worden (word(t)/worden** for the present and **werd/werden** for the imperfect); for the present perfect and past perfect use a form of the verb **zijn (ben(t)/is/zijn** or **was/waren**).

| present and imperfect | **word(t)/worden or werd/werden** + past participle |
| present perfect and past perfect | **ben(t)/is/zijn** or **was/waren** + past participle |

Exercise 10O
Write down what the following buildings are made of.

e.g. De Eiffeltoren is van staal/gietijzer gemaakt.

  a De British Library – baksteen
  b Een kas – glas
  c Het Parthenon – marmer
  d Veel moderne gebouwen – beton
  e Het Vikingschip – hout

Exercise 10P
Write a police report after you have been called to the scene of a rowdy party.

e.g. Alle flessen waren leeggedronken en waren in een hoek gegooid.

  a De tafel – bekrassen
  b De meeste glazen – breken
  c De vloer – met een laag viezigheid bedekken
  d De muur – met graffiti beschilderen
  e De hi-fi – hard aanzetten

Exercise 10Q
Wat moet er allemaal gedaan worden? You are organizing a large event and write out the tasks fully. Note that you use *er* with an indefinite subject.

e.g. Er moeten affiches ontworpen worden.

a de uitnodigingen versturen
b de burgemeester uitnodigen
c de caterer bestellen
d een band regelen
e een zaal huren

Exercise 10R
You are checking on the progress of the preparations. What hasn't been done yet that should have been? Use the list for Exercise 10Q. Note that with indefinite subjects you use *er*.

e.g. Er zouden affiches ontworpen worden.

Exercise 10S
Afterwards, you are evaluating your event. Write down points for future reference.

e.g. De uitnodigen zouden eerder verstuurd moeten worden.

a de beste rockband uitnodigen
b de wijn van tevoren ontkurken
c de zaal mooier versieren

10.5 The passive – use

There are various reasons why people would want to use the passive form instead of the active. The most common reasons are:

▶ **Context:** Sometimes the context calls for the passive, following on from previous information. For instance, imagine you are talking about Princess Diana:

Prinses Diana had niet veel *Princess Diana did not have much*
privacy in haar leven. *privacy during her life.*

In the next sentence you want to say that photographers were often following her. Since you are talking about Diana, you will almost automatically start the next sentence with her as a subject. But because she is undergoing the action, the sentence will have to be in the passive:

| **Zij werd vaak door fotografen achtervolgd.** | *She was often chased by photographers.* |

▶ Style: The passive can be used to add variation to texts. This is particularly used in formal written texts where it also functions to create some distance:

| **De passief wordt veel gebruikt in formele teksten.** | *The passive is used a lot in formal texts.* |

▶ Hiding the cause: Sometimes people want to 'hide' who the agent of the action was. This could be because they don't want to apportion blame for whatever reason, or because they want to emphasize the result of the action rather than the action itself. The passive is thus a useful tool for politicians, amongst others. Compare the following sentences:

De soldaten branden het dorp plat.	*The soldiers are burning the village down.*
Het dorp wordt platgebrand.	*The village is being burned down.*
Wij hebben fouten gemaakt.	*We have made mistakes.*
Fouten zijn gemaakt.	*Mistakes have been made.*

Exercise 10T
What follows? An active (A) or a passive (P) sentence?

a In New York zijn minstens 50 mensen ernstig ziek geworden door een virus.

A Niemand heeft dit virus eerder gesignaleerd.

P Dit virus is nog nooit eerder gesignaleerd.

b Uit onderzoek blijkt dat veel mensen stress ervaren op hun werk.
A Bazen, chefs en hoofden veroorzaken vaak deze stress.
P Deze stress wordt vaak veroorzaakt door bazen, chefs en hoofden.
c Steve McQueen heeft in 1999 de Turnerprijs gewonnen.
A Oude films van Buster Keaton hebben zijn werk beïnvloed.
P Zijn werk is beïnvloed door oude films van Buster Keaton.

Exercise 10U
Make these sentences active in order to create a more informal feel. Use the agent between brackets as the subject of the new sentence.

e.g. Er wordt vaker gescheiden in tijden van een slechte economie. (meer mensen)
Meer mensen scheiden in tijden van een slechte economie.

a Na ontvangst van betaling wordt het boek naar u opgestuurd. (wij)
b Een beslissing wordt nu elk moment verwacht. (ik)
c Uw klacht wordt onderzocht. (wij)
d Problemen worden gesignaleerd met het nieuwe computerprogramma. (sommige mensen)
e Dit kan op twee manieren geïnterpreteerd worden. (wij)

Exercise 10V
As a newspaper editor you don't want to be critical of the government. Which of the headlines would you choose?

a 1 NATO bombardeert Belgrado.
2 Belgrado wordt gebombardeerd.
b 1 Minister verhoogt belastingen.
2 Belastingen worden verhoogd.
c 1 Vluchtelingen worden teruggestuurd naar hun eigen land.
2 De regering stuurt vluchtelingen terug naar hun eigen land.

Things to remember

▶ In a conditional sentence, a condition has to be met before something else can happen. In English, this often involves an 'if' clause. In Dutch you use the subordinating conjunction **als**.

▶ The present tense or **zullen** + infinitive can be used in conditional sentences.

▶ To fantasize about a different present/future or to fantasize about a different past, **zou/zouden** can be used in conditional sentences.

▶ **Zou/zouden** are also used to ask polite questions, to give polite advice, or to indicate that you are uncertain about the truth of a statement.

▶ If a sentence starts with a word or phrase other than the subject, the finite verb has to follow in second position, meaning the finite verb is placed in front of the subject. This is called inversion.

▶ If there is more than one verb in a sentence, the finite verb takes the second position and the other verb/s is/are placed at the end of the sentence.

▶ If a question starts with a question word, the verb follows the question word in second position. If there is no question word, then the question starts with the finite verb. In both cases, inversion occurs.

▶ In relative clauses and sub-clauses all the verbs are moved to the end of the clause.

▶ Some words or phrases, such as prepositional phrases, can be placed after the verbs in final position.

▶ In the present and imperfect tenses, the passive is formed with the verb **worden** and a past participle. In the present and past perfect tenses, the passive is formed with the verb **zijn** and a past participle.

▶ When talking about people in general or if you don't know who is peforming the action, you use a passive sentence with er: **Er werd op de deur geklopt.** *Someone knocked on the door.*

11

Negation

11.1 Negatives – *geen* **and** *niet*

The two most common forms of negatives, apart from **nee** (no),
are **niet** and **geen**.

11.1.1 Form

In making a sentence negative you normally use either **niet**
or **geen**.

You don't have to add the verb *to do*, as you often do in
English.

Ik wil nog niet naar huis.	*I don't want to go home yet.*
Chris drinkt geen bier.	*Chris doesn't drink any beer.*

11.1.2 Niet

Niet is the most common form of making a negative. It simply
means not.

The most complicated thing about **niet** is the place it takes in the
sentence. It might be better to leave studying the next section until
you have a good grasp of word order.

11.1.3 The place of niet

Some general points:

▶ **Niet**, generally speaking, comes last in the sentence or the clause (but before the words which take the very last position such as the past participle, the infinitive or prepositional phrases):

U beantwoordt mijn vraag *niet*.	*You are not answering my question.*
Ik heb hem nog *niet* **gezien**.	*I haven't seen him yet.*

▶ **Niet** comes *before*:

– Prepositions:

Ik ga dit jaar *niet* **op vakantie**.	*I'm not going on holiday this year.*

– Adjectives which come after the noun:

Deze wijn is *niet lekker*.	*This wine is not nice.*
Die school is *niet erg modern*.	*That school is not very modern.*

– Adverbs:

Ik ben *niet gek*.	*I am not stupid.*
Hij werkt *niet erg hard*.	*He doesn't work very hard.*

11.1.4 Geen

Geen (*not a*, *not any*) is used in combination with nouns which refer to something in general (indefinite nouns). In the positive sentence these nouns have the article **een** or no article at all:

Heb je even tijd?	*Have you got a moment (of time)?*
Nee, sorry. Ik heb nu geen tijd.	*No, sorry. I haven't got any time now.*
Heb je een beetje melk?	*Have you got some milk?*
Nee, ik heb geen melk.	*No, I haven't got any milk.*

Insight

The opposite of **niet** and **geen** is **wel**. **Wel** is often used in combination with **niet** or **geen** to mark a contrast. In English, you usually only change your voice. For instance: **Jantien heeft geen auto, maar Drusilla wel.** *Jantien doesn't have a car, but Drusilla does.* Another example: **Willen jullie koffie? Ik niet, maar Jacob wel.** *Do you want coffee? I don't, but Jacob does.*

Exercise 11A
Explain the place of *niet* in the following sentences.

e.g. Ik ga niet met je mee. (niet comes before a preposition)

a Ik wacht niet op jou.
b Karin heeft haar schulden niet betaald.
c Ze hebben dat niet mooi gedaan.
d Ik begrijp die vraag niet.
e Die man is niet serieus.

Exercise 11B
Answer the following questions in the negative using a whole sentence and starting with the pronoun *ik*.

e.g. Neemt u die foto? Nee, ik neem die foto niet.

a Werkt u vanavond?
b Leest u de krant?
c Begrijp je de vraag?
d Vertrouw je hem?
e Heeft u onze brief ontvangen?
f Heb je dat programma gezien?
g Bent u uw cheques vergeten?
h Ga je zwemmen?
i Wil jij de auto wassen?
j Kunt u me helpen?
k Ga je straks naar de stad?
l Werk je in dat nieuwe gebouw?
m Ben je naar het theater geweest?
n Vindt u de voorstelling mooi?
o Hou je van Country 'n Western?
p Kom je morgen op de koffie?
q Ben je naar de kapper geweest?
r Heb je het koud?
s Ben je ziek?
t Heb je hard gewerkt?

Exercise 11C
Answer the following questions in the negative using a whole sentence and starting with the pronoun *ik*.

e.g. Heeft u een huisdier? Nee, ik heb geen huisdier.

<table>
<tr><td>a Heeft u een nieuwe auto?</td><td>e Heb je suiker in je koffie?</td></tr>
<tr><td>b Heb je dorst?</td><td>f Heb je pijn?</td></tr>
<tr><td>c Heeft u hoofdpijn?</td><td>g Heb je geld bij je?</td></tr>
<tr><td>d Heb je koffie?</td><td>h Drinkt u wijn?</td></tr>
</table>

Exercise 11D
Change the following statements into negative ones.

e.g. Ik ben moe. Ik ben niet moe.

<table>
<tr><td>a Petra wil stoppen met werken.</td><td>e Ik vind hem aardig.</td></tr>
<tr><td>b Er zit zand tussen mijn tenen.</td><td>f Jan gelooft mij.</td></tr>
<tr><td>c Het was een droom.</td><td>g Ik heb grijs haar.</td></tr>
<tr><td>d Wij zijn verdwaald.</td><td>h De minister heeft een besluit genomen.</td></tr>
</table>

11.2 Other negatives

11.2.1 Less explicit

There are various other, less explicit, ways of using the negative.

▶ The negative is still to happen – **nog niet, nog geen** (*not yet*):

Ik ben *nog niet* **klaar.**	*I'm not ready yet.*
Ik zie *nog geen* **verschil.**	*I don't see any difference yet.*

▶ The positive has ended: **niet meer, geen... meer** (*not any more*):

We werken *niet meer.*	*We aren't working any more.*
Ik heb *geen* **koffie** *meer.*	*I haven't got any more coffee.*

▶ To indicate gradation: **nauwelijks** (*hardly*), **zelden** (*seldom/hardly ever*).

Ik heb *nauwelijks* **kritiek gekregen.**   *I hardly got any criticism.*
Ik win *zelden* **een prijs.**   *I hardly ever win a prize.*

▶ To give a negative connotation (often equivalents of only). These words are thus not neutral: **nog maar, maar, pas, slechts.**

Ik heb *nog maar* **30 euro over.**   *I've only got 30 euros left.*
Zij heeft *maar* **30 katten.**   *She only has 30 cats.*
De film begint *pas* **om 8 uur.**   *The film doesn't start until 8 o'clock.*
Het kost *slechts* **1 miljoen.**   *It only costs a million.*

Slechts is only used in formal language.

Maar, pas, and **slechts** do not combine with the verb **moeten,** but use hoeven instead (see Section 6.2).

11.2.2 Other words

Some other words that are used to indicate negatives include: **nergens** (*nowhere*), **nooit** (*never*), **niemand** (*no one*), **niets** (*nothing.*)

These words take the same place in the sentence as **niet:**

Ik kan mijn bril *nergens* **vinden.**   *I can't find my glasses anywhere.*
Ik ben nog *nooit* **naar Rome geweest.**   *I have never been to Rome.*

Exercise 11E
Answer these questions in the negative with whole sentences using the equivalent expressions in Dutch of *not yet.*

e.g. Heb je dat formulier nu ingevuld? Nee, ik heb dat nog niet ingevuld.
Heb je al kinderen? Nee, ik heb nog geen kinderen.

a Heb je je huiswerk al gedaan?
b Is je vader al met pensioen?
c Heb je al een kadootje gekocht?
d Ben je al klaar met je studie?
e Is het eten al klaar?
f Heb je al antwoord gekregen op je brief?

Exercise 11F
Answer these questions in the negative as in Exercise 11E, using the equivalent expressions in Dutch of *not any more*.

e.g. Zijn er nog kaartjes? Nee, er zijn geen kaartjes meer.
Leeft zijn vader nog? Nee, zijn vader leeft niet meer.

a Gelooft je zoontje nog in Sinterklaas?
b Werk je nog bij het ziekenhuis?
c Heb je nog zin in koffie?
d Woon je nog bij je ouders?
e Ben je nog misselijk?
f Heb je nog tijd?

Exercise 11G
Answer these questions using the information in brackets indicating you think it is not very much.

e.g. Hoeveel flessen wijn heb je nog? (12) Ik heb nog maar 12 flessen.

a Hoeveel kinderen heb je? (5)
b Hoe laat gaat de bus? (om 3 uur)
c Hoe oud is je dochtertje (2 jaar)
d Hoeveel kaarten moet je nog schrijven? (15) (use hoeven te)

Exercise 11H
Answer the following questions using the negatives in brackets.

e.g. Heb je wel eens gelogen? (nog nooit) Ik heb nog nooit gelogen.

a Heeft iemand je met je werk geholpen? (niemand)
b Ben je wel eens in Bejing geweest? (nog nooit)
c Kun je de schaar vinden? (nergens)
d Heb je dat gemerkt? (niets)

Things to remember

▶ **Niet** is the most common form of making a negative. It simply means *not*.

▶ Generally speaking, **niet** comes last in the sentence or clause (but before the words which take the very last position such as the past participle, the infinitive or prepositional phrases).

▶ **Niet** is also placed before prepositions, adjectives preceding nouns and adverbs.

▶ **Geen** (not a, not any) is used in combination with indefinite nouns.

▶ Some less explicit negatives are: **nog niet/nog geen** (*not yet*), **niet meer/geen meer** (*not any more, 2 words*), **nauwelijks** (*hardly*), **zelden** (*hardly ever*), **maar, nog maar** (*only*), **pas** (*not until*).

12

·····

Prefixes and suffixes

Prefixes and suffixes are parts of words which can be added before
or after a base word.

12.1 Prefixes

Prefixes are added before words. These words can be verbs,
adjectives, adverbs or nouns. A prefix can be a preposition, as is
often the case with separable verbs (see Section 8.1), but frequently
a prefix is a short segment which is not a word in its own right,
and which changes the meaning of the base word. Some prefixes
in Dutch are borrowed from English. Here are some examples:

▶ Indicating an opposite meaning:

on-	**aardig**	*on***aardig** (*unkind*)
a-	**theïst**	*a***theïst** (*atheist*)
im-	**moreel**	*im***moreel** (*immoral*)
ir-	**rationeel**	*ir***rationeel** (*irrational*)
ont-	**wapenen**	*ont***wapenen** (*disarm*)

▶ Indicating something negative:

| wan- | **gedrag** | *wan***gedrag** (*misbehaviour*) |

▶ Location:

| onder- | **bewustzijn** | *onder***bewustzijn** (*subconscious*) |
| inter- | **nationaal** | *inter***nationaal** (*international*) |

▶ Time:

ex-	vriendje	*ex*vriendje (*ex-boyfriend*)
post-	nataal	*post*nataal (*post-natal*)

12.2 Suffixes

Suffixes are added to the end of a word, and are more important in changing the grammatical category than in changing the meaning of words. They are used for:

Making diminutives (see Section 2.10):

-je	kind	kind*je* (small, young child)

▶ Changing a word into an adjective or adverb. Some of these are -baar, -isch, -ig, -(e)lijk, -achtig

-baar	zicht	zicht*baar* (*visible*)
-ig	pracht	pracht*ig* (*gorgeous*)
-(e)lijk	vriend	vriend*elijk* (*friendly*)
-isch	fantast	fantast*isch* (*fantastic*)
-achtig	kind	kind*erachtig* (*childish*)

▶ Making into a noun:

-heid	mogelijk	mogelijk*heid* (*possibility*)

Insight

There are quite a few categories of prefixes and suffixes. It can be quite a chore to learn these. You may find it easier to use these categories as a reference and aid when you come across words with a prefix or suffix. This way you will gain a better understanding of the way words are formed in Dutch.

Exercise 12A

Which go together? Link the prefixes in the box to a word (adjective, noun or verb) from both columns to change its meaning. The meanings you need to aim for are given in English. The first one is done for you.

a- aseksueel asymmetrisch

beschadigd	(*undamaged*)	arm	(*underarm*)
titel	(*sub-title*)	vriendelijk	(*unfriendly*)
seksueel	(*asexual*)	begrip	(*misconception*)
populair	(*unpopular*)	vouwen	(*unfold*)
orde	(*disorder*)	symmetrisch	(*asymmetrical*)
bossen	(*deforestation*)	migratie	(*immigration*)

Exercise 12B
Fill in the grid. The first one is done for you. Use a dictionary if needed.

verb	noun	adjective
fantaseren	fantast	fantastisch
wanhopen	–	wanhopig
–	(aan)koop	verkoopbaar
(zich) verantwoorden	verantwoordelijkheid	–
geloven	–	–
–	zicht	–
–	–	mogelijk
(zich) interesseren	–	–
praktizeren	–	–

Exercise 12C
Correct the words in brackets by adding the appropriate suffix.

a Onze prijzen zijn (vergelijk) met die van de concurrent. (adjective)

b Het is bijna een (onmogelijk) om in het centrum te parkeren. (noun)

c Dat Afrikaanse land heeft eindelijk de (onafhankelijk) verkregen. (noun)

d Met (kracht) slagen zwom hij naar de overkant. (adjective)

e Wat een heerlijk (geur) kruidenthee. (adjective)

13

Er

13.1 *Er* – as a subject

In this section you will learn about the use of **er** in its function as a subject.

13.1.1 General information

The little word **er** is used frequently, but its application can be a little tricky. There are two main functions of the word. One of these functions is purely grammatical: its use as a subject or in combination with a subject. This is discussed in this section. The other function is one of substitution, to replace another word, and is discussed in Section 13.2.

13.1.2 Grammatical use

With grammatical use in this context we mean that the word **er** in the following situations does not have a meaning in its own right. There are two situations in which **er** has to be used purely for grammatical reasons. These two situations are:

1 In combination with an indefinite subject

De wedstrijd Ajax Barcelona is vanavond op tv.
The match between Ajax and Barcelona is on tv tonight.

▶ The subject is a specific one. We know which particular match we are talking about. But if you weren't certain which teams were playing, the subject would be indefinite. In that case you would say:

Er **is vanavond <u>een</u> voetbalwedstrijd op tv.**

▶ Indefinite subjects are normally subjects which have either no article at all or are preceded by **een**, **geen** or a counting word, including words like **weinig** and **veel**.

Er **is vanavond geen voetbal op tv.**	*There is no football on tv tonight.*
Er **zijn weinig kinderen op school vandaag.**	*There are not many children at school today.*

▶ Indefinite subjects can also be words like: **iets, niemand, iemand, wie, wat,** etc:

Er **komt straks iemand langs.**	*Someone will be around later on.*
Wie komt *er* **dan langs?**	*Who will be around then?*

2 As the subject in a passive sentence.

Passive sentences without a definite subject, describing human activities, start with er:

Er **mag hier niet gerookt worden.**	*Smoking is not allowed here.*
Er **wordt veel geschreven.**	*Much is being written.*

Exercise 13A
Make these definite subjects indefinite. This means you have to use *er*.

e.g. De koekjes zitten in de trommel.
　　　Er zitten koekjes in de trommel.

a Mijn man is in de tuin aan het werken.
b De trein vertrekt om 8 uur.
c Het boek ligt op de tafel.

d Het café is op de hoek van de straat.
e De natte kleren hangen aan de lijn.

Exercise 13B
Insert *er* in the correct position, but not at the start of the sentence.

e.g. Vanavond is geen yoga.
Vanavond is er geen yoga.

a Zit nog een beetje wijn in de fles?
b Wat is gebeurd?
c Op koninginnedag zijn veel mensen op straat.
d Morgen komt iemand op bezoek.
e Is een dokter in de zaal?

Exercise 13C
Describe some characteristics of the Netherlands making use of the picture below.

e.g. veel dijken Er zijn veel dijken.

a veel water **b** veel kerken **c** veel fietspaden

Exercise 13D
You are now describing activities which are often seen as being typically Dutch. Please note that some subjects are plural.

e.g. Veel gerookt. Er wordt veel gerookt.

a Veel drugs gebruikt.
b Veel koffie gedronken.
c Veel gefietst.
d Veel verjaarsfeestjes gevierd.

Exercise 13E

The sentences in Exercise 13D are too generalized. Change them into active sentences using the subject *sommige mensen*.

e.g. Sommige mensen roken veel.

13.2 *Er* – referring to things

In this section you will learn about the use of **er** to refer to things.

13.2.1 Place

The word **er** can be substituted for a place. In this situation **er** simply means **there**:

Ken je Amsterdam goed?	*Do you know Amsterdam well?*
Nee, ik ben *er* **maar een keer geweest.**	*No, I've only been there once.*
Wat een kleine keuken heb jij.	*What a small kitchen you've got.*
Ik kan *er* **niks vinden.**	*I can't find anything (there).*

NB The stressed form of **er** is **daar** and often comes at the start of the sentence: *Daar* ben ik maar een keer geweest.

13.2.2 With quantity

You also use **er** to refer to something in combination with a counting word.

Ik heb nu vijf kinderen in huis; ik heb *er* **zelf twee en mijn nieuwe partner heeft** *er* **drie.**	*I now have five children at home; two of them are my own and my new partner has got three.*
Heb je een fiets? Ja, ik heb *er* **een.**	*Have you got a bike? Yes, I've got one.*

13.2.3 With a preposition

Normally when you refer to an object or idea, you use an object pronoun, e.g. **hij, hem, ze, het** etc. However, when combined with a preposition the object pronoun cannot be used. Instead you must use **er**. Compare the following sentences:

Heb je dat programma nog gezien?	*Did you see that programme?*
Nee, ik heb het niet gezien.	*No, I didn't see it.*
Kijk jij vanavond naar dat programma?	*Will you watch that programme tonight?*
Nee, ik ga *er* **niet** *naar* **kijken.**	*No, I won't watch it.*

Note the following two points:

▶ **Er** + preposition is written as one word if not separated by other words.

Ik hou *ervan.*	*I love it.*
Ik hou *er* **erg veel** *van.*	*I love it a lot.*

▶ You can also use **daar** for stressing the point. It normally comes at the beginning of the sentence:

Daar **ga ik niet naar kijken.**	*I won't watch that.*

Insight

When learning Dutch you may find it easiest to focus first on the use of **er** with an indefinite subject: whenever a sentence has an indefinite subject, start your sentence with **er** (see 13.1.1). Then focus on the other uses: in passive sentences (13.1.2), the relatively straightforward use of **er** when it means *there* (13.2.1), and referring to things (13.2.2 and 13.2.3).

Exercise 13F
Answer the following questions using the information in brackets. Replace the underlined places with *er*. Note that the words in italics should not be used in the answer.

e.g. Ben je *wel eens* in Brussel geweest? (een keer)
Ik ben er een keer geweest.

a Kom je *vaak* in de bibliotheek? (regelmatig)
b Hoe lang woon je nu in Utrecht? (drie jaar)
c Zit je elke dag in je werkkamer te werken ? (bijna elke dag)
d Ben je *al* bij je ouders geweest? (gisteren)
e Ben je gisteren *nog* naar die astrologiecursus geweest? (niet)

Exercise 13G
Answer the following questions using the information between brackets. Refer to the underlined words with *er*.

e.g. Hoeveel planten heb je? (ongeveer zes)
Ik heb er ongeveer zes.

a Heb je een computer? (één)
b Hoeveel fietsen heeft Eef? (vier)
c Heeft u een auto? (twee)
d Heb jij een euro voor de automaat? (zelfs drie)
e Heeft u een televisie? (geen een)

Exercise 13H
Use *er* in answering the following questions.

e.g. Gelooft u in spoken?   Ja, ik geloof **erin**.
Nee, ik geloof er niet **in**.

a Houdt u van strandvakanties?
b Heeft u een hekel aan huisdieren?
c Ben je bang van spinnen?
d Ben je tevreden over je werk?
e Ben je goed in surfen?
f Heeft u goede herinneringen aan de vakantie?
g Verlang je naar de zomer?

13.3 *Er* – position

In this section you will learn what position **er** usually takes in the sentence.

13.3.1 Grammatical use

If **er** is used as a subject or in combination with a generalized subject, it usually comes at the start of the sentence:

Er **was eens een prinses...**	*Once upon a time there was a princess.*
Er **werd niet veel gelachen in haar huis.**	*There was not much laughter in her house.*

However, **er** can also come after the finite verb if the sentence starts with another element:

Veel werd **er** niet gelachen in haar huis.

13.3.2 Referring

▶ **Er** generally comes straight after the finite verb:

Jantien *heeft er* **geen zin meer in.**	*Jantien doesn't fancy it any more.*

▶ **Er** generally comes after the subject in sentences with inversion:

Gisteren *is* **Floris** *er* **geweest.**	*Yesterday Floris went there.*

▶ If you use **er** as a term of reference (whether in relation to place, quantity or with a preposition) you cannot place it at the start of the sentence, because **er** in this situation is always unstressed.

If you want to stress the reference you are making, you need to use the word **daar**:

Ik heb *er* **niet veel van**   *I didn't understand much of it.*
  begrepen.
Daar **heb ik niet veel van begrepen.**

▶ A reflexive pronoun (Section 9.1) takes precedence over **er** and thus comes straight after the finite verb and before **er**:

Ik maak *me er* **geen zorgen over.**   *I am not worried about it.*
Ik verheug *me erop* **om hem**   *I am looking forward to*
  te zien.   *seeing him.*

▶ An object or object pronoun also takes precedence over **er**:

Ik geef *hem er* **twee.**   *I'll give him two of them.*
Paul geeft *Petra er* **drie.**   *Paul gives three of them to Petra.*

▶ In a sub-clause (Section 15.1) **er** comes straight after the subject or after the reflexive pronoun:

Hij zegt dat *hij er* **nooit naar**   *He says he never watches it.*
  kijkt.
Ik denk dat zij *zich er* **niet**   *I think she is not ashamed of it.*
  voor schaamt.

Exercise 13I
Insert *er* in the correct position.

e.g. is een nieuwe jongen in de klas   Er is een nieuwe jongen in
                                           de klas.
    veel fouten zijn niet gemaakt   Veel fouten zijn er niet
                                           gemaakt.

a zijn te veel auto's op de weg
b (Pas op!) ligt veel hondenpoep op straat
c gisteren was een feest bij de buren

d waren veel mensen
e werd veel gelachen en gedronken
f waarschijnlijk komt een nieuw hoofd op school

Exercise 13J
Answer the following questions twice. Use *er* in your first answer
and *daar* in your second one to refer to the underlined noun.

e.g. Hebben jullie aan de loterij meegedaan?
We hebben er (niet) aan meegedaan.
Daar hebben we (niet) aan meegedaan.

a Kijk jij naar Big Brother op tv?
b Bel jij Hans vanavond over die afspraak?
c Is Leontien blij met haar cadeautje?
d Kom je uit die som?
e Wacht u op het antwoord van de directeur?
f Bent u naar de begrafenis geweest

Exercise 13K
Replace the underlined nouns by *er* and place it in the correct
position in the sentence. Add *-toe* and *-vandaan* if needed
(see Section 13.4).

e.g. Ik ga een paar keer per jaar naar Amsterdam. (add *-toe*)
Ik ga er een paar keer per jaar naartoe.

a Op kantoor heb ik twee computers.
b Carrie is ontevreden over het nieuwe programma.
c Pam gaat drie middagen per week naar school. (add *-toe*)
d Nico geeft Ineke twee doosjes bonbons.
e Tineke schaamt zich voor haar laatste show.
f U komt zeker net van de tentoonstelling? (add *-vandaan*)
g Ik geloof niet dat hij van klassieke muziek houdt.
h Joop zegt dat hij zich over het examen geen zorgen maakt.

13.4 *Er* – some other considerations

This section lists some extra points about the use of **er**.

13.4.1 Referring to things with a preposition

When referring to something in combination with a preposition, you only use **er** when referring to an *object* or *idea*. When you refer to *people* you use an object pronoun:

Ik denk nooit meer aan *hem.* **(mijn ex-vriendje)**	*I never think about him anymore. (my ex-boyfriend)*
Ik denk *er* **nooit meer aan.** **(mijn vakantie)**	*I never think about it anymore. (my holiday)*

The prepositions **met** and **tot** change into **mee** and **toe** respectively, when they are combined with **er** or **daar**:

> **Werk jij weleens** *met* **Power Point? Ja, ik werk** *er* **vaak** *mee.*

It is important not to confuse the prefix of a separable verb with the preposition which is combined with **er**:

> **Kijk je weleens** *in* **dat boek? Nee, ik kijk** *er* **bijna nooit in.**
> *Do you ever look in that book? No, I hardly ever look in it.*
> **Heb je dat boek** *uit* **(gelezen)? Nee, ik heb** *het* **nog niet uit.**
> *Did you finish that book? No, I haven't finished it yet.*

Uit belongs to the separable verb, so you need to refer to the book with **het** rather than with **er**.

13.4.2 Direction

If a direction is indicated, you need to add the suffixes **-naartoe**, **-heen**, or **-vandaan**:

Ik ga *ernaartoe.* **Ik ga** *erheen.*	*I am going there.*
Ik kom *ervandaan.*	*I am coming from there.*

These words can be split up:

Ik ga er **nu** naartoe.　　　　　*I am going there now.*

13.4.3 More than one *er*

In the following example the first **er** has a grammatical function, the second **er** is used because it refers to something in combination with a counting word:

Er **zijn** er **nog een paar.**　　*There are still a few (left).*

Occasionally **er** can refer to two things at once:

Heb je boven nog een stoel?　*Have you got another chair upstairs?*
Ja, er **staat** er **nog een.**　　*Yes, there is still one there.*

The second **er** refers to both the chair and to upstairs.

Exercise 13L
Substitute the underlined words with either the object pronouns *hem*, *haar* or *hen/ze* or use *er*.

e.g. We wachten op <u>antwoord</u>.
　　　We wachten erop.

  a We wachten op <u>Maria</u>.
  b Ik ben bang van <u>mijn baas</u>.
  c Herman is bang van <u>onweer</u> (*thunder and lightning*).
  d Niemand gelooft meer in <u>een vreedzame</u> (*peaceful*) <u>oplossing</u>.
  e We hopen op <u>mooi weer</u>.
  f We drinken op <u>jullie gezondheid</u>.
  g Hannes luistert nooit naar <u>Janette</u>.
  h Onze club speelt tegen <u>het thuiselftal</u> (*home team*).

Exercise 13M
Fill in *met*, *mee*, *tot* or *toe*, as appropriate.

a Heb je hem aangemoedigd ___ stoppen met roken?
b Nee, ik heb hem er niet ___ aangemoedigd.
c Kook jij wel eens ___ walnootolie?
d Ja, daar kook ik regelmatig ___
e Schrijf jij vaak ___ een vulpen?
f Nee, ik schrijf er eigenlijk nooit ___

Exercise 13N
Fill in the correct words which indicate you are going or have just been somewhere.

a Ga je vaak naar de bibliotheek?
   Ja, ik kom ___ net ___
b Ga je nog wel eens naar Ikea?
   Ik ben ___ gisteren ___ geweest.
c Zullen we vanavond naar de bioscoop?
   Laten we ___ morgen ___ gaan.
d Wil je naar het orgelconcert in de Grote Kerk?
   Ja, ik wil ___ wel ___

Things to remember

▶ **Er** is used when a sentence has an indefinite subject (**Er is een wedstrijd op tv.** *There is a match on tv.*)

▶ **Er** is used in passive sentences describing human activities when there is no specific subject (**Er mag hier niet gerookt worden.** *Smoking isn't allowed here.*)

▶ **Er** can refer to a place (**Ik woon er al een jaar.** *I've lived there for a year.*).

▶ **Er** can refer to something in combination with a counting word (**Ik heb er vijf.** *I have five of them.*).

▶ When referring to an object or idea with an object pronoun, in combination with a preposition, the object pronoun is replaced by **er** (**Kijk jij naar het programma?** *Are you watching the programme?* **Nee, ik kijk er niet naar.** *No, I'm not watching it.*).

▶ When **er** is used to refer to something, it generally comes straight after the finite verb, though reflexive pronouns, objects and object pronouns are placed in front of **er**.

▶ Combined with **er**, the prepositions **met** and **tot** change into **mee** and **toe** (**ermee, ertoe**).

▶ If a direction is indicated in a sentence where **er** refers to a place, **er** is combined with the suffixes **-naartoe, -heen** or **-vandaan** (**ernaartoe, erheen, ervandaan**).

14

Prepositions

14.1 Prepositions – general

Prepositions are words such as *at*, *in*, *to*, etc.

14.1.1 Function

Prepositions are important words in a sentence because they generally show the relationship between things. This relationship is frequently to do with place, direction, time, cause and reason and means. Use of the wrong preposition can make the sentence difficult to understand and can even change the meaning entirely.

NB Prepositions are often part of a separable verb. This is a completely separate category. Information in this section will not apply to those prepositions.

14.1.2 Meaning

Prepositions do not translate easily. Even though prepositions often have a literal meaning,which might translate well, the way in which prepositions are used depends on the context. The use of prepositions in English is not necessarily the same as in Dutch.

14.1.3 Fixed expressions

There are many expressions which have a fixed preposition. It is best to learn these expressions with their preposition as you come across them. See Section 14.4.

14.1.4 Place in sentence

▶ Prepositions normally come before a noun:

Ik ga straks *naar* **de stad.**　　*I'll go up to town in a minute.*

▶ Sometimes they are used before adverbs:

Ik ga *naar* **beneden.**　　*I'm going downstairs.*

▶ Occasionally prepositions are used after a noun:

Francien loopt de trap *af*.　　*Francien walks down the stairs.*

▶ Prepositions are sometimes combined with **er, hier, daar, waar**. They might then be written as one word e.g. **eraan, hierin, daarop, waarover** etc.

▶ Prepositional phrases (a combination of words which start with a preposition, such as **met onze vrienden**), can come after the last verb position in the sentence (see Section 17.3):

We gaan uit eten met onze　　*We're going out for a meal with*
vrienden.　　　　　　　　　*our friends.*

14.1.5 The prepositions *met* and *tot*

The prepositions **met** and **tot** change into **mee** and **toe** respectively when you use them with **er, hier, daar** and **waar**, e.g. **ermee, ertoe, hiermee, daartoe** etc.

Exercise 14A
Find the ten prepositions in this story.

Een man zit te vissen aan een brede sloot in Noord-Holland.
Zijn vishaak komt vast te zitten aan iets zwaars. Voorbijgangers
komen de man helpen en tenslotte halen zij met z'n allen het
lichaam van een man naar boven. Het blijkt een postbode te zijn
die al een dag of tien werd vermist. Hij heeft zijn tas nog om.
In de tas zit een brief. Deze is geadresseerd aan de man die hem
heeft opgevist.

Adapted from: *Broodje Aap* by Ethel Portnoy

Exercise 14B
Identify the prepositional phrases.

a Dinsdag gaan we met z'n allen naar de film.
b De trein was gelukkig op tijd.
c Ik kom uit het zuiden.
d Ze droeg zo'n rare hoed met echte bloemen erop.
e Ze zijn heel gelukkig met z'n tweeën.
f Remi staat altijd een uur onder de douche.

Exercise 14C
Insert the prepositions in brackets into the right place.

a Er dreef een vlieg een vol glas water. (in)
b Mijn broek en mijn riem hingen een stoel. (over)
c Het rook benauwd de kamer. (in)
d Ik stond op, opende de deur en keek een donkere gang. (in)
e Twee hielen schoten de hoek. (om) (hiel = heel)
f Ik zweette en zocht verkoeling het balkon. (op)
g Buiten was het stikdonker, alleen geluiden, krekels, de zee,
maar mijn gevoel richting was ik kwijt. (voor)
h Ik rilde de kou. (van)

Source: *Palmwijn* by Adriaan van Dis

Exercise 14D

Choose the correct preposition from these given in brackets.

a Ik ga ___ Albert mee. (met, mee)
b Ik loop mee ___ je huis. (tot, toe)
c Wil je me hier ___ helpen? (met, mee)
d Hoe ben je ___ die beslissing gekomen? (tot, toe)
e Hoe ben je er ___ gekomen? (tot, toe)

14.2 Prepositions – space and location

By far the largest group of prepositions express some relation to space or location.

The table contains a list of the most common prepositions of location and space. Note however, that many of these prepositions can also be used to indicate other relationships or meanings.

in	Het zit *in* mijn tas.	It is *in* my bag.
op	Suiker staat *op* de tafel.	Sugar is *on* the table.
onder	Je tas staat *onder* je bureau.	Your bag is *under* your desk.
	Hillegom ligt iets *onder* Haarlem.	Hillegom is a little *south* of Haarlem.
voor	De auto staat *voor* het huis.	The car is *in front of* the house.
achter	Ik loop wel *achter* je.	I'll walk *behind* you.
naast	Kom je *naast* me zitten?	Will you come and sit *next to* me?
over	Je moet *over* de brug, dan links.	Go *over* the bridge, then left.
	Leg een kleed *over* de bank.	Put a throw *over* the sofa.
tussen	Ik wil niet *tussen* jullie komen.	I don't want to come *between* you.
	Het kastje past precies *tussen* die stoelen.	The cupboard fits exactly *in between* those two chairs.
tegen	Zet je fiets niet *tegen* het huis.	Don't put your bike *against* the house.

tegenover	Ik woon *tegenover* **het park.**	I live *opposite* **the park.**
aan	**Blijf nog even** *aan* **tafel zitten.**	**Stay** *at* **the table for a while.**
	Wat hangt er *aan* **de muur?**	**What's hanging** *on* **the wall?**
bij	**Ze staan** *bij* **de deur.**	**They are** *near* **the door.**
	Hij woont *bij* **een vriend.**	**He lives** *at* **a friend's.**
door	**Je moet** *door* **het poortje.**	**You need to go** *through* **the archway.**
op	**Ik zit** *op* **mijn kamer.**	**I'm** *in* **my room.**
uit	**Ik kom** *uit* **Nederland.**	**I come** *from* **Holland.**

Exercise 14E

Are the prepositions in bold used in a literal sense to indicate
location or space or are they used figuratively?

a Achter ons huis ligt een groot bos.
b Hij stopte zijn camera **onder** zijn regenjas.
c **Onder** tieners is er weinig interesse voor politiek.
d **In** het vliegtuig voelde hij zich ziek.
e Gebruik je zoetjes **in** je koffie?
f **Over** een paar weken gaan we weg.
g Zij had een baby **op** haar schoot.
h Wij gaan altijd een weekje weg **in** het najaar.
i **Op** donderdag komt de schoonmaakster.
j Thea ging **tegenover** mij zitten.

Exercise 14F

Complete these instructions for an assault course by filling in the
correct preposition.

kruip ____ de tunnel   spring ___ het water   klim ___ de boom,
                                                  ___ het huis

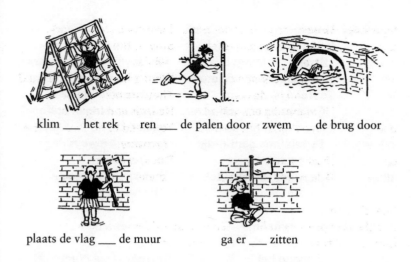

klim ___ het rek   ren ___ de palen door   zwem ___ de brug door

plaats de vlag ___ de muur   ga er ___ zitten

14.3 Prepositions – other types

In this section you will find prepositions that express relationships
between things other than space and location.

14.3.1 Directions, movement

naar	**Wanneer gaan jullie** *naar* **Antwerpen?**	When are you going *to* Antwerp?
uit	**Hij is** *uit* **de voorstelling weggelopen.**	He left the performance.
tot	**Ik loop mee** *tot* **de hoek.**	I'll walk with you *to* the corner.
langs	*Langs* **het huis loopt een drukke weg.**	*Alongside* the house is a busy road.
op	**Hij loopt snel die berg** *op*.	He is walking quickly *up* that mountain.
af	**Remi rent de trap** *af*.	Remi is running *down* the stairs.
voorbij	**Er kwam net een oude auto** *voorbij*.	An old car just came *past*.

14.3.2 Time

tot	Ik blijf *tot* morgen.	I'm staying *until* tomorrow.
na	Kim komt pas *na* vieren.	Kim is not coming until *after* four (o'clock).
om	Chris komt *om* half zeven.	Chris is coming *at* half past six.
onder	De telefoon gaat altijd *onder* het eten.	The phone always rings *during* dinner.
tijdens	Ze waren ondergedoken *tijdens* de oorlog.	They were in hiding *during* the war.

14.3.3 Cause, reason

uit	Ik vraag het *uit* belangstelling, niet *uit* nieuwsgierigheid.	I'm asking *out of* interest, not *out of* curiosity.
door	*Door* hard te werken heeft hij zijn examen gehaald.	*By* working hard he passed his exam.
vanwege	*Vanwege* de drukte op de wegen zijn er lange files.	*Because of* the road works there are long traffic jams.
van	Ik ben bijna doof *van* al dat lawaai.	I'm almost deaf *from* all that noise.

14.3.4 Opinion

tegen	Ik ben *tegen* dat voorstel.	I'm *against* that proposal.
volgens	*Volgens* Julie gaat hij gauw met pensioen.	*According to* Julie he will retire soon.

14.3.5 Means

met	Ik ga meestal *met* de bus.	I normally go *by* bus.

14.3.6 Possession

van	**Sorry hoor, maar dat is** *van* **mij.**	**Sorry, but that is mine** (*from* **me**).
voor	**Wat heb je** *voor* **Hester gekocht?**	**What did you buy** *for* **Hester?**

Insight

Prepositions are notoriously difficult to learn in foreign languages. One of the reasons is that in other languages you rarely use the litteral translation of the preposition which you use in your mother tongue. Often it seems that there is no logic in which preposition has to be used. However, if you persist and learn which preposition is to be used in a particular context, you will soon find it starts to pay off, and the learning process becomes easier and easier.

Exercise 14G

What do the prepositions in bold express? Choose one of the following: a) direction/movement; b) time; c) cause/reason; d) opinion; e) possession; f) means; g) figurative use.

1 Hij zong **met** een bedroefde stem.
2 's Morgens **om** half elf ging ik boodschappen doen.
3 Hij haalde de brief **uit** zijn zak.
4 Hij liep **langs** me heen zonder me te zien.
5 **Volgens** Jasmijn is hij opnieuw getrouwd.
6 Ze durfde niet **naar** de anderen te kijken.
7 Herman reed **naar** zijn werk.
8 Ze begon te huilen **uit** pure frustratie.
9 Ik heb iets **voor** je meegebracht.
10 **Door** de sneeuwval in Zuid-Duitsland staat het water in de IJssel nu erg hoog.
11 Ik loop **met** je mee **tot** de supermarkt.

Exercise 14H

You are preparing a treasure hunt for a children's party. Complete the clues by adding the correct preposition.

Loop de trap ___

en ga de deur ___

Ga ___ rechts

loop ___ het hek

steek de weg ___

loop ___ de boom en pak de envelop

haal de brief ___ de envelop

Ga ___ het adres dat wordt genoemd

14.4 Fixed prepositions (1)

Sometimes prepositions are used with verbs or within expressions where you'd often not expect them – these are fixed prepositions.

14.4.1 Expressions

There are many expressions in Dutch which always have the same preposition – normally not used in a literal sense (some of these expressions also have a preposition as part of a separable verb).

afhangen *van*	*to depend on*
antwoorden *op*	*to answer*
zich bemoeien *met*	*to stick one's nose in*
bewondering hebben *voor*	*to admire/feel admiration for*
bezig zijn *met*	*to be busy with*
denken *aan*	*to think of*
het (niet) eens zijn *met*	*to (not) agree with*
zich ergeren *aan*	*to feel irritated by*
feliciteren *met*	*to congratulate (on)*
genieten *van*	*to enjoy*
gaan *over*	*to be about, concern*
een hekel hebben *aan*	*to dislike*
houden *van*	*to like/to love*

NB Often the English equivalent does not have a preposition.

14.4.2 Example sentences

Heb je nu al geantwoord *op* **die brief?**	*Have you answered that letter yet?*
Bemoei je er niet *mee.*	*Don't stick your nose in.*
Ik ben bezig *met* **een nieuw project.**	*I'm busy with/working on a new project.*
Ik ben het niet *met* **je eens.**	*I don't agree with you.*
Ik erger me *aan* **zijn maniertjes.**	*His manners irritate me.*
Gefeliciteerd *met* **je verjaardag.**	*Congratulations on your birthday.*
Waar gaat dat boek *over***?**	*What's that book about?*

Exercise 14I
Fill in the correct preposition.

e.g. Denk je nog wel eens __ me?
Denk je nog wel eens aan me?

a Geniet maar lekker __ je vakantie.
b Sorry hoor, maar ik geef geen antwoord __ die vraag.
c Gefeliciteerd __ jullie baby.
d Of we naar de politie gaan, hangt af __ jou.
e Ik heb een hekel __ computerspelletjes.
f Jan houdt __ watersporten.
g Weet jij waar die film __ gaat?
h Ik heb grote bewondering __ mensen die met kleine kinderen
werken.

Exercise 14J
The following verbs all have *met* as a fixed preposition. Fill in *met*
or *mee* as appropriate.

e.g. Doe jij mee __ de loterij?
Doe jij mee met de loterij?

a Zullen we beginnen __ de eerste vraag?
b Zullen we er nu maar __ stoppen?
c Even wachten, ik ben nu bezig __ koken.
d Mijn collega's zijn het nooit eens __ elkaar.
e Nou, gefeliciteerd er __
f Mijn baas bemoeit zich altijd __ de kleinste details.
g Veel plezier er __
h We zijn tegelijk __ jullie aangekomen.

Exercise 14K
Fill in the correct preposition. You might have to refer to the
dictionary.

e.g. Ik ben benieuwd __ zijn beslissing.
Ik ben benieuwd naar zijn beslissing.

a Ludwien is gek __ drop.
b Lex verdiept zich __ antropologie.

c Ik ben slecht ___ sport.
d Marijke heeft zin ___ een lekker broodje kaas.
e Rosa heeft spijt ___ haar gemene opmerking.
f Herinner je me er ___ dat ik straks moet werken?

14.4.3 Here are some more examples of expressions with fixed prepositions

zich interesseren *voor*	*to be interested in*
geïnteresseerd zijn *in*	*to be interested in*
kwaad zijn *op* **(iemand)**	*to be angry with (someone)*
kwaad zijn *over/om* **(iets)**	*to be angry about (something)*
luisteren *naar*	*to listen to*
praten *over*	*to talk about*
zich schamen *voor*	*to be ashamed about*
solliciteren *naar*	*to apply for (a job)*
tevreden zijn *met/over*	*to be satisfied about*
twijfelen *aan*	*to doubt*
verliefd zijn *op*	*to be in love with*
zich vergissen *in*	*to be mistaken about*
verwijzen *naar*	*to refer to*
wachten *op*	*to wait for*
zoeken *naar*	*to look for*
zich zorgen maken *over/om*	*to be worried about*

14.4.4 Example sentences

Ik ben geïnteresseerd *in* **quantumtheorie.**	*I'm interested in quantum theory.*
Joost is heel kwaad *op* **Peter.**	*Joost is really angry with Peter.*
Waar praten jullie *over***?**	*What are you talking about?*
Ik solliciteer hierbij *naar* **de baan van manager**	*I am applying herewith for the job of manager.*
Lena twijfelt *aan* **zichzelf.**	*Lena is doubting herself.*
Ik ben verliefd *op* **een getrouwde man.**	*I'm in love with a married man.*
Ik heb me *in* **jou vergist.**	*I've been mistaken about you.*

Exercise 14L
Describe someone you like, using some of the expressions below.

houden van	bewondering hebben voor
genieten van	blij zijn met to be *happy with*
verliefd zijn op	plezier hebben in to *enjoy*
zich interesseren voor	gek zijn op to be *fond of*
belangstelling hebben	dromen van to *dream of*
voor to be *interested in*	

e.g. Ik hou van Melissa. Ik heb bewondering voor haar intelligentie.
Zij heeft belangstelling voor politiek en economie en zij geniet
van een goed gesprek. *I love Melissa. I admire her intelligence.*
She is interested in politics and economics and she enjoys a
good conversation.

Exercise 14M
Describe someone you don't like using some of the expressions
below.

zich ergeren aan to *get annoyed with*	zich bemoeien *met* to *interfere with*
zich vergissen *in* to *be mistaken about*	een hekel hebben aan to *dislike*
zich schamen voor to *be ashamed of*	denken aan to *think of*
twijfelen aan to *doubt*	de schuld geven van to *blame*
kritiek hebben op *to criticize*	

e.g. Ik erger me aan Michael. Hij bemoeit zich met mijn zaken. Hij
heeft overal kritiek op. Hij geeft anderen de schuld van zijn
fouten. *Michael irritates me. He sticks his nose in my affairs.*
He criticizes everything. He blames others for his mistakes.

Exercise 14N
Fill in the correct preposition. You might have to refer to a dictionary.

e.g. Ik blijf mijn hele leven __ je wachten.
Ik blijf mijn hele leven op je wachten.

a Anneke is bang __ grote honden.
b Douwe solliciteert __ de baan van hoofdredacteur.
c De meisjes praten __ de jongens.
d Niemand luistert __ me.
e Ik ben kwaad __ de prijsverhoging.
f Ze zoeken nog steeds __ een oplossing.

Things to remember

▶ Prepositions are normally placed in front of a noun (**op school** *at school*), but are sometimes also used in front of an adverb (**naar beneden** *(to go) upstairs*), or after a noun (**de trap af** *down the stairs*).

▶ Prepositional phrases can be placed after the last verb position in a sentence.

▶ The prepositions **met** and **tot** change into **mee** and **toe** when used with **er**, **hier**, **daar** and **waar**, e.g. **ermee**, **ertoe**, **hiermee**, **daartoe**, etc.

▶ Frequently used prepositions relating to space or location are: **in** *in*, **op** *on*, **voor** *in front of*, **achter** *behind*, **naast** *next to*, **tussen** *between*, **aan** *at/on*, **bij** *near/at*, **uit** *from*.

▶ Frequently used prepositions relating to direction or movement are: **naar** *to*, **tot** *(up) to*, **langs** *along*, **op** *up*, **af** *down*.

▶ Frequently used prepositions relating to time are: **tot** *until*, **na** *after*, **om** *at*, **tijdens** *during*.

▶ Frequently used preposition relating to cause or reason are: **door** *by*, **vanwege** *because of*, **van** *from*.

15

Clauses and conjunctions

15.1 Basic information on clauses

15.1.1 General information

A clause is (a part of) a sentence which has at least one verb and normally a subject. There are three different kinds of clause: main clause, sub-clause and relative clause. The relative clause is discussed separately (see Section 15.6), although this is also a kind of sub-clause. Most simple sentences have only a main clause. More complex sentences often consist of two or more clauses, at least one of which will normally be a main clause.

There are two reasons why you need to know what kind of clause a particular sentence part is. Depending on the kind of clause:

▶ the verb takes a certain position in the sentence
▶ certain linking words are used (see Sections 15.3–15.5).

15.1.2 Main clause

Most sentences have at least one main clause. A main clause is (a part of) a sentence which can stand on its own. It could be short or slightly longer:

Ik werk hard.	*I'm working hard*
Ik ga vanavond met mijn zus en haar man ergens in de stad wat drinken.	*I'm going to town for a drink with my sister and her husband this evening.*

In a main clause the finite verb is the second item in the sentence, except when the sentence is a yes/no question or an order.

15.1.3 Sub-clause

A sub-clause is a part of a sentence which normally cannot be used on its own. It needs to be combined with a main clause.

Ik denk (*main clause*) **dat ik vanavond vroeg naar bed ga**
(*sub-clause*).
I think that I'll be going to bed early tonight.

A sub-clause has two characteristics:

▶ the verb goes to the end of the clause, and
▶ the sub-clause always starts with a special linking word (see Sections 15.3–15.4):

Ik weet *dat* **ik soms moeilijk ben.**
I know I'm not the easiest of people. (lit: *I know that I am sometimes difficult.*)

If there is a second verb in the sub-clause, this verb also goes to the very end. If it's a past participle, it can come before or after the finite verb.

Je weet toch dat ik het nooit heb geprobeerd.	*You know I have never tried it.*
Je weet toch dat ik het nooit geprobeerd heb.	

Exercise 15A
Identify the various main and sub-clauses in the weather forecast.

a Het blijft de komende dagen zacht, maar de zon blijft weg.
b Bovendien valt er af en toe regen.
c De kans op regen zal na het weekeinde toenemen, omdat er
een lagedrukgebied boven Nederland ligt.
d De temperatuur zal overdag rond de 9 graden liggen en 's
nachts zal deze dalen tot 4 graden boven nul.
e Verder in Europa is het weer wisselvallig, maar in de Alpen is
het zonnig op de skipistes.
f Volgende week zal het zacht blijven in Nederland, terwijl het
in de Alpen goed skiweer blijft.

> **lagedrukgebied** *area of low pressure*   **wisselvallig** *changeable*

Exercise 15B
You have the following information on hearsay. You want to
present it as your own.

e.g. Zij zegt dat Sieme een nieuwe auto heeft.
Sieme heeft een nieuwe auto.

a Zij zegt dat de benzineprijzen volgende maand zullen dalen.
b Zij zegt dat nieuwe auto's schoner zijn.
c Zij zegt dat Sieme echt een auto nodig heeft.
d Zij zegt dat hij soms ook met de trein reist.
e Zij zegt dat Reint altijd met het openbaar vervoer reist.
f Zij zegt dat Reint erg milieubewust is.

> **milieubewust** *environmentally aware*

Exercise 15C
Where else can the verb go? Use an alternative word order.

e.g. Ik geloof dat ze zich heeft bezeerd.
Ik geloof dat ze zich bezeerd heeft.

a Jari vindt dat hij geluk heeft gehad.
b Je weet toch dat Bernlef veel prijzen heeft gewonnen?
c Remi zegt dat hij geen tv heeft gekeken.

d Maar Chris zegt dat hij dat wel heeft gedaan.
e Ik ben bang dat ik me heb verslapen.
f Ik heb gehoord dat Kim een nieuwe band heeft opgericht.

15.2 Conjunctions: linking similar clauses

Many sentences consist of more than one clause. These clauses are linked by special linking words: conjunctions.

15.2.1 Linking two or more main clauses

When you want to combine two main clauses, i.e. two sentence parts each of which could also stand on its own as a sentence, you can do this by using a linking word. These linking words are called co-ordinating conjunctions.

15.2.2 Form

The word order in the linked clauses remains exactly the same as if they were separate sentences.

15.2.3 Use

Co-ordinating conjunctions do more in a sentence than just a grammatical linking; they indicate the relation between the two sentence parts. Their use corresponds with the equivalent English conjunctions:

▶ **en** (*and*) summing up information:

Jane heeft twee kinderen en ze heeft een volle baan.	*Jane has two children and she has a full-time job.*

▶ **of** (*or*) indicating alternatives:

Ga jij naar die vergadering of zal ik gaan?	*Are you going to that meeting or shall I go?*

▶ **maar** (*but*) indicating a contradiction:

Ik heb niet veel tijd, maar ik   *I haven't got much time, but*
  zal toch gaan.   *I will go.*

▶ **want** (*because*) indicating a reason:

Ik heb niet veel tijd want ik   *I haven't got much time since*
  moet dit nog afmaken.   *I still have to finish this.*

▶ **dus** (*so, thus*) indicating a conclusion:

Ik moet morgen weg, dus ik   *I've got to go away tomorrow,*
  moet dit nu afmaken.   *so I've got to finish this now.*

15.2.4 Linking two sub-clauses

In a similar manner two or more sub-clauses can be linked:

Ik geloof niet dat hij dat boek   *I don't believe that he has stolen*
  heeft gestolen of dat hij het   *that book or that he has taken*
  koffiegeld heft weggenomen.   *the coffeemoney.*

These co-ordinating conjunctions can, as in English, also be used to link separate words or phrases: **de zon** *en* **de maan; niet Jupiter,** *maar* **Mars.**

Exercise 15D
Link the following sentence with the correct conjunction to the second clauses.

Ik heb een hekel aan koken ....

> of   want   dus   en   maar

a   ik vind het wel leuk een kerstdiner klaar te maken.
b   ik heb een hekel aan schoonmaken.

c ik haal altijd kant-en-klaar maaltijden. (kant-en-klaar, *ready-made*)

d ik laat altijd alles aanbranden.

Note that one conjunction will remain unused.

Exercise 15E
Link these sub-clauses by using the appropriate co-ordinating conjunction.

a Ria zegt dat ze een pop van Sinterklaas wil ___ dat ze geen chocolade letter hoeft.

b Ik heb geen zin om op vakantie te gaan ___ ik blijf deze zomer gewoon thuis.

c Wil je nu die jurk kopen ___ wacht je tot de uitverkoop?

Exercise 15F
Link each pair of sentences with the appropriate co-ordinating conjunction. Each conjunction is used only once.

a Van Goghs schilderijen waren iets nieuws.
Hij schilderde op een expressieve manier.

b Hij voelde zich mislukt in zijn werk.
Hij voelde zich mislukt in zijn persoonlijk leven.

c In het begin gebruikte hij vooral donkere en bruine kleuren.
Later schilderde hij met felle en intense kleuren.

d Zijn schilderijen zijn nu wereldberoemd.
Ze zijn veel geld waard.

e Is van Gogh beroemd omdat zijn werk zo vernieuwend was?
Is hij beroemd omdat hij zijn oor heeft afgesneden?

15.3 Linking main and sub-clauses – general

Sub-clauses have to be linked to a main clause with a special linking word: a subordinating conjunction.

15.3.1 Examples

There are many of these subordinating conjunctions. It is easiest to divide them into three groups:

▶ **Question words:** The sub-clause starts with a question word and in effect becomes an indirect question. These words are often combined with the verbs **weten, zeggen, (zich af)vragen** etc.:

wat *what*	**hoe** *how*	**wanneer** *when*	**welk(e)** *which*
wie *who*	**waar** *where*	**waarom** *why*	

Weten jullie *waar* **ik het plakband kan vinden?**	*Do you know where I can find the sticky tape?*
Tom weet echt niet *hoe* **hij zijn schulden moet afbetalen.**	*Tom really doesn't know how to pay off his debts.*
Ik vraag me af *waarom* **die man altijd zo chagrijnig is.**	*I wonder why that man is always so grumpy.*

▶ **dat, of: Dat** (*that*) is perhaps the most frequent of all linking words and is often combined with verbs such as **vertellen, geloven**, zeggen, **weten, beloven** etc. The sub-clause functions as an indirect statement.

Of (*whether, if*) is used frequently with the verb **vragen**, and must not be confused with the co-ordinating conjunction **of** meaning **or**. It indicates uncertainty.

Ik begrijp *dat* **je wat in de war bent.**	*I understand (that) you are somewhat confused.*
Henk heeft gevraagd *of* **wij morgen bij hem komen eten.**	*Henk asked whether we are coming to dinner tomorrow.*

▶ **Subordinating conjunctions** are linking words that determine the relation between two sentence parts. The next section (15.4) will give some examples.

Exercise 15G
You're in a pondering mood and are asking the following questions of yourself. Start each question with the phrase
Ik zou weleens willen weten... (*I would like to know...*).

e.g. Wat was de eerste taal?
Ik zou weleens willen weten wat de eerste taal was.

a Waarom heeft een giraf een lange nek?
b Wat is de zin van het leven?
c Waarom heb ik nooit genoeg geld?
d Hoe leren kinderen hun moedertaal?
e Waar komen sterren vandaan?
f Wie was de eerste popster?
g Welke oceaan is het diepste?

Exercise 15H
You're conducting a questionnaire about people's opinions. Write out the questions using the statements given. Start each question with
Denkt u dat...

e.g. Moet iedereen een vreemde taal leren?
Denkt u dat iedereen een vreemde taal moet leren?

a Bestaat er leven op andere planeten?
b Moeten studenten collegegeld betalen?
c Moeten supermarkten 24 uur open zijn?
d Moet de werkweek uit 4 dagen bestaan? (bestaan uit, *consist of*)
e Moeten mensen met veel geld meer belasting (*tax*) betalen?
f Moeten alle kinderen thuis een computer hebben?

Exercise 15I

Your boss has given you a list with various questions on it. Discuss these in a meeting with your colleagues. Start each question with:

Thea heeft gevraagd of...
and change the pronoun *jullie* to *wij*.

e.g. Zijn jullie met het project bijna klaar?
Thea heeft gevraagd of we met het project bijna klaar zijn.

a Hebben jullie alle gegevens (data) verzameld?
b Hebben jullie het rapport geschreven?
c Hebben jullie de conferentie georganiseerd?
d Hebben jullie de sprekers uitgenodigd?
e Vinden jullie het werk nog steeds leuk?

15.3.2 Place in sentence

A subordinating conjunction does not necessarily have to come *in between* the two parts of the sentence. The sub-clause (starting with the conjunction) can come before the main clause. If this is the case you get inversion: the main clause will not start with the subject – the subject will come after the verb. Compare:

Janine heeft **nog steeds geen vriendje**, *terwijl* **ze toch zo'n leuke meid is.**	*Janine still hasn't got a boyfriend, even though she is such a nice girl.*
Terwijl **ze toch zo'n leuke meid is,** *heeft Janine* **nog steeds geen vriendje.**	

15.4 Linking main and sub-clauses – functions

In this section we will look at subordinating conjunctions indicating various relationships between main and sub-clause.

15.4.1 Functions – time

Subordinating conjunctions can be grouped according to the relationship they express between the two sentence parts. One of these functions is time:

als	*when (at that time)*	**terwijl**	*while, whilst*
toen	*when (in the past)*	**nu**	*now*
wanneer	*when (at that time)*	**sinds**	*since*
voordat	*before (that)*	**zodra**	*as soon as*
nadat	*after (that)*	**zolang**	*as long as*
totdat	*until (that)*		

NB **Toen** can only be used with the imperfect or past perfect tenses. If **toen** means *then* it is not a subordinating conjunction, but an adverb.

15.4.2 Example sentences

Weet je nog hoe verlegen je was, *toen* **je hier voor het eerst kwam?**	*Do you remember how shy you were when you came here for the first time?*
Hij heeft 20 jaar in dezelfde fabriek gewerkt, *totdat* **hij werd ontslagen.**	*He worked in the same factory for 20 years until he got sacked.*
Nu **je met je studie klaar bent, kun je me wat vaker helpen.**	*Now that you've finished your studies you can help me more often.*
Ze waren nog maar net getrouwd, *toen* **de ruzies al begonnen.**	*They were only just married, when the arguments started.*

Exercise 15J
Rewrite the following sentences starting with the underlined sub-clause. Think about inversion.

e.g. Ik bel je <u>zodra ik klaar ben</u>.
    Zodra ik klaar ben, bel ik je.

a Ik zit hard te werken <u>terwijl jij niks zit te doen</u>.
b Ik zie Chantal nooit meer <u>nu ze kinderen heeft</u>.
c Ik zet nog even koffie <u>voordat je weg gaat</u>.
d De hond zal niet bijten <u>zolang je hem niet aanraakt</u>.
e Ik logeerde vaak bij mijn opa en oma op de boerderij <u>toen ik klein was</u>.

Exercise 15K

Link the two sentences together using the subordinating conjunction between brackets. Think about the place of the verb in the sub-clause.

e.g. Je kunt hier komen logeren. (totdat)
Je hebt een nieuw huis gevonden.
Je kunt hier komen logeren **totdat** je een nieuw huis **hebt** gevonden/gevonden **hebt**.

a Ik heb zoveel tijd voor mezelf. (nu)
Mijn jongste kind zit op school.
b Vera komt. (zodra)
Ze is beter.
c Je zult weinig leren. (zolang)
Je doet je best niet.
d Ik heb hoofdpijn. (sinds)
De televisie staat aan.
e Wil je een fles wijn voor me meebrengen. (wanneer)
Je gaat naar de supermarkt?
f Voeten vegen. (voordat)
Je komt binnen.

Exercise 15L

Take the same sentence pairs as in Exercise 15K. Now link the sentences starting with the sub-clause.

e.g. Totdat je een nieuw huis hebt gevonden, kun je hier komen logeren.

15.4.3 Conditions

tenzij	*unless*
als	*if, in case of*
als ... dan	*if... then*
Je kunt geen diploma krijgen, *tenzij* **je al je opdrachten af hebt.**	*You can't get a certificate, unless you have finished all your tasks.*

15.4.4 Comparisons

alsof	*(as)... if*
zoals	*as*
(net zo/even)... als	*just as*
(hetzelfde/dezelfde) ... als	*just as*
Je moet net zo mooi zingen *als* **je tijdens de auditie deed.**	*You have to sing just as beautifully as you did during the audition.*

15.4.5 Cause/reason

doordat	*because*
omdat	*because*
zodat	*so that*
Er komt weinig zonlicht in mijn kamer, *omdat* **mijn raam op het noorden ligt.**	*There is not a lot of natural light in my room, because it faces north.*

15.4.6 Contrast

ondanks (het feit dat)	*despite (the fact that)*
terwijl	*while/whilst/even though*
hoewel	*even though*
Ondanks **het feit dat Ko een ernstige blessure heeft, gaat hij toch skiën**	*Despite the fact that Ko has got a serious sports injury, he will still go skiing.*

15.4.7 Several meanings

Note that some conjunctions can have different meanings, depending on the context, e.g. **terwijl** and **als**.

> **Insight**
>
> The most important thing to learn about sub-clauses is that the verbs are moved to the end of the sub-clause. The other important thing to learn are the most frequently used subordinating conjunctions: **en** *and*, **of** *or*, **maar** *but*, **omdat** *because*, **dat** *that*, **want** *because*.
>
> Beware that, although the verbs in a sub-clause move, they don't necessarily move to the end of the whole sentence. Often the sub-clause is only part of a longer sentence. When a sentence starts with a sub-clause, the verbs at the end of the sub-clause actually end up in the middle of the sentence as a whole. In this example the verbs of the sub-clause are underlined: **Omdat Gerda haar werk gisteren niet <u>had</u> <u>afgemaakt</u>, moest ze vandaag vroeg beginnen.** *Because Gerda hadn't finished her work yesterday, she had to start early today.*

Exercise 15M
Link the two sentences together using the subordinating conjunction in brackets.

a Ik kan het niet. (zoals)
   Hij doet het.
b Hij kan het niet uitleggen. (hoewel) (uitleggen, *to explain*)
   Hij begrijpt het goed.
c Wij vertrekken. (als)
   Het weer klaart op. (klaart op, *gets better*)
d Ik blijf morgen een dagje thuis. (omdat)
   Ik voel me niet lekker.
e Ik ga je niet helpen. (tenzij)
   Je betaalt me meer.

Exercise 15N
Which sentence parts go together?

a	Het is een goede film	**1**	als Johanna het heeft.
b	Hij heeft me veel pijn gedaan	**2**	omdat ik hem heb gemaakt.
c	Je mag binnenkomen	**3**	doordat hij me niet serieus nam.
d	Ik wil mijn haar net zo laten knippen	**4**	als je belooft je netjes te gedragen.

Exercise 15O
Choose the correct subordinating conjunction from the box to complete the sentence.

> doordat   tenzij   als   alsof   zoals   terwijl

a ___ we dit afhebben, gaan we naar de kroeg.
b ___ jij je gedraagt, kan echt niet door de beugel. (*won't do*)
c Ik ga niet naar die verjaardag ___ Karien ook komt.
d Wij hebben zulk mooi weer gehad, ___ het in Frankrijk stormde.
e ___ de rente zo hoog is, kopen weinig mensen een nieuw huis.
f Paulien gedraagt zich ___ ze de baas is.

15.5 Linking with adverbs

15.5.1 General information

Clauses (whether main or sub-clauses) can also be joined together using adverbs. As with the conjunctions, these 'linking adverbs' (*conjunctive adverbs*) indicate the relationship between the parts of the sentence. They can also link sentences together. These adverbs are used as often in speaking as in writing, but it is particularly helpful to use them in writing as they often make a piece of writing easier to read.

15.5.2 Word order

Conjunctive adverbs are part of the main clause. As they are the first word in the sentence you will get inversion: the subject will then come after the verb. These adverbs can also be used as normal adverbs, which means they will come in the middle of the sentence (see Sections 16.1–16.3).

15.5.3 Exceptions

There are a few exceptions to this rule. A few examples are **tenminste** (*at least*), **althans** (*that is to say*), **trouwens** (*besides*), and **integendeel** (*on the contrary*). If these words are used to link sentences they are followed by a comma and there is no inversion:

Alida verdient een kapitaal, *althans,* **dat zegt ze.**	*Alida earns a fortune, at least, that's what she says.*

15.5.4 Use

The 'linking adverbs' can be grouped according to their function. Some of these functions are time, cause, reason and conclusion. (The next section will give examples of other functions.)

Time	Cause	Reason/conclusion
daarna *after that*	**daardoor** *because of*	**daarom** *because*
daarvoor *before that*		**daartoe** *for that (purpose)*
toen *then*		**dus** *so, thus*
dan *then, after that*		
nu *now*		

▶ **Toen** cannot be used with the present tense. Do not confuse **toen** as an adverb, meaning *then*, with **toen** as a subordinating conjunction, meaning *when* (see Section 15.4).

▶ **Dus** as an adverb means the same as when used as a coordinating conjunction (see Section 15.2), but as an adverb, inversion is optional.

Kijk op deze foto; *toen* **was jij twee jaar oud**. *Dus* **ging je nog niet naar school.**	*Look at this picture; you were 2 years old then. So you didn't go to school yet.*

Exercise 15P
Link these two clauses into one sentence, using the adverb in brackets. Note the change in word order.

e.g. Eerst moet je de tekst lezen (dan) Je moet de oefening doen.
Eerst moet je de tekst lezen, dan moet je de oefening doen.

a Die psychopaat lijkt zo normaal (daarom)
Het is juist zo'n enge man.
b De brug was open (daardoor)
We kwamen te laat op school.
c Maandag kan ik niet komen (dan)
Mijn ouders komen op bezoek.
d Eerst gingen we ergens wat drinken (toen)
We gingen naar de voorstelling en (daarna)
Ik bracht hem weer terug naar het station.
e We hebben lang genoeg gewacht (nu)
We gaan.

Exercise 15Q
Combine the following sentences, using the words in the box.

> tenminste   althans   trouwens   integendeel

e.g. Ik ben gek op lasagne. Al het Italiaanse eten is lekker.
Ik ben gek op lasagne. Trouwens, al het Italiaanse eten is lekker.

a Jan is helemaal niet moe.
Hij barst van de energie.
b Het gaat heel goed met haar.
Ze heeft een nieuw vriendje.

c Nederlanders zijn erg gelukkig.
Dat stond in een artikel in de krant.

d Ik heb geen zin om naar de bioscoop te gaan.
Ik heb er ook geen geld voor.

15.5.5 Daar + preposition

Many adverbs consist of a combination with **daar** + preposition.
These adverbs are frequently used in similar ways as the
prepositions on their own. Some relate to time, some to location
etc. (See Sections 14.2 and 14.3.)

▶ Time: e.g. **daarna** *after that/next/then*
              daarvoor *before that.*
▶ Location: e.g. **daarnaast** *next to that, besides it/besides*
              daarvoor *in front of that*
              daartegenover *opposite that etc.*
▶ Direction: e.g. **daarlangs** *alongside it etc.*:
Zie je de bakker?   *Can you see the bakery?*
Daartegenover zit de kapper. *Opposite that is the*
                                 hairdresser's.

15.5.6 Condition

Some adverbs indicate a condition: **anders**, *otherwise*, (**als**)... **dan**
if... then:

Ik wil 15% van de winst, *anders* **verdien ik er niets aan.**
I want 15% of the profit, otherwise I won't benefit.

15.5.7 Contrast or alternative

Some adverbs indicate a contrast or alternative: **toch** *still*, **nietemin**
nevertheless:

Het is geen goede school, (maar) *toch* **stuurt ze haar kinderen
ernaartoe.**
It is not a good school, (but) she still sends her children there.

15.5.8 Summing up

Some adverbs are used for summing up information: **ook** *also/ as well*, **tevens** *at the same time/also*, **verder** *further/furthermore*, **bovendien** *besides/moreover*:

> **We hebben een goede winst gemaakt.** *Bovendien* **zijn onze klanten tevreden.**
> *We made a good profit. Moreover, our customers are satisfied.*

Exercise 15R
Link these sentences, making them more cohesive. Choose the most appropriate adverb from those given in brackets. Also use adverbs from the previous section. Note the word order.

e.g. Ons bedrijf bestaat 100 jaar. Wij hebben een fantastische aanbieding voor u. (daarop, toch, daarom)
Ons bedrijf bestaat 100 jaar. Daarom hebben wij een fantastische aanbieding voor u.

a Wij bieden kwalitatief hoog onderwijs in de Nederlandse taal. Wij bieden een interessant cultureel programma. (daarvoor, daardoor, daarnaast)
b Heeft u nog niet on line uw boodschappen gedaan? U moet snel onze gids voor 'on line shopping' aanvragen. (toen, dan, anders)
c Wij zoeken een vlotte verkoopassistent. Mensen zonder ervaring kunnen solliciteren. (ook, dan, daarna)
d Onze stichting wil jonge mensen met drugsproblemen helpen. Wij hebben praatgroepen voor drugsverslaafden. (daarop, daartoe, daarnaast)

Exercise 15S
Choose from the adverbs in the box to fill in the gaps in this notice from the police.

> daarop dus anders daarom dan toch daarnaast daarvoor

Na een inbraak weten mensen vaak niet precies wat er is gestolen ___ is het belangrijk dat u uw eigendommen registreert ___ weet u precies wat u mist na een inbraak. ___, vul nu de bon in, ___ bent u uw gestolen eigendommen voor altijd kwijt. In deze folder zit een formulier. ___ kunt u al uw gegevens invullen.

....
:   :
:   eigendom *property*   inbraak *burglary*   :
....

Exercise 15T
The following information is a report by the school council. Link the sentences together to sum up the information. Note that there might be more than one possibility. Also note the word order.

e.g. Op de vergadering hebben we besproken dat de koffieautomaat in de kantine alweer kapot is.

  a We hebben het gehad over het aantal leerlingen dat ziek is.
  b We hebben gediscussieerd over de grote hoeveelheid huiswerk die leerlingen krijgen.
  c De organisatie van het grote schoolfeest is besproken.

_____

15.6 Relative clauses

A relative clause starts with a relative pronoun e.g. which/that or who(m). In this section we will discuss two of the Dutch pronouns: **die** and **dat**.

15.6.1 General information

A relative clause is a part of a sentence which gives added information about a person or thing: the antecedent. Often the relative clause comes straight after the antecedent it refers to. In the following examples the relative clauses are underlined and the antecedents are in italics:

De studenten **die het hardste werken**, krijgen vaak de hoogste cijfers.	*The students who work hardest often get the highest marks.*
Het idee **dat je hebt**, is interessant.	*The idea (that) you have is interesting.*

Sometimes the relative pronoun does not come straight after the antecedent so that the sentence flows better:

Ik heb gisteren *dat boek* **gekocht** *I bought that book yesterday*
  dat Rita me had aangeraden.   *which Rita had recommended.*

NB Unlike in English, the relative pronoun (**die** or **dat**) must always be used.

15.6.2 Place of verb

A relative clause is a kind of sub-clause; the verb goes to the end of the sentence, as you can see from the previous examples.

15.6.3 Die or dat?

Which one you need depends on the article of the noun you are referring to:

- ▶ **Die:** de-words (including plural words); personal pronouns and names of people; words referring to people such as **iedereen** (*everyone*), **niemand** (*no one*), **sommigen** (*some*).
- ▶ **Dat:** het-words.

NB The rule for using **die** or **dat** applies even if there is no article or the indefinite article **een** is used, so you have to know whether a particular noun is a **de**-word or a **het**-word:

Kinderen *die* **vragen worden overgeslagen.**	*Children who ask miss a turn.*
Water *dat* **vervuild is, kan je maar beter niet drinken.**	*You'd better not drink water which is polluted.*
Iemand *die* **dat doet is gek.**	*Anyone who would do that is mad.*

Exercise 15U
1) Underline the antecedent in the following sentences. 2) Point out why either *die* or *dat* is used. 3) Underline the relative clauses.

a Wij zijn een bedrijf dat u kunt vertrouwen.

b De fietsen die ze daar verhuren, zijn erg oud.

c Ik heb nog wat van die oranje verf over die ik voor die muur heb gebruikt.

d Er is niemand die zoveel voor onze school heeft gedaan als de conciërge.

e Het computerspelletje dat mijn kinderen willen hebben, is idioot duur.

f Er zijn weinig Nederlanders die geen vreemde talen spreken.

g Zij wilde een jasje kopen dat van Diana was geweest.

Exercise 15V
Fill in the appropriate relative pronoun *die* or *dat*.

a Het huis ___ we net gekocht hebben, is nu al veel meer waard.

b De engste film ___ ik heb gezien was de originele versie van 'Vanishing'.

c Stress is de prikkel ___ je nodig hebt om te presteren.

d De computers ___ we twee jaar geleden gekocht hebben, zijn nu al verouderd.

e Het leven ___ we tegenwoordig leiden is erg gehaast.

f Het huiswerk ___ we voor morgen moeten doen, is wel erg gemakkelijk.

Exercise 15W
What did you buy? Describe the items you bought by formulating sentences using relative clauses.

e.g. De stof/zacht rose
De stof die ik gekocht heb, is zacht rose.

a De auto/rood.

b De appels/niet lekker.

c De kaas/erg pittig.

d Het kastje/bijna 100 jaar oud.

e Het vloerkleed/fel gekleurd.

f De sjaal/van goede kwaliteit.

15.6.4 Indefinite antecedent

If you refer to something unspecific which cannot be clearly defined, you need to use the relative pronoun **wat**. You also use **wat** if you refer to a whole sentence:

Alles *wat* **daar ligt is 5 euro.**	*Everything (which is) there is 5 Euros.*
Hij heeft een verhouding met zijn secretaresse, *wat* **iedereen weet.**	*He is having an affair with his secretary, (which is) something everyone knows.*

15.6.5 No antecedent

If you refer to something in general without a clear antecedent you use: **wie** if you refer to people, **wat** if you refer to things.

Wie het weet mag het zeggen.	*Those who know may say so.*
Wat ik niet begrijp, is …	*What I don't understand is…*

15.6.6 With prepositions

If you refer to an antecedent in combination with a preposition you use the following combinations: preposition + **wie** if you refer to people, **waar** + preposition if you refer to things.

Dat is de jongen *over wie* **ik je heb verteld.**	*That is the boy about whom I told you.*
Het vak *waaraan* **ik de grootste hekel had op school, was godsdienst.**	*The subject (that) I disliked most at school was religious education.*

NB Even though the grammar rules tell you to use **wie** when you refer to a person, many Dutch people are not aware of this rule and they will frequently refer to people using **waar** in combination with a preposition. Note also that the prepositions **met** and **tot**

change into **mee** and **toe,** respectively, but only when combined with **waar:**

> **De collega** *met wie* **ik dat project doe, is verschrikkelijk eigenwijs.**
> *The colleague with whom I'm doing that project is terribly cocksure.*
> **De collega** *waarmee* **ik dat project doe...**

15.6.7 Waar + preposition

Waar + preposition can be written as one word or it can be split up:

> **De stoel** *waar je op* **zit, is**   *The chair on which you are sitting*
> **van m'n opa geweest.**   *used to be my grandfather's.*

Splitting it up sounds snappier and is used more frequently in speech.

Exercise 15X

Fill in the appropriate pronoun *wie* or *wat.*

a Hij is toch voor zijn examen geslaagd, ___ me erg verbaasde.
b Dat is wel erg veel, ___ je me daar geeft.
c ___ ik niet begrijp, is waar hij al dat geld vandaan haalt.
d ___ het niet begrijpt moet het nu zeggen.
e Er is iets ___ ik graag wil hebben voor mijn verjaardag.
f Ik heb eindelijk gezegd waarom ik boos ben, ___ me erg opluchtte.
g ___ mee wil op excursie, moet zich nu opgeven.

Exercise 15Y

Finish the sentence. Remember the verb goes to the end.

e.g. Ik hou het meest van Londen. De stad ___
De stad waar ik het meest van hou, is Londen.
De stad waarvan ik het meest hou, is Londen.

a Ik heb de grootste hekel aan wiskunde. Het vak ___
b Ik hou het meest van jazz. De muziek ___

c Ik heb de grootste hekel aan voetbal. De sport ___
d Ik hou het meest van lasagne. Het eten ___
e Ik heb de grootste hekel aan melk. De drank ___

Exercise 15Z

Use the expressions in the box to indicate your attitude to the following people and things. Use *wie* when referring to people.

een hekel hebben aan	*to dislike*
medelijden hebben met	*to feel sorry for*
jaloers zijn op	*to be jealous of*
(geen) aandacht besteden aan	*to pay (no) attention to*
bewondering hebben voor	*to feel admiration for*
(niet) geïnteresseerd zijn in	*to (not) be interested in*

e.g. De minister-president is iemand...
De minister-president is iemand voor wie ik bewondering heb.

a De Europese politiek is iets ...
b Computers zijn dingen...
c De koningin van Engeland is iemand ...
d Mijn buurman is iemand ...
e Voetbal is iets...
f Astrologie is iets ...
g Mijn manager is iemand ...

Things to remember

▶ A clause is (a part of) a sentence which has at least one verb and normally a subject. There are three different kinds of clauses: main clauses, sub-clauses and relative clauses.

▶ A main clause is (a part of) a sentence which can stand on its own. In a main clause the finite verb is the second item in the sentence, except when the sentence is a yes/no question or an order.

▶ A sub-clause is a part of a sentence which normally cannot be used on its own, but needs to be combined with a main clause.

▶ Sub-clauses start with a subordinating conjunction and all verbs in the clause are placed in final position.

▶ Co-ordinating conjunctions link two or more main clauses or two or more sub-clauses and indicate the relation between the sentence parts (**en** *and*, **of** *or*, **maar** *but*, **want** *because*, **dus** *so/thus*).

▶ Subordinating conjunctions link main and sub-clauses.

▶ Examples of subordinating conjunctions are question words (e.g. **wat** *what*, **hoe** *how*, **wie** *who*, **waarom** *why*), **dat** *that*, **of** *whether*, **als** *when (at that time)*, **toen** *when (in the past)*, **nadat** *after (that)*, **als** *if/in case of*, **omdat** *because*, **zodat** *so that*, **hoewel** *although*, **ondanks** *despite*.

▶ Clauses can also be linked using adverbs such as **daarna** *afterwards*, **dan** *then*, **nu** *now*, **anders** *otherwise*, **toch** *still*, **niettemin** *nevertheless*, **bovendien** *moreover*.

▶ A relative clause gives added information about a person or thing (the antecedent) and starts with a relative pronoun. All verbs in a relative clause are placed at the end.

▶ The relative pronoun **die** is used to refer to **de**-words, personal pronouns, names of people and words for people; the relative pronoun **dat** is used to refer to **het**-words.

▶ When a relative clause refers to something which cannot be clearly defined, or if you refer to a whole sentence, the relative pronoun **wat** is used.

▶ If you refer to an antecedent in combination with a preposition, preposition + **wie** is used when referring to people, and **waar** + preposition when referring to things.

16

Adverbs

16.1 Adverbs – general

Adverbs tell you when, how and where the main action of the sentence takes place.

16.1.1 What are adverbs?

Adverbs are words which tell you if, when, how, where, how often, and to what extent, something is happening. Here are some examples: **absoluut** (*absolutely*), **morgen** (*tomorrow*), **snel** (*quickly*), **hier** (*here*), **vaak** (*often*), **helemaal** (*completely*). An adverbial phrase consists of an adverb plus other words.

16.1.2 Form

As you can see from the examples just given, in English you can make an adverb from an adjective by adding -ly (e.g., *quick* becomes *quickly*). Sometimes the form of the adverb is completely different (*good* becomes *well*). Dutch is much simpler; you don't add anything and there are no irregular forms like *well* (**goed** can mean either *good* or *well*).

Hij loopt *snel* **naar het station.**   *He walks quickly to the station.*
Goed **gedaan!**   *Well done!*

Some adverbs have a comparative and superlative form (**snel, sneller, snelst**). These are discussed in Section 2.6.

16.1.3 Types of adverb

As indicated above, you can divide adverbs into several categories according to the type of information they provide. In this book we use the following categories:

- ▶ Time – adverbs of time give information about when something takes place.
- ▶ Manner – adverbs of manner indicate how something takes place.
- ▶ Place – adverbs of place tell you where something takes place.
- ▶ Frequency – adverbs of frequency indicate how often something takes place.
- ▶ Degree – adverbs of degree say to what degree something takes place.
- ▶ Sentence – sentence adverbs give information about a whole sentence, and usually express an opinion.

You can find more information about the various categories in Sections 16.2 and 16.3 in this section.

Exercise 16A
Underline the adverbs/adverbial phrases in the following sentences.

- **a** Mieke staat vroeg op.
- **b** Ze eet niets maar ze drinkt gauw een kopje koffie.
- **c** Daarna loopt ze vlug naar het station.
- **d** Ze gaat met de trein van 7.45 naar de stad.
- **e** In de stad koopt ze altijd een krant.
- **f** Op haar werk groet Mieke vrolijk de portier.
- **g** Mieke leest eerst haar emails.
- **h** Dan heeft ze een lange vergadering.
- **i** Ze heeft meestal niet veel tijd om te lunchen.

Exercise 16B
In the following sentences, you will find the adverbs underlined.
Indicate what types of adverbs they are (e.g. an adverb of time? or
of place? or frequency?, etc.).

a Joshua kan <u>redelijk</u> goed zingen.
b <u>Gelukkig</u> hoef ik vandaag niet te werken.
c Wie wil <u>daar</u> nou wonen?
d Tante Marie gaat <u>vaak</u> op vakantie naar Limburg.
e Heb je de afwas <u>al</u> gedaan?
f Mijn vriendin was <u>heel</u> kwaad dat ik te laat was.
g Je moet het pakje <u>voorzichtig</u> openmaken.
h Joachim gaat vrij <u>regelmatig</u> voor z'n werk naar het
   buitenland.
i Het was een leuk feest maar toch is ze <u>heel vroeg plotseling</u>
   naar huis gegaan.

16.2 Adverbs – types

Adverbs of time, manner and place give information about when,
how and where something takes place.

16.2.1 Time

Adverbs of time provide information about when the action
described in a sentence takes place. Examples of such adverbs are:

vandaag	*today*	**plotseling**	*suddenly*	**nog**	*still*
gisteren	*yesterday*	**gauw**	*soon*	**al**	*already*
nu	*now*	**daarna**	*afterwards*	**pas**	*yet*
's ochtends	*in the morning*		**'s avonds**	*in the evening, etc.*	
's winters	*in the winter*		**'s zomers**	*in the summer, etc.*	

NB 's comes from the archaic form **des** (*of the*) and is always
lower case.

16.2.2 Manner

Adverbs of manner tell you about the way in which something is done or the way in which it takes place. Examples are:

snel	*quickly*	**goed**	*well*	**graag**	*gladly*
langzaam	*slowly*	**slecht**	*badly*	**voorzichtig**	*carefully*
stom	*stupidly*	**mooi**	*beautifully*	**kwaad**	*angrily*

This can also take the form of a prepositional phrase like **met mijn vrienden: Ik ga vanavond met mijn vrienden naar de bioscoop.**

16.2.3 Place

Adverbs of place give information about where something takes place. Often adverbs of place take the form of a prepositional phrase:

Ik heb *daar* **vier jaar gewoond.**	*I lived there for four years.*
Wilt u *hier* **zitten?**	*Would you like to sit here?*
Jantien gaat naar *Barcelona.*	*Jantien is going to Barcelona.*

16.2.4 Time, manner, place

When you use adverbs of time, manner and place in one sentence, you generally put them in exactly that order: time – manner – place. The following example shows you the difference with English:

Ann-Sofie gaat morgen (time) / met de trein (manner) / naar München (place).	*Ann-Sofie is going to Munich by train tomorrow.*

As in English, this order is not set in stone and can be changed (see Section 16.3). For instance:

Nee, ze gaat naar München　　*No, she's going to Munich by car!*
met de auto!

In this sentence, **met de auto** is stressed by putting it last.

Exercise 16C
Put the adverb in the right place in the sentence.

e.g. Geert moet met het vliegtuig naar Londen. (morgen)
　　 Geert moet morgen met het vliegtuig naar Londen.

a	nu	Je moet snel naar huis, anders kom je te laat.
b	naar Frankrijk	We gaan over twee weken op vakantie.
c	goed	Dat heb je niet gedaan.
d	graag	Ik ga altijd naar Antwerpen.
e	slecht	Ajax heeft verleden week gespeeld.

Exercise 16D
Rearrange the adverbs or adverbial phrases in these sentences to the standard order of time–manner–place.

a We gaan met de buren naar Oostenrijk op vakantie
　　volgend jaar.
b Marloes heeft het werk snel gisteren afgemaakt.
c Lees jij ook graag 's ochtends de krant?
d Ik eet langzaam altijd maar mijn vrouw eet meestal snel.
e Die man staat altijd in de tuin al vroeg te werken.
f Kees heeft heel hard de laatste paar weken gewerkt.

Exercise 16E
Rewrite the sentences with the adverbial information regarding time–manner–place.

e.g. Jan kijkt TV vanavond – met zijn vriendin – thuis
　　 Jan kijkt vanavond met zijn vriendin thuis tv.

	Time	Manner	Place
a Remco speelt voetbal	zaterdag	met zijn elftal	in Volendam
b Ik ga op vakantie	in juni	lekker	naar Australië
c Kom je eten?	morgen	met je vriend	bij mij
d Gré heeft gekookt	gisteren	heerlijk	–
e Han schildert als hij tijd heeft	's zomers	vaak	in de tuin
f Het was mooi weer	vanochtend	–	bij ons
g Waarom ga je niet uit eten?	vanavond	met Sofie	in de stad

16.2.5 Frequency

Adverbs of frequency tell you how often something takes place; they give the answer to the question 'how often?'.

altijd	always	**meestal**	usually	**regelmatig**	regularly
nooit	never	**vaak**	often	**soms**	sometimes
ooit	ever	**bijna altijd**	nearly always	**zelden**	seldom

16.2.6 Degree

Adverbs of degree tell you the degree or extent to which something is true: <u>vrij</u> mooi weer (*quite nice weather*) or <u>erg</u> mooi weer (*very nice weather*) for instance. As you can see, adverbs of degree often modify the meaning of an adjective (**mooi** in the example).

heel	very	**vrij**	quite	**helemaal**	entirely
erg	very	**redelijk**	reasonably	**absoluut**	absolutely
zeer	very	**graag**	gladly	**compleet**	completely

NB If the adverbs **heel** or **erg** are used to modify an adjective, and the adjective is given an extra -e (which can happen in front of a noun – see Section 2.3), they get an extra -e, but usually only when speaking – not in writing: **hel<u>e</u> mooi<u>e</u> schoenen** (*very beautiful shoes*).

16.2.7 Sentence adverbs

Sentence adverbs give information about a whole sentence. Often sentence adverbs express the opinion of the speaker, for instance regarding the likelihood of something happening: **ongetwijfeld** (*undoubtedly*) or **misschien** (*perhaps*).

misschien	*perhaps*	**mogelijk**	*possibly*	**ongetwijfeld**	*undoubtedly*
blijkbaar	*clearly*	**waarschijnlijk**	*probably*	**gelukkig**	*luckily*
zeker	*surely*	**natuurlijk**	*of course*	**duidelijk**	*obviously*

Insight

The adverbs **heel, erg** and **zeer** all translate as *very*. However, sometimes **zeer** can be perceived as a little more formal and old fashioned than **heel** and **erg**, which are generally used more often. **Heel mooi** *very beautiful*. **Erg duur** *very expensive*. **Zeer langzaam** *very slow*.

Note that **erg** can also mean *terrible*, and is used in expressions such as **Erg, hè?** *It's terrible, isn't it?*

16.3 Adverbs – place and order

This section tells you what order to place adverbs in when you use more than one.

16.3.1 Where?

You usually place the adverbs discussed in this section as closely behind the finite verb as possible.

Ze gaan *meestal* **'s zaterdags naar de bioscoop.**
They usually go to the cinema on Saturday.

Maar morgen gaan ze *waarschijnlijk* **uit eten.**
But tomorrow they're probably going out for dinner.

Exercise 16F
Indicate the function of the underlined adverbs or adverbial phrases, i.e. are they adverbs of frequency or degree or sentence adverbs?

a Hij zegt dat hij <u>zelden</u> ziek is.
b Ik loop ook in de herfst en de winter <u>graag</u> op het strand.
c <u>Misschien</u> is hij wel te laat omdat hij in een file staat.
d Ik had <u>gelukkig</u> mijn creditcard bij me dus ik kon het toch kopen.
e Vond jij die laatste Brad Pitt film ook eigenlijk <u>heel</u> slecht?
f <u>Soms</u> heb ik gewoon geen zin om te werken. Ken je dat gevoel?

Exercise 16G
Look at the following activities and indicate how often you engage in them. Use an appropriate adverb of frequency.

e.g. tennis spelen
Ik speel **vaak** tennis; ik speel **nooit** tennis.

a koken
b internetten
c overwerken
d een DVD huren
e op vakantie gaan

f voetballen
g een boek lezen
h Nederlands oefenen

Exercise 16H

Read the following list of things that Miriam might do over the weekend. Reorder the sentences by putting the thing she's most likely to do at the top and the least likely at the bottom.

a Miriam gaat misschien naar het fitness-centrum.
b Ze gaat ongetwijfeld boodschappen doen.
c Waarschijnlijk gaat Miriam iets drinken met een stel vriendinnen.
d Ze gaat zaterdag mogelijk haar huis opruimen.

16.3.2 Time, manner, place

When you're using more than one adverb in a sentence, the most important thing to remember is that the standard sequence in Dutch is: time–manner–place.

Jantien gaat morgen te voet naar Haarlem.
Jantien's going to Haarlem on foot tomorrow.

16.3.3 Emphasis

To highlight one piece of information over another, you can move a particular item to the front or back. To stress that Jantien is walking to Haarlem, for instance, you can place the adverb of manner (**te voet**) at the beginning:

Ze gaat te voet naar Haarlem morgen.
She's going on foot to Haarlem tomorrow.

16.3.4 Frequency, degree, sentence

Other adverbs are usually placed as closely behind the finite verb of the sentence as possible (see Section 16.2). In the following example, **waarschijnlijk** (*probably*) comes straight after the verb **gaat**:

Ze gaat waarschijnlijk morgen in Haarlem winkelen
She's probably going shopping in Haarlem tomorrow.

16.3.5 Inversion

For emphasis, you can also start a sentence with an adverb:

Waarschijnlijk gaan we volgend jaar naar Thailand.
We're probably going to Thailand next year.

In this way, adverbs can also link a sentence to a previous sentence. Don't forget, however, that the finite verb must always be the second item in a Dutch sentence. In other words, you must put the verb immediately behind the adverb (in the example **gaan** comes directly after **waarschijnlijk**).

Exercise 16I
In the following sentences, the adverbs don't follow the standard order of time–manner–place. This is done to emphasize certain pieces of information. Indicate which information has been emphasized.

e.g. Het was op de weg vandaag heel rustig.
op de weg (adverbial phrase of place) has been emphasized by placing it forward of its usual position.

a Ga je naar je werk op zaterdag?
b Met jou wil ik helemaal niet op vakantie!
c We kunnen aanstaande zaterdag naar oma met de auto of met de trein.
d Hij wil dit jaar met zijn vriendin een huis kopen in Leiden.

e Na de koop geven ze misschien wel een groot feest in hun nieuwe huis.

f Je bent met mijn broer getrouwd gisteren!?

Exercise 16J

Re-write the following sentences by starting the sentences with the underlined adverbs/adverbial phrases to emphasize this information (note that inversion will take place).

e.g. Hij zingt <u>hard en vals</u>.
Hard en vals zingt hij!

a Dat krantenartikel is <u>heel goed</u> geschreven.

b Je ziet beroemde Hollywood-acteurs <u>zelden</u> op straat lopen in Amsterdam.

c Ik heb Harry Mulisch, de Nederlandse schrijver, <u>één keer</u> in de tram zien zitten.

d Ik heb je nu verdorie <u>al meer dan tien keer</u> geroepen. Kom uit je bed!

e Die stomme printer is <u>altijd</u> kapot en die computer doet het ook nooit!

f Die films van Hitchcock zijn <u>fantastisch</u>, vind je ook niet?

Exercise 16K

Insert the adverbs on the left into the sentences.

a	misschien	Kan jij even boodschappen voor me doen?
b	waarschijnlijk	We gaan in juni twee weken op vakantie.
c	ongetwijfeld	Karin heeft alles voor ons geregeld.
d	blijkbaar	De medicijnen hebben niet erg goed geholpen.

Things to remember

▶ Adverbs are words which tell you if, when, how, where, how often, and to what extent. In Dutch, adverbs (**mooi** *beautifully*) do not look different from adjectives (**mooi** *beautiful*): **mooi geschilderd** *beautifully painted*, **een mooi schilderij** *a beautiful painting*.

▶ Adverbs of time give information about when the action in a sentence takes place. For instance: **vandaag** *today*, **morgen** *tomorrow*, **nu** *now*, **gauw** *soon*, **pas** *not/yet/until*, **al** *already*.

▶ Adverbs of manner tell you about the way in which something is done or the way in which it takes place. For instance: **snel** *quickly*, **goed** *well*, **slecht** *badly*, **stom** *stupidly*, **voorzichtig** *carefully*, **graag** *gladly*.

▶ Adverbs of place tell you where something takes place – often these are prepositional phrases. For instance: **daar** *there*, **hier** *here*, **naar Barcelona** *to Barcelona*, **op het strand** *at the beach*.

▶ Adverbs of frequency tell you how often something takes place. For instance: **altijd** *always*, **nooit** *never*, **soms** *sometimes*, **regelmatig** *regularly*.

▶ Adverbs of degree tell you the degree or extent to which something is true. For instance, **erg** *very*, **heel** *very*, **vrij** *quite*, **redelijk** *reasonable*, **compleet** *completely*.

▶ Sentence adverbs give information about a whole sentence. For instance: **misschien** *perhaps*, **mogelijk** *possibly*, **blijkbaar** *clearly*, **natuurlijk** *of course*, **zeker** *surely*.

▶ Adverbs are usually placed as closely behind the finite verb as possible. Adverbs of time, manner and place are usually put in exactly that order: time, manner, place.

17

Word order

17.1 Word order: main clauses

17.1.1 General

Word order in Dutch sentences can be one of the most difficult things to come to grips with for English-speaking learners. It is helpful to think about a sentence as consisting of six sections:

1	2	3	4	5	6
First position	Verb	Subject (if not first)	Middle part	Last verb place	Final position

17.1.2 The first position

The first position can be taken up by: the subject, the object, adverbs (those indicating time or place are most frequently used), question words: **waar, wat, waarom**, etc., an entire sub-clause.

1	2	3	4	5	6
Frieda	studeert	–	wiskunde in Leiden.	–	–
Soms	zit	ze	de hele dag in de bibliotheek	te werken.	–

(Contd)

1	2	3	4	5	6
Waarom	komt	Janneke	morgen niet met ons	mee?	–
Bij het ongeluk	zijn	vier mensen	om het leven	gekomen.	–
Dat boek van Mulish	heb	ik	in één keer	uitgelezen.	–
Als ik 65 ben,	koop	ik	een boerderijtje in Frankrijk.	–	–
–	Is	dat	wel veilig?	–	–

17.1.3 The second position

The second position is always taken up by the *verb*, although when giving orders or asking a 'yes/no' question the first position remains empty (so the sentence starts with the verb). The verb in this position is the finite (or main) verb, which changes its form depending on the subject and tense of the sentence.

Exercise 17A
1) Look at the example sentences in 17.1.2. Identify for each of these sentences what the subject is.

2) Identify now for each of these sentences which of the following has taken up the first sentence position: a) subject; b) adverb; c) question word; d) prepositional phrase; e) object; f) sub-clause.

Exercise 17B
'Unjumble' the sentences below and put the sections in the correct boxes. Note that for this exercise you don't have to use the last box. There might be various possibilities, but note whether the sentence is a question, statement, or order.

First position	Verb	Subject (if not first)	Middle part	Last verb place	Final position

a de trein – gemist – alweer – jullie – hebben?
b Jacob – op zaterdag – werkt – bij Albert Heijn
c sparen – hij – wil – veel geld
d je fiets – wel – zet – op slot (NB this is an imperative)
e een nieuw huis – kopen – jullie – gaan?
f gescoord – hoeveel – doelpunten – Ajax – heeft?
g de verkoop – behoorlijk – gestegen – is – door onze actie
h word – ik – soms – wakker – met een gevoel van angst

17.1.4 The third position

The **third position** is the **subject** of the sentence if this did not come in first position. If the subject is put behind the verb this is called inversion.

17.1.5 The fourth position

The **fourth position** is taken up by the **middle part** of the sentence. This can contain all the other possible sentence parts: the object,

object pronouns, adverbs, **er**, **niet**, etc., prepositional phrases, relative clauses, etc.

17.1.6 The fifth position

The **fifth position** holds the **last verb** place. This will contain: the past participle, infinitive(s), the prefix of a separable verb.

NB See Section 10.3 for information on the order among verbs themselves.

17.1.7 The sixth position

There are a few items which can come here: prepositional phrases, sub-clauses, **om** + **te** + infinitive. See the next section for more information.

1	2	3	4	5	6
Daarom	hoef	je	het niet	te doen	–
Over enkele ogenblikken	zullen	wij	op Schiphol	landen	–
U	kunt	–	hier meer	te weten, komen	over de natuur
Ze	interesseren	–	zich er niet meer voor	–	–
De dokter	geeft	–	het kindje een injectie	–	–
Wat	moet	je	–	doen	om het probleem op te lossen?

Exercise 17C
In which of the example sentences in 17.1.7 is there inversion?

Exercise 17D
Put the following sentences into the appropriate boxes.

e.g. Zie je die man die daar loopt?

–	Zie	je	die man die daar loopt?		

e.g. Het zou een heerlijke dag zijn geweest om een eindje te fietsen.

Het	zou	–	een heerlijke dag	zijn geweest	om een eindje te fietsen

First position	Verb	Subject (if not first)	Middle part	Last verb place	Final position

a Als we gaan verhuizen, wil ik de grootste slaapkamer hebben.
b Jij mag dan de slaapkamer met balkon nemen.
c Een dagje naar Disneyland is ontzettend duur.
d Dan kan je maar beter een dagje naar de Efteling gaan.
e De trein waarmee ik elke dag naar mijn werk reis, rijdt vanochtend niet.
f Je moet je wel verzekeren als je op reis gaat.

Exercise 17E

Put the following jumbled up sentences in the correct order.

a jij – naar Mirjams feestje – geweest – ben?
b vermaakt – heb – je – je er?
c terug – geef – mijn fiets (NB teruggeven is a separable verb)
d jij – steek – aan – de kaarsjes?
e heb – jij – wat – die kip lekker – klaargemaakt!
f heb – ik – er de hele dag naar – gekeken.

17.2 Word order: sub-clauses

This section describes the word order in sub-clauses.

17.2.1 General information

The main differences in word order between a main clause and a sub-clause are the first position in the sentence and the place of the finite (the main) verb.

For more information on all the various grammatical categories and structures look in the relevant sections.

Sub-clauses have the following sentence positions:

1	2	3	4	5	
Another (normally a main) clause	Linking word: sub-ordinating conjunction	Subject	Middle part	Finite verb + other verbs	Final position

17.2.2 The first position

The first position is always taken up by a subordinating conjunction, **dat** or **of**, a question word in an indirect question, a relative pronoun.

17.2.3 The second position

The second position is normally taken up by the subject.

17.2.4 The third position

The third position is taken up by the same kind of words as the middle position in the main clause. These are: object and object pronouns, prepositional phrases, relative clauses (if part of object), reflexive pronouns, prepositional phrases, adverbs and so on. Look in the relevant sections for more information about these various categories and words.

17.2.5 The fourth position

The fourth position is always taken up by the finite verb. If there are other verbs in the sub-clause (e.g. an infinitive, or a past participle) these will come either just before or after the finite verb (see Section 10.3 for the order among verbs in this position).

17.2.6 The fifth position

The fifth position can be taken up by a few structures, including a main clause or another sub-clause. If the main clause comes in this final position, it will start with the verb as you will get inversion.

	1	2	3	4	5
Ik weet	dat	je	geen tijd	hebt	om te komen
Ik vraag me af	of	Joost	wel	weet	dat zijn zoontje bij ons is

Exercise 17F
Put the following sentences into the correct boxes.

e.g. Matthijs vindt dat zijn plaatselijke voetbalclub de beste is.

Matthijs vindt	dat	zijn plaatselijke voetbalclub	de beste	is

1	2	3	4	5	
Another (normally a main) clause	Linking word: sub-ordinating conjunction	Subject	Middle part	Finite verb + other verbs	Final position

a Roland kan niet komen, omdat hij een opdracht van een klant moet afmaken.

b hoewel ze veel geld hebben, leven ze heel zuinig.

c als hij niet zo jong was gestorven, zou hij veel meer boeken hebben geschreven.

d Irma woont nog steeds bij haar ouders, zodat zij voor haar moeder die ziek is, kan zorgen.

e Lieve heeft haar huis laten verbouwen, toen ze in verwachting was van haar jongste.

Exercise 17G

Make sentences by putting the jumbled up sections in the correct order. Note that the word order in the main clause will give you a clue about whether the sentence starts with the main or the sub-clause.

e.g. wist ik wel – dat – een beetje vreemd – waren – haar kinderen
Dat haar kinderen een beetje vreemd waren, wist ik wel.

a maar ik wist niet – haar man – haar – sloeg – dat

b ze – zo'n slecht gebit – heeft – omdat – zij durft niet te lachen

c waren haar kinderen de erfenis aan het verdelen – terwijl – doodziek op bed – lag – hun moeder

d ik voel me heel blij – ik – omdat – een mooie diamanten ring – heb gekregen – voor de kerst

e ze wilde haar dochter geven – wat – had gemist – zelf – ze

17.3 Word order: final position in sentence

This section describes which elements can come in the final position in a sentence.

17.3.1 General information

Early on in most language courses and grammar books (this one being no exception) you are told that many forms of the verb go to the end of the sentence or the clause.

In practice, however, the Dutch frequently place other elements after this last verb place. These can be: prepositional phrases, constructions with **om + te + infinitive**, and comparisons.

17.3.2 Prepositional phrases

Generally speaking, prepositional phrases (a group of words which starts with a preposition) can come either before or after the last verb position in the sentence:

Ik ben op vakantie geweest met Jannie.   *I have been on holiday with Jannie.*

Ik ben met Jannie op vakantie geweest.

This also applies to sub-clauses:

Wist je dat ik op vakantie ben geweest met Jannie?   *Did you know I have been on holiday with Jannie?*

Wist je dat ik met Jannie op vakantie ben geweest?

NB Which of these is preferable depends on the information structure of a sentence (see Section 18.6).

In some cases, however, the prepositional phrase needs to go before the verb(s). This is particularly the case when the verb is closely

connected with the phrase, e.g. **van mond tot mond gaan** *to go around (a rumour)*:
Dat verhaal is van mond tot mond gegaan.

17.3.3 Om + te + infinitive

This construction always comes after the last verb place:

Ik hoef niets te doen *om* **mooi slank** *te blijven.*
I don't have to do anything to stay nice and slim.
Dries moet hard werken *om* **de beste van de klas** *te zijn.*
Dries has to work hard to remain top of the class.

17.3.4 Comparisons

These often come after the last verb place:
Ik ben altijd avontuurlijker geweest *dan mijn broer.*
Tim is nog nooit zo ziek geweest *als nu.*

Exercise 17H
Rewrite the following sentences with the prepositional phrase in another position.

e.g. Hij is met Marieke wezen lunchen.
Hij is wezen lunchen met Marieke.

a Edith heeft het besproken met Nellie.
b Tja, dat hangt af van jou.
c Ik ben nog nooit zo kwaad geweest op iemand.
d Ik heb al zo lang niets van Janna gehoord.
e We hebben allemaal hard gewerkt aan het project.
f Ze heeft een uur zitten wachten op je.

Exercise 17I
Write these jumbled up sentences in the correct order. Start all sentences with the subject.

a ik – gewerkt – altijd alleen – om geld te verdienen – heb
b Saskia – zegt – om te ontspannen – dat ze wijn moet drinken
c Dirk – om ervaring op te doen – gewerkt – heeft – bij ons
d heeft – zij – zo goed – als nu – nog nooit – geacteerd (acteren, to act)
e Arjen – nog even bij ons – om dat boek te lenen (to borrow) – is – langs geweest (visited)
f gisteren – mijn moeder – om het nieuws te vertellen – langsgekomen (dropped by) – is
g zin – om met de trein te komen – had – geen – ik

Insight
Word order can seem quite a lot to come to grips with. However, on the whole it isn't too complicated. These are the most important rules: the finite verb comes in second position (except in questions that don't start with a question word) and all other verbs are moved to the end of a clause. In subclauses all verbs are moved to the end.

Note that prepositional phrases can move about quite freely. They can start a sentence, but they can also come after the verb(s) in final position. This means that you will come across prepositional phrases indicating time (**om acht uur** *at eight o'clock*), manner (**met m'n vrienden** *with my friends*) and place (**in Maastricht**) in different places. This may seem confusing at first, but they are always easily recognizable and the underlying word order of the clause or sentence always adheres to the main rules.

Things to remember

▶ The first position of a main clause can be taken up by the subject, the object, adverbs, questions words or a sub-clause.

▶ The second position of a main clause is always taken up by the finite verb, although when giving orders or asking a yes/ no question, the first position remains empty, so the sentence starts with the finite verb.

▶ If a sentence starts with something other than the subject, the subject is moved behind the fiinite verb into the third position of the main clause.

▶ The fourth position of a main clause can be taken up by all other possible sentence parts.

▶ The fifth position is the last verb place and can contain the past participle, infinitive(s) or the prefix of a separable verb.

▶ The sixth position can hold several items: prepositional phrases, sub-clauses, **om** + **te** + infinitive.

▶ Word order in sub-clauses differs from main clauses with respect to: the first position, which is always taken up by a subordinating conjunction, **dat** or **of**, a question word or a relative pronoun; the second position, which is taken by the subject; the fourth position, which is always taken by the finite verb, with any other verbs directly preceding or following it; the fifth position, which can be taken up by a main clause or another sub-clause.

▶ Verbs other than the finite verb (and in a sub-clause or relative clause even the finite verb itself) should be moved to the end of a sentence or clause. However, in practice, other elements are often placed after the last verb(s). These can be prepositional phrases, constructions with **om** + **te** + infinitive, and comparisons.

18

....

Style

_____

18.1 Formal and informal

What's the difference between formal and informal Dutch, and how do you know when to use which?

18.1.1 Differences

The difference between formal and informal language shows in various ways.

▶ **U/je/jij:** One of the most important signals of formal language in Dutch is the word **u** (in formal writing sometimes a capital U), which is used to address people directly (English you). Informally the words **je** and **jij** are used (see Section 4.1).
▶ **Vocabulary:** Formality or informality is also expressed by the words you use. **Café**, for instance, is a more neutral/formal word for bar/café than **kroeg**.
▶ **Grammar:** The kind of grammatical structures that you use can also be an indication of formal and informal. Passive structures, for instance, are often used in more formal situations than active structures, and are seen a lot, for instance, in more formal kinds of writing. Using a lot of long, complex sentences with sub-clauses can also create a formal feeling.

18.1.2 Informal?

Whether to be formal or informal depends on the type of environment you are in and the people you are with. On the whole, however, the Dutch will move to a first name basis with one another more quickly than, say, the French. This is not generally true of Flemish people, who don't use **je** and **jij** as much. In the south the form **ge** exists, which is considered to be extremely formal north of the border and isn't used there.

In the Netherlands there is a strong trend towards informality amongst young people in particular. Many children at primary school, for instance, call their teachers by their first names, and often do the same with their grandparents.

18.1.3 How do I know?

It can be difficult to decide whether to be formal or informal. The thing to remember is that it's less easy to offend people by being formal, so sometimes it's best to start off more formal and assess the situation before becoming more informal. Often the introduction provides a clue – if someone introduces themselves with their first name, you're obviously being invited to be informal. If in doubt, you can always ask: **Mag ik 'je' zeggen?** *May I say 'je'?*

Exercise 18A
Indicate whether the following dialogues/pieces of text are formal or informal, and also say why.

   a Hoe laat ga jij 's morgens naar je werk?
      Ik ga meestal om een uur of 8 van huis.
   b Vriendelijk bedankt voor alle hulp!
      Geen dank, laat me weten als ik meer voor je kan doen.
   c Zin om vanavond te gaan stappen?
      Nee, ik ben deze week elke avond al naar de kroeg geweest.
   d Prettig kennis te maken, mijn naam is Van Daernesloot.
      Eensgelijks, Laveloos is de naam.

e Voor verdere informatie kan contact worden opgenomen met de afdeling inlichtingen op het volgende telefoonnummer...

f Nou, tot morgen dan!
Ja, de mazzel!

Exercise 18B
Fill in the correct form of the verb in brackets, using *u* or *je* as appropriate.

e.g. 'Mijn papa heeft een hele grote auto.'
'Dan (moeten) de auto van mijn papa eens zien!'
'Dan moet je de auto van mijn papa eens zien!'

a Beste mevrouw Metselaar, hoe (maken) het?

b (*amongst friends*) Remco wil naar de Italiaan. (vinden) dat goed?

c (*to a shop assistant*) Pardon, maar (weet) hoeveel dit boek kost?

d Om lid te worden van onze sportclub (hebben) een geldig legitimatiebewijs nodig en twee foto's.

e Hoe laat (willen) morgen eten, schat?

f Van mij (mogen) de auto wel lenen, maar (moeten) het eerst aan je moeder vragen.

g (*in a letter*) Lieve Koningin, hopelijk (hebben) een ogenblik om naar mijn probleem te luisteren...

18.2 Foreign words

This section will give you some examples of the use of foreign words in Dutch.

Throughout the ages, Dutch has been influenced by a large number of different languages through all sorts of contact with countries around the world. However, the strongest influence has been exerted by the languages found relatively close to home: German, French and English, and many words from these languages have been adopted into Dutch. This assimilation is more acceptable in the Netherlands than in Flanders, where Dutch speakers historically have had to fight a hard battle for their language and are consequently more protective of it.

▶ **German:** Dutch and German share many features (together with English, both are part of the same family of languages) but there is only a relatively small number of actual German words in use in Dutch, not least because of the relative unpopularity of German due to historical reasons. Of these **überhaupt** (at all, anyway) is the most often heard.

   Daar kijk ik überhaupt nooit naar. *I never watch that anyway.*

▶ **French:** The greatest number of French words entered the Dutch language during Napoleon's occupation of the Low Countries. Many French words are used every day, some in a slightly altered form: **trottoir** (*pavement*), **paraplu** (*umbrella*), **restaurant, cadeau** (*present*), **bureau** (*desk*).

▶ **English:** In the twentieth century, English in particular influenced Dutch greatly. Especially among the generations growing up with American television series and pop music, a great many English words have been adopted into everyday usage. Many of these refer to new technological developments, such as the computer (**computer** in Dutch). Some examples:

ticket, **printer** (for a computer), **e-mail, videorecorder, mobieltje** (*mobile phone*).

Lots of words from the sporting world have also been adopted: **team, trainer, hockey, tennis**, etc. The most popular of these, football, has been given Dutch spelling: **voetbal**. It is very common in Dutch to take foreign words like these (not just with sports) and make them into verbs by adding **-en**. To play football, for instance, is **voetballen**, to train is **trainen**, and to score is **scoren**. Similarly: **pushen, coachen, shoppen, rugbyen**, etc. Adding a t/d to past participles and the imperfect is based on how the last letter of the stem *sounds* rather than how it is spelled.

Exercise 18C
Fill in the correct form of the verbs in brackets.

e.g. Karel (tennissen) in het park.
Karel tennist in het park.

a Als je die kinderen zo (coachen), winnen zo nooit.
b Hoe vaak (trainen) jullie per week?
c Heb je dat televisieprogramma gisteravond (tapen)?
d Hebben jullie die brief al (faxen)?
e (Bridgen) hij vaak?
f Ik (joggen) elke ochtend in het park.

Exercise 18D
Underline all the words derived from foreign words in this text.

In de rood-blauwe armstoel (1918) van Rietveld zijn de principes van De Stijl goed te zien. Het is een constructie van horizontale en verticale lijnen. De zitting en leuning van de stoel zijn geschilderd in de primaire kleuren rood, geel en blauw. Het constructieve deel van de stoel is zwart. De stoel was een radicale breuk met de traditie; een stimulans voor nieuwe experimentele ideeën; en een inspiratie voor meubeldesign, grafisch ontwerp en de schilderkunst.

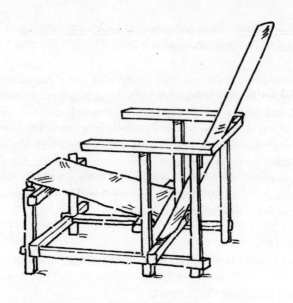

18.3 Exclamations

Exclamations add extra force to what you are saying.

18.3.1 What is it?

Any sentence which is spoken (or written) with extra force is an exclamation. You use exclamations more often in conversations than you do in writing:

Pas op! Er komt een auto aan! *Watch out! A car is coming!*

18.3.2 Function

Exclamations normally express particular emotions such as surprise, disgust, delight. Some of these are just sounds:

au	*ouch*	**Au, dat doet pijn!**	*Ouch, that hurts!*
bah	*yuck*	**Bah, wat vies!**	*Yuck, how dirty/how horrible!*

hoera	*yippee*	**Ik ben jarig, hoera!**	*It's my birthday, yippee!*
hé/ha	*hey*	**Ha, leuk dat je er bent!**	*Hey, glad you could make it!*

18.3.3 Other sounds and words

Not all of these sounds have an English equivalent. The following sounds express:

brrr	*shivering with cold*	**Brr, wat koud.**	*It's so cold.*
hè	*disappointment/ displeasure*	**Hè, wat jammer.**	*Oh, what a shame.*
hè, hè	*relief*	**Hè, hè, eindelijk**	*Finally…*
Jee…zeg/tjee	*expresses surprise, or admiration as in Really?/Gee!*		
Nou ja!	*expresses resigning oneself as in Oh well… or exasperation as in Goodness me!*		
Vooruit dan maar!	*expresses concession as in OK then!*		

Many exclamations, of course, come under the category of 'strong language' (see Section 18.5), or are interjections (see Section 18.4).

18.3.4 Wat, dat, zo'n

Often an exclamation starts with the words **wat** (*what*), **dat**, **da's** (**dat is**) (*that is*), **zo'n** (*such a*).

Wat een saaie boel hier!	*It's so boring here!*
Wat een mooi huis heb je!	*What a nice house you've got!*
Wat interessant!	*How interesting!*
Wat een leuk mens, zeg!	*She is such a nice woman!*
Wat een vent!	*What a man!*
Zo'n leuke les was dat!	*That was such a nice lesson!*
Zo'n lieve man is dat!	*He is such a sweet man!*
Da's (dat is) me ook wat moois.	*Charming!*

Exercise 18E
What particular emotion is expressed in the following exclamations?

e.g. Bah, deze appel is verrot! (*disgust*)

a Hoera, je bent geslaagd! Gefeliciteerd!
b Hé, ik dacht dat jij op vakantie was!
c Hè, hè; ik heb het eindelijk afgekregen!
d Tjee, wat een mooie auto!
e Jee zeg, waarom heeft-ie dat nou gedaan?
f Mag ik een koekje mama? Nou, vooruit dan maar!

Exercise 18F
Which word would you add to make these statements into exclamations?

e.g. ___wat vervelend dat je ziek bent.
Hè, wat vervelend dat je ziek bent!

a ___, deze aardappels zijn niet lekker!
b ___, 't vriest minstens 10 graden!
c ___, dat is mijn lievelingswijn. Dank je wel.
d ___, ik ben blij dat we er eindelijk zijn.
e ___, hij is zijn auto nu voor de 3e keer deze week aan het wassen!
f ___, die man hiernaast heeft alweer de radio te hard staan!

Exercise 18G
Exclaim your opinion about the following, making use of the words in the box below. Start with *wat*.

e.g. the daughter of your friend: Wat een leuke meid!

a a neighbour
b a film/pop star
c someone you work with
d a painting of Picasso

Exercise 18H
Change the exclamations from Exercise 18G into exclamations starting with *zo'n*.

e.g. Zo'n leuke meid is dat!

18.4 Interjections

18.4.1 What are they?

Interjections are little words which are used very frequently by native speakers. These words are normally difficult to translate because their meanings are subtle and depend largely on the context in which they are used. Some of these meanings can only be expressed in English by changing your tone of voice.

18.4.2 Function

Interjections have a communicative function: they often 'oil' the conversation and frequently soften a statement, order or question, or make it sound more polite. Other functions are establishing contact, urging, reassuring etc.

18.4.3 Place in sentence

There is no rule for this as some interjections tend to be used only at the beginning or at the end of a sentence, and others tend to be inserted into the middle of a sentence. Sometimes the place of the interjection determines its function or meaning. Check in the examples where the interjections come in the sentence.

18.4.4 Some examples

Zeg	▶ establishing contact with other speaker:	
(lit.: say)	**Zeg, heb je het al gehoord?**	*Hey, have you heard?*
	▶ emphasizing statement:	
	Wat een ellende, zeg!	*I say, such a misery!*
Hoor	▶ reassuring other speaker after giving a yes/no answer:	
	(see toch) **Ja, hoor.**	*Yes, sure.*
Toch	▶ showing concern in a question:	
	Je hebt je moeder toch wel gebeld?	*You did phone your mum, didn't you?*
	Je bent toch niet ziek?	*You aren't ill, are you?*

NB The answer to these questions would be **Ja, hoor** and **Nee, hoor** respectively.

▶ showing irritation (when part of an order):

Loop toch wat sneller!	*Walk a bit faster, will you?*

▶ indicating a contrast:

Wat je ook zegt, hij luistert toch niet.	*Whatever you say, he won't listen.*

▶ checking that your information/assumption is correct:

Jij komt toch ook?	*You are coming, aren't you?*

NB In English you would use a tag to do this, e.g. *isn't he? are you?*

Exercise 18I
Where would you insert *zeg*? At the beginning or end?

e.g. Weet jij wie dat is?
Zeg, weet jij wie dat is?

a Jij hebt toch ook dat boek over Hannibal Lecter gelezen?
b Wat een troep hier!
c Ga jij wel eens naar de kerk?
d Dat is verschrikkelijk!

Exercise 18J
Answer the questions below in a reassuring manner.

e.g. Je hebt de deur toch wel op slot gedaan?
Ja, hoor!

a Je hebt Nita toch wel bedankt, hè?
b Je hebt het hem toch niet verteld, hè?
c Je bent toch niet naar de kroeg geweest, hè?
d Je komt toch wel met me mee naar de dokter, hè?

Exercise 18K
What is the function of *toch* in these sentences below?

a Je gaat toch wel naar de schoolmusical?
b U bent toch meneer van Wijngaarden?
c Zet de televisie toch wat zachter!
d Hij werkt ontzettend hard en toch waarderen zijn collega's hem niet.
e In België spreken ze toch ook Nederlands?

Exercise 18L
How would you express the following? Make use of the appropriate interjection.

e.g. Order someone to stop (ophouden), it isn't working anyway (niet werken)

Hou toch op, 't werkt toch niet.

a Check that the time is indeed 10.30. (**half elf**)
b Urge your son to eat his food. (**bord leeg eten**)
c Tell your partner kindly to go to sleep. (**gaan slapen**)
d Check that your guest takes milk in his coffee. (**melk in je koffie**)

18.4.5 More examples

Maar	▶	softening an order or changing an order into an invitation:

        Kom *maar* **bij me.**   *Come to me!*

▶ giving advice, especially when combined with **zouden**:

        Ik zou dat *maar* **doen, als ik** *I would do that, if*
        jou was.   *I were you.*

▶ expressing a contrast or surprise (as in English *but*):

        Maar **wat wil je dan?**   *But what do you want then?*

Even/ eventjes ▶ softening a question, or order; being polite (**eventjes** has an even stronger softening effect):

        Wil jij *even(tjes)* **koffie** *Would you mind getting me*
        voor me halen?   *a coffee?*

▶ to indicate something will only take a little while:

        Even(tjes) **wachten!**   *Just a moment, please.*

        Even(tjes) **kijken, hoor!** *I'll just have a look!*

Eens ▶ expresses an irritation (often part of an order):

        Ga nu *eens* **je huiswerk** *Go and do your homework*
        maken!   *now!*

        Kom *eens* **even hier!**   *Come here, will you?*

Gewoon ▶ expresses how simple something is (as in just):

        Ik heb *gewoon* **de**   *I just followed the*
        instructies gevolgd   *instructions.*

▸ expresses a negative attitude of the speaker:

Hoe heb je dat gedaan?   *How did you do that?*

Nou, *gewoon***!**   *Well, I just did!*

Ze is *gewoon* **huisvrouw.**   *She is only a housewife.*

▸ expresses the speaker feels he/she is right:

Dat is *gewoon* **zo!**   *That's how it is!*

Eigenlijk   ▸ softening a negative answer (as in **actually**):

Ik kan *eigenlijk* **niet.**   *Actually, I can't make it.*

▸ expresses a change of plan (as in **actually**):

We wilden *eigenlijk* **naar Japan, maar het was te duur.**

Actually, we wanted to go to Japan, but it was too expensive

Zeker   ▸ expresses an assumption:

Geert heeft *zeker* **weer te veel gedronken?**   *Geert has drunk too much again, hasn't he?*

Exercise 18M
What is the function of the interjection in bold?

Maar dat kan toch niet? *Expressing contrast and surprise.*

a Stop **maar**! Je hebt genoeg gedaan.
b Ik zou hem **maar** wat geld geven. Hij heeft niks.
c Hebt u even **een** ogenblikje?
d Wil jij **eventjes** mijn nek masseren?
e Laat je werk **eens** zien!
f De Engelsen zijn **toch** gewoon beleefder?
g Roel is **gewoon** weggelopen.
h Zij is **gewoon** dom!
i Ik ben het er **eigenlijk** niet mee eens.
j Ik wilde eerst **eigenlijk** die rode bank kopen, maar ik heb toch maar die blauwe gekocht.
k Je hebt **zeker** de loterij gewonnen?

Exercise 18N

Rewrite these sentences with the appropriate interjection.

a Make the order sound less harsh
Doe het raam open.
b Express that this is the truth
Ik ben beter in communiceren dan jij!
c Express that you think this will happen
Je komt vanavond weer laat thuis, hè?
d Express your irritation
Stop met schrijven!
e Soften the following statement
Ik heb geen zin om vanavond te koken.

Exercise 18O

What is the difference in meaning between the two sentences?

a 1 Ik wil eigenlijk niet naar de verjaardag van je baas.
2 Ik wil gewoon niet naar de verjaardag van je baas.
b 1 Je hebt gewoon een slechte jeugd gehad.
2 Je hebt zeker een slechte jeugd gehad?
c 1 Stop eens met werken.
2 Stop maar met werken.
d 1 Ik wil dit eerst even afmaken.
2 Ik wil dit eigenlijk eerst afmaken.

Insight

Exclamations and interjections make you sound like a native speaker. Learn one or two of these and listen out for their use. Try to use them as often as possible. **Hè** can be useful to start with because it can be used in many situations. Also, besides the uses outlined above, **hè** is also used to ask *what?* Do note that it is very short and informal, and is not considered particularly polite.

18.5 Strong language

What's the attitude towards strong language in Dutch?

18.5.1 General

Dutch is generally quite colloquial in its spoken form. Written Dutch is on the whole more formal. The use of strong language used to be defined by social classes, where it was more acceptable to use strong language in the lower classes than in the higher social classes.

18.5.2 Social groups

With very little of a class system remaining in the Low Countries, the use of strong language is now mostly determined within various social groups. Among students – in the past mostly part of the higher social classes – and young people, for instance, strong language has become very much part of accepted, and often expected, social behaviour.

18.5.3 Boundaries

You could say that the boundaries of what is acceptable and non-acceptable strong language in Dutch are not as clearly defined as in some other languages, like English. For a large part of Dutch speakers there are practically no words which are considered too shocking or rude to use – even within the media and on television, which are part of a relatively liberal environment, particularly in the Netherlands. However, don't forget that statements like this are always generalizations and that strong language is not acceptable to everyone.

18.5.4 'Shit'

In recent years, English has had a strong influence on Dutch. Within the context of strong language, *shit* is an appropriate example. From the mid- to late 1980s this English word has been adopted by Dutch speakers (particularly in the north), but isn't as strong as it is in English, and has a meaning between *oh*, *dear* and *damn*.

18.5.5 Less strong?

What is true for the adoption of the English *shit* is true in general for a lot of other strong language in Dutch; on the whole the meaning of rude words is less strong than their literal translation which you find in the dictionary. This is less true in Belgium, where speakers of Dutch tend to be less openly colloquial and strong language is less generally acceptable.

Don't forget, however, that, as in most places, there is a considerable part of the population in the Netherlands which does not accept such language. (In public places in the Netherlands, you can frequently see advertisements against swearing.)

Exercise 18P
Identify the strong language in the following sentences, taken from quality newspapers and magazines.

  a 'Ach, verdomme', klonk het uit de keel van de jongen.
  b Wat is die professor toch een zak.
  c Als iemand een echte lul is, zeg ik dat ook.
  d Dat is iemand die veel shit produceert.
  e Als ik dat hele zootje overzie, ben ik heel gelukkig.
  f Het was moeilijk in het begin, maar het is goed voor je als je een paar keer flink op je bek gaat.
  g Donder op, zeg ik dan!

18.6 Topic – comment

This section discusses how to order information in Dutch sentences.

18.6.1 Order

The grammatical rules for word order help you to speak and write correctly, but not necessarily logically or clearly. Without thinking about how to present information, you might sound quite stilted. An example (Berlage was a Dutch architect):

Berlage bouwde in 1903 in Amsterdam een nieuw beursgebouw. Berlage's politieke ideeën zijn erin gereflecteerd. Het is ook een mooi gebouw.

> **bouwen** *to build* **beursgebouw** *stock exchange (building)*

Compare this with the following:

In 1903 bouwde Berlage in Amsterdam een beursgebouw. De beurs is niet alleen een mooi gebouw, maar ook reflecteert het Berlage's politieke ideeën.

> **de beurs** *stock exchange*

In the latter example, the second sentence starts with information linking it to the previous sentence. The main information of the first sentence is the fact that a new stock exchange was built. The second sentence starts with that 'old' information (**de beurs**) and continues to give more information about the building: it is beautiful and it also reflects the political ideas of the architect.

18.6.2 Clarity

Starting a sentence with 'old' information and thereby linking it to what was written or said before improves communication and makes texts or conversations flow better.

18.6.3 Topic/Comment

The 'old' information, which was referred to before, is called the **topic**. The rest of the sentence, giving 'new' information about the topic, is called the **comment**. The example shows that it is often advisable to start your sentence with the topic. (Not all sentences have both a topic and comment, but many do.)

This sometimes means that you have to start your sentence with an **object** rather than a subject. This means you will get *inversion*:

Die film van Cameron vond <u>ik</u> zo mooi!
Dit boek is niet voor kinderen. **Hun** heeft <u>het</u> niets te bieden.

18.6.4 Be a rebel!

For the sake of emphasis, contrast or attention seeking, you may also want to flaunt these guidelines on topic and comment sometimes, and start with new information:

Een schitterend meesterwerk is die nieuwe film van Scorsese.

Exercise 18Q
Indicate the topic and the comment in the following sentences.

e.g. Die afspraak die we gemaakt hebben, moet verzet worden.
   topic = die afspraak die we gemaakt hebben; comment = moet verzet worden.

a De reorganisatie op zijn werk veroorzaakt (*causes*) veel stress.
b Het konijntje dat jullie me hebben gegeven, is gisteren doodgegaan.
c Die manager van jou is een verschrikkelijk mens, hè?
d Arie komt morgen om mijn wasmachine te maken.
e Die tentoonstelling van Pollock die vorig jaar in Londen was, heb ik in Amsterdam gezien.

f We zijn gisteren een dagje naar Brussel geweest.

g Ik heb die vacature (*job ad*) waar je het gisteren over had uit de krant geknipt.

h Dat huis dat Lisette en Hans hebben gekocht is nu een kapitaal waard.

Exercise 18R
Read the following text and indicate how the various sentences are linked.

In juli '42 moest Anne Frank met haar ouders en haar zus onderduiken. Het gezin zat in het Achterhuis tot 1944. Tijdens deze periode hield Anne een dagboek bij. Hierin beschreef zij haar leven en emoties. Haar laatste notitie was gedateerd 1 augustus 1944. Drie dagen later werd het gezin door de nazi's opgepakt.

Na de oorlog besloot haar vader, Otto Frank, haar dagboek te publiceren. Het boek is nu, ruim een halve eeuw later, nog steeds een bestseller.

> **onderduiken** *go into hiding* **hield...bij** *kept*
> **beschreef** *described*
> **opgepakt** *arrested* **besloot** *decided*

Exercise 18S
Read the following text and change word order if appropriate to follow the conventions of structuring old (topic) before new (comment) information (there is usually more than one solution).

Kinderen zijn tegenwoordig geen kinderen meer. De psycholoog professor Kuip zei dat. Om te leren lezen en schrijven gingen kinderen vroeger naar school. Toegang tot de wereld van volwassenen kregen ze op die manier. Kinderen krijgen die toegang nu via computer, televisie en internet.

> **toegang** *access*

18.7 Style

In this section we look at the effects of grammar on style.

18.7.1 What is it?

Style is a particular way of writing (or speaking) which people change and adapt according to the circumstances, such as who you write (or speak) to and why. You will write a letter to a friend in a different style from a letter to the editor of a newspaper. Stylistic differences can be formal, informal, poetic, dry, lively, dramatic and so on.

18.7.2 How?

You can change your style to a large degree by your choice of vocabulary. Choosing unfamiliar, difficult words will create a more formal style than using familiar and colloquial words: **u attenderen op** (*to draw your attention to*) is more formal than **je laten weten** (*to let you know*).

But grammar can also affect style.

18.7.3 Grammar and style

There are various ways in which grammar can affect style. One of these is by the type of words you use:

▶ **Nouns or verbs:** Using many nouns where you could use verbs instead tends to create a formal and static style. The use of verbs gives a sentence a more dynamic feel. In the following example the nouns are underlined:

Ons <u>doel</u> is <u>het creëren</u> van meer <u>werk</u>.	*Our aim is the creation of more work.*
Wij willen meer <u>werk</u> creëren.	*We want to create more work.*

► **Adjectives:** Using adjectives will make your sentences more descriptive. Depending on the kind of adjectives used, you create a style which is poetic, dramatic, positive, feminine, etc.:

Hij leest altijd voor uit hetzelfde *versleten* **boek, in die** *geheimzinnige, onverstaanbare* **taal.**	*He always reads to us from the same worn book, in that mysterious, incomprehensible language.*
Deze *fascinerende* **biografie geeft een** *dynamisch* **beeld van het leed en de passies van deze** *hartstochtelijke* **vrouw.**	*This fascinating biography gives a dynamic picture of the suffering and passions of this ardent woman.*

Exercise 18T
Which of these words/expressions in the following pairs is more formal?

a	café	kroeg
b	reageren op	een reactie geven op
c	mijn ervaring is dat dit goed werkt	ik heb gemerkt dat dit goed werkt
d	uitnodiging	invitatie
e	er zal worden gestreefd naar een oplossing	wij proberen dit op te lossen
f	gauw	in de nabije toekomst
g	beslissen	een beslissing nemen
h	steun verlenen aan	steunen
i	ik ben verkouden	ik heb een verkoudheid
j	ik bewonder dat mens	ik heb bewondering voor die vrouw

Exercise 18U
Add the adjectives in the box to the text. How does that effect the style?

....
:   **geweldig** *hard* **fel** *bright* **donker** *dark*   :
:   **religieus** *religious* **streng** *strict* **zwijgzaam** *silent*   :
: **gepolijst** *polished* **zwart** *black* **glimmend** *shiny* **vilten** *felt* :
....

a Op dat moment hoorde ik een _____ knal en zag ik een _____ lichtflits in de _____ straat.

b Mijn moeder kwam uit een _____ gezin. Zij was een _____ en _____ vrouw voor wie het personeel een beetje bang was. In gedachten zie ik mijn ouders altijd door iets gescheiden, een _____ tafel, een _____ vleugel, en de _____ parketvloeren, waar iedereen op _____ pantoffels liep.

Adapted from: *De witte stad* by Bernlef

---

in gedachten *in my mind*　　　**gescheiden** *separated*
vleugel *grand piano*　　　**parketvloer** *parquet flooring*
pantoffels *slippers*

Besides your choice of words, style is influenced by various grammatical points. Here are some of the most important ones:

18.7.4 Simple/complex sentences

Short simple sentences can create a sense of speed and drama. Longer complex sentences make a text more difficult and formal. Compare:

Hij liep naar binnen, trok zijn pistool en schoot ze neer.
He walked in, pulled his gun and shot them.
Nadat hij het gebouw was binnengelopen, haalde hij uit zijn jas zijn pistool tevoorschijn en schoot hij vervolgens iedereen neer.
After he had walked into the building, he pulled his gun out of his coat and proceeded to shoot everyone.

18.7.5 Passive/active

Using passive structures creates a more formal style and has a distancing effect. (see Sections 10.4 and 10.5 for passive sentences.)

18.7.6 Interjections

Inserting little words can 'oil' your sentences and create a conversational style in writing (see Section 18.4).

Moeten we vanmiddag *eigenlijk* **niet even vergaderen?**

18.7.7 Word order

Varying the place where certain word patterns come in a sentence can make your style more lively (see Section 18.6 for topic/comment).

18.7.8 Linking and referring

To create a clear style of writing it is particularly important that you link sentences with a correct linking word (see Sections 15.2–15.5). You can also link sentences logically through the ideas you express in them. You express this partly through word order (see Section 17.3). In order to refer clearly to previous ideas, you make use of object pronouns, **er, hier, daar, dat** and relative pronouns (check the corresponding sections for more information).

Exercise 18V
Compare the following two texts. What are the main stylistic differences between the texts and how is this difference achieved?

Als jij ziek zou worden, ga je naar een dokter of het ziekenhuis. En om te voorkomen dat je ziek wordt, heb je allerlei injecties gekregen.
Als jij de kraan opendraait, komt er schoon drinkwater uit. En als jij trek krijgt, komt er eten op tafel.
Voor miljoenen kinderen in ontwikkelingslanden is dit helemaal niet zo vanzelfsprekend. Ze hebben vaak geen schoon water. Ze kunnen niet naar school, omdat ze de hele dag moeten werken en als ze ziek worden, zijn er vaak geen dokters en ziekenhuizen.
Nog veel erger is het dat er soms niks te eten is.

voorkomen	*to prevent*
kraan	*tap*
ontwikkelingslanden	*developing countries*
vanzelfsprekend	*(can be) taken for granted*

Geachte mevrouw/meneer

Zoals u weet, zijn er in de binnenstad parkeermeters. Deze meters zijn vooral bedoeld voor bezoekers, zodat ze in de directe nabijheid van hun bezoekadres kunnen parkeren. Tevens zijn ze bedoeld om te kunnen parkeren in de buurt van winkels. Wellicht heeft u gelezen dat het gebruik van deze parkeermeters in onze stad niet zonder problemen is verlopen. Sommige meters gaven de incorrecte tijd of accepteerden bepaalde munten niet. Deze meters zijn inmiddels vervangen door nieuwe exemplaren.

Met vriendelijke groet

binnenstad	*city centre*	**nabijheid**	*vicinity*
tevens	*furthermore*	**wellicht**	*perhaps*
verlopen	*occurred*	**vervangen**	*replaced*
inmiddels	*in the meantime*		

Things to remember

▶ Formality or informality is indicated by form of address (**je** and **jij** *you* are informal and **u** is formal), vocabulary (some words are considered more formal than others) and grammar (some grammatical structures are considered more formal than others).

▶ People in the Netherlands tend to be more informal more quickly towards one another than people in Flanders.

▶ Exclamations add force to what you are saying. Examples are: **au** *ouch*, **bah** *yuck*, **hé/ha** *hey*.

▶ Many exclamations start with the words **wat** *what*, **dat** *that*, **dat is/da's** *that is*, **zo'n** *such a* (**wat interessant** *how interesting*).

▶ Interjections are difficult to translate because their meaning depends on the context in which they are used. Examples are **zeg** (**Wat een rotmuziek, zeg.** *That's really terrible music.*), **hoor** (**Ja, hoor.** *Yes, sure.*), **maar** (**Ga maar zitten.** *Do sit down.*)

▶ It is often advisable to start a sentence with 'old' or 'known' information (the topic) and then give new information in the rest of the sentence (the comment).

▶ Grammatical choices (using lots of nouns instead of verbs, using complex sentences or not, using the passive, word order, etc.) influence the style of your language use.

Best of the rest

19.1 Punctuation and accents

When do you use commas in Dutch, and what accents can you use?

19.1.1 Punctuation marks

In general, punctuation marks in Dutch are used much as in other neighbouring languages such as German, English and French. For this reason, we will leave full stops, exclamation marks, question marks and colons, etc. and only look at the comma.

19.1.2 Comma

The general rule in Dutch is that you use a comma only if it facilitates the reading process. This means that you usually need a comma if there's a short pause when reading out loud. The two most important situations in which it is advisable to use a comma are:

▶ Verb verb verb: If you put two or more verbs next to each other and they belong to different clauses, it's usually a good idea to separate them by a comma. This often happens when a sub-clause with verb in final position precedes a main clause.

Als je het goed vindt, ga ik even liggen.
If it's OK with you, I'll lie down for a while.

▶ Relative clauses, which give extra information about nouns, often end in a comma to separate the verbs of the relative clause and the main clause. However, only non-restrictive relative clauses (which don't add vital new information) also start with a comma; restrictive relative clauses (which do add vital new information) don't.

Sinaasappels, die oranje zijn, zijn lekker.	*Oranges, which are orange, are nice.*
Sinaasappels die groen zijn, zijn verrot.	*Oranges which are green are rotten.*

19.1.3 Accents

▶ Accents ´ and ` are mainly used on French words, but can also indicate stress (1) or pronunciation (2 and 3):

1	**Ik zei niet droog maar hóóg.**	*I didn't say dry but high.*
2	é is long and open: **Hé jij daar!**	*Hey you there!*
3	è is short and closed: **Hè, wat zeg je?**	*What's that you're saying?*

▶ A **trema** (two dots ¨) indicates the start of a new syllable when it isn't clear whether a sequence of vowels is one sound. **Tweeëntwintig** is therefore pronounced **twee-en-twin-tig**.

NB Accents aren't used on capital letters in Dutch.

Exercise 19A
Insert commas into the following sentences where and if appropriate.

e.g. Als je het te laat vindt moet je naar huis gaan.
Als je het te laat vindt, moet je naar huis gaan.

  a Vliegtuigen die meer dan twintig jaar oud zijn moeten goed worden gecontroleerd.
  b We gaan morgen met mijn ouders in de stad eten.

c Kangoeroes die alleen in Australië voorkomen vind ik zulke grappige beesten.

d Mijn hond zei de jongen is twee jaar oud.

e Als je morgen tijd hebt kom ik even langs om over dat werk te praten.

f Ze hebben hun huis pas verbouwd dacht ik.

g Heb jij enig idee waar ze naartoe zijn verhuisd?

h Hoewel het vreselijk slecht weer was zijn we toch gegaan.

i Als jullie willen kan ik een tafel voor ons reserveren.

j Mijn vrouw vindt dit soort films vulgair dom en infantiel.

Exercise 19B

What is the difference in meaning between the following pairs of sentences?

a 1 Ton de tuinman en zijn vrouw komen morgen op bezoek.
  2 Ton, de tuinman en zijn vrouw komen morgen op bezoek.

b 1 Zijn baas vroeg hem opnieuw, het aanbod in overweging te nemen.
  2 Zijn baas vroeg hem, opnieuw het aanbod in overweging the nemen.

c 1 Ze zegt, niet met hem te willen trouwen.
  2 Ze zegt niet, met hem te willen trouwen.

d 1 Heb ik je dat boek en die CD van Barbra Streisand al teruggegeven?
  2 Heb ik je dat boek, en die CD van Barbra Streisand al teruggegeven?

19.2 Dictionaries

What to look for in a dictionary.

19.2.1 A great help

When you're learning a foreign language it is always important to have a good dictionary. Any dictionary is a help, but a Dutch–English dictionary is particularly important, as it will help you understand language which you didn't understand before and, unlike an English–Dutch dictionary, it will help you think in the foreign language.

19.2.2 Buying a dictionary

When buying one, don't opt for any old dictionary. Make sure you get your money's worth and that it contains most of the following information:

▶ Each entry should have different meanings; words rarely have only one meaning.

▶ Each entry should list several examples to illustrate the various meanings. This will help you decide in which contexts a word can be used.

▶ For nouns it should say whether a word is feminine or masculine (and therefore a **de**-word) or neuter (a **het**-word). This is often indicated with **v** (**vrouwelijk** = *feminine*), **m** (**mannelijk** = *masculine*) or **o** (**onzijdig** = *neuter*). (For gender see Section 2.1.)

▶ A good dictionary often also indicates where the stress lies on a word, often by an apostrophe in front of the stressed syllable. This will not only help your pronunciation, but also tell you whether verbs with a prefix are separable or not (if the prefix is stressed they are).

▶ Some dictionaries may even give you the past forms of (irregular) verbs, which is a great help of course.

19.2.3 Dutch–Dutch

After you have become more familiar with the basics of Dutch, you will find it a great help to have a Dutch–Dutch dictionary. A good single language dictionary often contains more detailed information about the different meanings of the entries and, vitally, usually lists more examples.

Exercise 19C

Look up the following words in your dictionary and find out whether they are nouns, verbs or adjectives.

a	magnetron	**i**	burger
b	koper	**j**	beheren
c	vies	**k**	gezellig
d	servies	**l**	leugen
e	verkopen	**m**	kleurrijk
f	schoon	**n**	schoon
g	zichtbaar	**o**	oorzaak
h	puinhoop	**p**	planning

Exercise 19D

Find out which of the following nouns take the article *het* and which take the article *de*.

a	ontwerper	**i**	zaal
b	toilet	**j**	konijn
c	kleding	**k**	agenda
d	land	**l**	koffiezetapparaat
e	wandeling	**m**	identiteit
f	toneelstuk	**n**	naam
g	ster	**o**	programma
h	televisie	**p**	grapjas

Exercise 19E

Find out at least two different meanings for the following words.

a	jagen
b	nagaan

c beeld
d patroon
e optreden
f maat
g bus

19.3 Using dictionaries

This section discusses how to look up words in dictionaries.

19.3.1 Different forms

Dictionaries are wonderful books for looking up all sorts of words, but unfortunately not all the words you may want to look up appear in the dictionary exactly as you come across them. As you can see in many sections in this book, words change and can have many different forms. Here are some of the main word categories and how to look them up.

19.3.2 Regular verbs

Verbs are listed under only one of their many forms, the infinitive, so it is important that you know how to find the infinitive. For most verbs this is quite easy because all their forms consist of the stem of the verb plus one or more letters added at the end (a suffix) or beginning (a prefix). The stem of regular verbs is usually the infinitive minus -en, so once you've found the stem, simply add this -en back on and you'll know where to look in the dictionary. Some examples:

	stem	infinitive
Je kookte	kook	koken
Het heeft gewaaid	waai	waaien

19.3.3 Separable verbs

With separable verbs you should remember that they come with a prefix which may be separated from the verb, and can normally be found at the end of the sentence. With past participles, the prefix comes before **ge-**. So, in the sentence **Je stelt me teleur**, you should look up **teleurstellen**.

19.3.4 Irregular verbs

Irregular verbs often don't base their forms on the stem. The best advice is to try and learn their forms by heart.

19.3.5 Adjectives

Adjectives are entered in the dictionary under their basic form, so all you have to do is chop off the extra **-e** which is added in some cases.

19.3.6 Nouns

Nouns are entered in dictionaries under their singular form. If you have a plural noun, simply take away **-en** or **-s** to get the singular form. However, don't forget that there are some irregular forms as well.

19.3.7 Spelling

Don't forget the various spelling rules which apply, for instance, to the doubling of consonants or vowels, or **s/z** and **f/v** – see Sections 1.4 and 1.5.

Exercise 19F
Give the infinitive of the underlined verbs in the following phrases and look up their meaning in a dictionary.

  a Ik <u>vind</u> dit boek erg mooi.
  b Hij <u>woonde</u> in die tijd in een klein huisje in York.

c Heb je je moeder al <u>opgebeld</u>?
d Peter en Marcus <u>tafeltennisten</u> de hele dag.
e Wie heeft dat schilderij <u>geschilderd</u>?
f Mijn collega heeft die brief voor je <u>gefaxt</u>.
g <u>Kijk</u> even dit document voor me <u>door</u>.
h Wist jij dat hij ook <u>vertaalde</u>?
i Ik <u>stuur</u> dat pakket morgenochtend vroeg <u>op</u>.
j Ze <u>bediscussieert</u> dat soort dingen altijd heel agressief.
k Hoeveel <u>levert</u> dit werk ons <u>op</u>?
l Dat portret heeft mijn vader <u>geschilderd</u>.
m De buren zijn naar Australië <u>verhuisd</u>.
n Aan wie <u>geef</u> je dat enorme cadeau?

Exercise 19G
Find out the infinitives of the following underlined irregular verb forms.

a Ben je wel eens in Rome <u>geweest</u>?
b Vroeger <u>kocht</u> mijn vriendin veel dure kleren.
c Waarom <u>ga</u> je al zo vroeg naar huis, Jacqueline?
d Je <u>kan</u> dat werk natuurlijk ook morgen doen.
e Hanna <u>moest</u> vanochtend de hond uitlaten.

Exercise 19H
What are the singular forms of the following plural nouns, and what do they mean?

a huizen
b brillen
c horloges
d vragen
e kinderen
f politici
g glazen
h uren
i boekensteunen
j bomen

19.3.8 What does it mean?!

Dutch, like almost any other language, uses lots of set expressions, or figurative ways of speech, the meaning of which you can't deduce simply by looking at the individual words that are used. The thing to do is to look up the most important or central word in the expression and then to check the examples given in your dictionary.

19.3.9 Examples

▶ Take the expression **de kat uit de boom kijken**. You will probably have guessed that this doesn't mean to *look the cat out of the tree*. If you look up **kat** in a good Dutch–English dictionary, you will find that it means to wait and see which way the wind blows. A good dictionary will also tell you that there are plenty more figurative expressions with the word **kat** in it, like:

leven als kat en hond	*to be at loggerheads*
een kat in de zak kopen	*to buy a pig in a poke*

▶ Another expression is **te veel hooi op de vork nemen**. Again it is advisable to look up the first noun, **hooi**. You will find that it means *to bite off more than you can chew*.

▶ Here are some expressions (the words to look up in the dictionary are in underlined):

iets onder de <u>knie</u> krijgen	*to get the hang of something*
ergens geen <u>kaas</u> van gegeten hebben	*not know the first thing about something*
ergens geen <u>bal</u> van snappen (colloquial)	*to not understand something*
de <u>buik</u> vol hebben van iets	*to be fed up with something*
iets <u>zat</u> zijn	*to be fed up with something*

de <u>mist</u> ingaan	*to go completely wrong*
<u>rood</u> staan	*to be in the red (financially)*
over de <u>rooie</u> gaan (colloquial)	*to lose self-control/become angry*
een <u>blauwtje</u> lopen	*to be dumped/jilted(colloquial)*
over de <u>brug</u> komen	*to pay up*
goed voor de <u>dag</u> komen	*to make a good impression*
op het <u>punt</u> staan	*to be about (to do something)*
op het <u>nippertje</u>	*in the nick of time*
aan de <u>orde</u> komen	*to come up (for discussion)*
iets niet kunnen <u>maken</u>	*you can't do that (It's not done)*
uit je <u>dak</u> gaan (colloquial)	*to go wild (with enthusiasm)*

Exercise 19I

Look at the following expressions and underline the word under which you should look in the dictionary.

e.g. Dat kan niet door de beugel.
beugel

a de deur platlopen
b iets van de grond krijgen
c hoogte nemen van
d er is iets aan de hand
e iemand de hand reiken
f aan de bel trekken
g iemand op zijn donder geven
h een kater hebben
i op je tenen lopen
j Je bent er geknipt voor

Exercise 19J

Look up the meaning of the expressions in Exercise 19I in your dictionary.

Dat kan niet door de <u>beugel</u>.
That won't do.

een kater hebben

19.4 Abbreviations

In this section you'll find the most commonly used abbreviations
in Dutch.

19.4.1 Abbreviation mad?

As you will see from the number of entries that follow, Dutch
speakers are keen users of abbreviations. As in most languages, lots
of abbreviations exist within particular professions as part of the
jargon. However, below we've only included abbreviations which
you will find used in everyday Dutch.

19.4.2 Full stops

In general, abbreviations of a single word only get a full stop at the
end of the abbreviations. If the abbreviation refers to more than
one word, each letter is usually separated by a full stop.

▶ General

enz. = **enzovoort**	*etcetera*	**p.** = **pagina**	*page*
etc. = **etcetera**	*etc.*	**blz.** = **bladzijde**	*page*
bv. = **bijvoorbeeld**	*for example*	**par.** = **paragraaf**	*para.*
t/m = **tot en met**	*up to and including*	**N.B.** = **nota bene**	*NB*
z.o.z. = **zie ommezijde**	*p.t.o.*	**a.u.b.** = **alstublieft**	*please*
i.v.m. = **in verband met**	*re*	**s.v.p.** = **s'il vous plaît**	*please*

m.a.w. = **met andere woorden** *in other words*

▶ **Dates** In dates you can use the following abbreviations:
jl. (**jongstleden** = last) and **a.s.** (**aanstaande** = next). These
abbreviations always come after the date:

24 december jl.	*24th of December last*
17 mei a.s.	*17th of May next*

▶ **Titles** You will usually address women as **mevrouw** in Dutch,
which can be abbreviated to **mevr.** You usually address men as
meneer, which has the slightly strange abbreviation **dhr.** (from
de heer, or *the gentleman*).

The following titles are professional or academic titles and are
always put in front of people's names:

prof. = **professor**   **mr.** = **meester** (*from the legal profession*)
drs. = **doctorandus** (equivalent to a masters degree)

▶ **Addresses** The following abbreviations are common in Dutch
addresses.

a/d = **aan de**	on the	Alphen a/d Rijn
a/z = **aan zee**	on sea	Egmont a/z
hs = **huis**	ground floor	Kwerelijnlaan 33hs

Exercise 19K

e.g. Abbreviate the expressions in bold according to the conventions.

De toegangsprijs is 10 euro per persoon.
De toegangsprijs is 10 euro p.p.

a Fietsen niet tegen het raam plaatsen **alstublieft**.
b Het Concertgebouworkest staat **onder leiding van** Mariss Jansons (*led/conducted by*).
c Wij zullen u de boeken **zo spoedig mogelijk** (*as soon as possible*) sturen.
d Wij willen **door middel van** (*by means of*) bezuinigingen 10% op onze uitgaven besparen.
e De huur zal **met ingang van** (*as of*) 1 januari **aanstaande** met 50 euro **per maand** worden verhoogd.
f Je kunt je sollicitaties richten aan 'Talentrecruitment' **ter attentie van** (*attention of*) Marieke Wagemaker.

Exercise 19L

Write out the following abbreviations in full.

a Op 15 augustus jl. is ons filiaal in Haarlem geopend.
b Voeten vegen s.v.p.
c Wij hebben i.v.m. uw aanvraag tot verlenging van uw huurcontract besloten dit contract niet te vernieuwen, m.a.w., wij willen dat u uit ons huis weggaat.
d Zou u zo vriendelijk willen zijn ons d.m.v een briefje z.s.m. antwoord te geven?
e Etage te huur voor max. 1 jaar. Liefst 1 pers. 550 euro p.m. incl.

Exercise 19M

You are writing to the following people. Write their names on the envelope and follow the conventions.

a M. Harskamp (has a degree)
b J. Aleman (a lawyer)
c L. Krosse (a professor)
d Mr. Vanderbilt
e Mrs. Hetjes

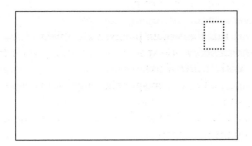

19.4.3 Politics

In the Netherlands and Belgium, most of the names of political parties consist of abbreviations. Here are the most important ones.

In the Netherlands:

CDA	=	Christen Democratisch Appèl (*Christian Democrats*)
PvdA	=	Partij van de Arbeid (*Socialist/Labour*)
VVD	=	Volkspartij voor Vrijheid en Democratie (*Conservative*)
SP	=	Socialistische Partij (*left wing*)
PVV	=	Partijd voor de Vrijheid (*Conservative, right wing*)
GL	=	GroenLinks (*Green, left wing*)

In Belgium/Flanders:

SP	=	socialistische partij (*Labour*)
CVP	=	Christelijke Volkspartij (*Christian Democrats*)
VLD	=	Vlaamse Liberalen en Democraten (*Conservative*)
VU	=	Volks Unie (*moderate nationalist platform*)

19.4.4 Work

The Dutch also like abbreviations in work-related issues, which can make some news reports, for instance, difficult to understand. These are the main ones:

VUT = **vervroegde uittreding** (*early retirement*)
ADV = **arbeidsduurverkorting** (*shortening of the number of hours people work*)
CAO = **centrale arbeidsovereenkomst** (*collective labour agreement*, which determines salaries and working conditions within particular industries)

19.4.5 Education

Educational systems abroad can be difficult to understand at the best of times, but in the Netherlands the situation isn't helped by the many abbreviations, particularly relating to secondary education, or **voortgezet onderwijs** (from ages 12–18). The three main types are:

mavo = **middelbaar algemeen voortgezet onderwijs** (*middle ability*)
havo = **hoger algemeen voortgezet onderwijs** (*higher ability*)
vwo = **voortgezet wetenschappelijk onderwijs** (*top ability*)

Exercise 19N
The following texts contain abbreviations. Use the context to identify whether they are abbreviations of: a) names of an institution or an organization, b) names of a political party, c) names of a particular law, d) an abbreviated word/expression, e) an educational level or f) a transport system. Then look them up in your dictionary or in the key.

Text 1

Het slechte weer heeft volgens de VVV's en de ANWB nog geen invloed gehad op het toerisme naar Nederland. Volgens het NBT, de ANWB en de VVV's, is er nog geen reden tot klagen.

Text 2

Op 18 december 1974 besloten de socialistische vakcentrale en de katholieke vakbond om toe te treden tot de FNV.

Text 3

HSL: minder files op de wegen, meer mensen in het openbaar vervoer.

Text 4

Buitenschoolse Opvang Utrecht
Wij zoeken m.i.v. 15 september a.s.
DIRECTEUR m/v
eisen: **min.** diploma op **MBO**-niveau en
management diploma op **HBO**-niveau
salaris: conform de **CAO**-welzijn
c.v. richten aan: **BSO** Utrecht
t.a.v. mevr. Meier

19.5 Irregular verbs

In this section you will find the imperfect and perfect forms of irregular verbs.

19.5.1 Forms

In this section you will find a list of irregular verbs. In the first column you'll find the infinitive plus a translation (e.g. **kopen** *to buy*); in the second column you'll can find the singular and plural forms

of the imperfect (**kocht, kochten**) and in the last column the past
participle (**gekocht**).

19.5.2 Present perfect

If only the past participle is given in the third column, like
gekocht, it is assumed that the present perfect is formed with a
form of the verb **hebben**. If you need a form of the verb **zijn** in the
present perfect, it is added in front of the past participle (e.g. **zijn
geweest**). If (**zijn**) is given in brackets, the verb can be used with
zijn or **hebben** in the present perfect (often in different contexts –
see Section 7.3).

19.5.3 Irregular and strong

The section includes irregular and strong verbs. Strong verbs form
their (im)perfect forms according to a pattern. However, there
are many different groups of strong verbs and we believe that
you will find this list easier to use if we simply list all the verbs
alphabetically.

infinitive	imperfect	present perfect
bakken *to bake*	bakte, bakten	gebakken
barsten *to burst*	barstte, barstten	zijn gebarsten
beginnen *to begin*	begon, begonnen	zijn begonnen
begrijpen *to understand*	begreep, begrepen	begrepen
bekijken *to look at, examine*	bekeek, bekeken	bekeken
besluiten *to decide*	besloot, besloten	besloten
bestaan *to exist*	bestond, bestonden	bestaan
bevallen *to give birth, please*	beviel, bevielen	zijn bevallen
bewegen *to move*	bewoog, bewogen	bewogen
bewijzen *to prove*	bewees, bewezen	bewezen
bezoeken *to visit*	bezocht, bezochten	bezocht
bieden *to offer, bid*	bood, boden	geboden

infinitive	imperfect	present perfect
binden *to bind*	bond, bonden	gebonden
blijken *to prove (to be)*	bleek, bleken	zijn gebleken
blijven *to remain, stay*	bleef, bleven	zijn gebleven
breken *to break*	brak, braken	gebroken
brengen *to bring, take*	bracht, brachten	gebracht
denken *to think*	dacht, dachten	gedacht
doen *to do*	deed, deden	gedaan
dragen *to carry, wear*	droeg, droegen	gedragen
drinken *to drink*	dronk, dronken	gedronken
eten *to eat*	at, aten	gegeten
gaan *to go*	ging, gingen	zijn gegaan
gelden *to apply (to)*	gold, golden	gegolden
geven *to give*	gaf, gaven	gegeven
hangen *to hang*	hing, hingen	gehangen
hebben *to have*	had, hadden	gehad
helpen *to help*	hielp, hielpen	geholpen
heten *to be called*	heette, heetten	geheten
hoeven *to (not) have to*	hoefde, hoefden	gehoeven
houden *to hold*	hield, hielden	gehouden
kiezen *to choose*	koos, kozen	gekozen
kijken *to look*	keek, keken	gekeken
klimmen *to climb*	klom, klommen	(zijn) geklommen
komen *to come*	kwam, kwamen	zijn gekomen
kopen *to buy*	kocht, kochten	gekocht
krijgen *to get, receive*	kreeg, kregen	gekregen
kunnen *can, be able to*	kon, konden	gekund
lachen *to laugh*	lachte, lachten	gelachen
laten *to let, have (something done)*	liet, lieten	gelaten
lezen *to read*	las, lazen	gelezen
liggen *to lie*	lag, lagen	gelegen
lijden *to suffer*	leed, leden	geleden
lijken *to appear, seem*	leek, leken	geleken
lopen *to walk*	liep, liepen	(zijn) gelopen
moeten *must, to have to*	moest, moesten	gemoeten

(Contd)

infinitive	imperfect	present perfect
mogen *may, to be allowed*	mocht, mochten	gemogen
nemen *to take*	nam, namen	genomen
onthouden *to remember*	onthield, onthielden	onthouden
ontmoeten *to meet*	ontmoette, ontmoetten	ontmoet
ontslaan *to dismiss, sack*	ontsloeg, ontsloegen	ontslaan
ontstaan *to come into being*	onstond, ontstonden	zijn ontstaan
overlijden *to die*	overleed, overleden	zijn overleden
raden *to guess*	raadde, raadden ried, rieden	geraden geraden
rijden *to ride, to drive*	reed, reden	(zijn) gereden
roepen *to call*	riep, riepen	geroepen
ruiken *to smell*	rook, roken	geroken
scheiden *to separate, divorce*	scheidde, scheidden	(zijn) gescheiden
scheppen *to create*	schiep, schiepen	geschapen
scheren *to shave*	scheerde, scheerden	geschoren
schijnen *to appear, seem*	scheen, schenen	geschenen
schrijven *to write*	schreef, schreven	geschreven
schrikken *to be startled*	schrok, schrokken	zijn geschrokken
slaan *to hit*	sloeg, sloegen	geslagen
slapen *to sleep*	sliep, sliepen	geslapen
sluiten *to close*	sloot, sloten	gesloten
smijten *to throw, hurl*	smeet, smeten	gesmeten
snijden *to cut*	sneed, sneden	gesneden
spreken *to speak*	sprak, spraken	gesproken
springen *to jump*	sprong, sprongen	(zijn) gesprongen
staan *to stand*	stond, stonden	gestaan
steken *to stab, stick, put*	stak, staken	gestoken
stelen *to steal*	stal, stalen	gestolen
sterven *to die*	stierf, stierven	zijn gestorven
stinken *to stink*	stonk, stonken	gestonken
treffen *to hit, meet*	trof, troffen	getroffen

infinitive	imperfect	present perfect
trekken *to pull*	trok, trokken	getrokken
vallen *to fall*	viel, vielen	zijn gevallen
vangen *to catch*	ving, vingen	gevangen
varen *to sail*	vaarde, vaarden	(zijn) gevaren
verbergen *to hide*	verborg, verborgen	verborgen
verdwijnen *to disappear*	verdween, verdwenen	zijn verdwenen
vergelijken *to compare*	vergeleek, vergeleken	vergeleken
vergeten *to forget*	vergat, vergaten	(zijn) vergeten
verliezen *to lose*	verloor, verloren	(zijn) verloren
vertrekken *to depart*	vertrok, vertrokken	zijn vertrokken
vinden *to find*	vond, vonden	gevonden
vliegen *to fly*	vloog, vlogen	(zijn) gevlogen
vragen *to ask*	vroeg, vroegen	gevraagd
vriezen *to freeze*	vroor, vroren	gevroren
waaien *to blow (wind)*	waaide, waaiden	gewaaid
wassen *to wash*	waste, wasten	gewassen
wegen *to weigh*	woog, wogen	gewogen
werpen *to throw*	wierp, wierpen	geworpen
weten *to know*	wist, wisten	geweten
wijzen *to point, indicate*	wees, wezen	gewezen
worden *to become*	werd, werden	zijn geworden
zeggen *to say*	zei, zeiden	gezegd
zenden *to send*	zond, zonden	gezonden
zien *to see*	zag, zagen	gezien
zijn *to be*	was, waren	zijn geweest
zingen *to sing*	zong, zongen	gezongen
zitten *to sit*	zat, zaten	gezeten
zoeken *to look for, seek*	zocht, zochten	gezocht
zwemmen *to swim*	zwom, zwommen	(zijn) gezwommen
zwijgen *to be/remain silent*	zweeg, zwegen	gezwegen

Things to remember

▶ Use a comma between verbs in Dutch if two or more adjacent verbs belong to different clauses (**Als je het goed vindt, ga ik even liggen.** *If it's all right with you, I will lie down for a bit.*).

▶ Relative clauses often end in a comma, to separate the verbs of the relative clause and the main clause. However, non-restrictive relative clauses (which don't add vital new information) also start with a comma; restrictive relative clauses (which do add vital new information) don't.

▶ A trema (two dots on a letter, such as ë) indicates the start of a new syllable.

▶ A Dutch dictionary should indicate whether a noun is feminine or masculine (a **de**-word) or neuter (a **het**-word). A **v** often indicates feminine (**vrouwelijk**), an **m** masculine (**mannelijk**) and **o** neuter (**onzijdig**).

▶ Some of the most often used abbreviations in Dutch are: **enz.** (**enzovoort** *etcetera*), **blz.** (**bladzijde** *page*), **bv.** (**bijvoorbeeld** *for example*), **t/m** (**tot en met** *upto and including*), **a.u.b.** (**alstublieft** = *please*), **s.v.p.** (**s'il vous plaît** *please*), **mevr.** (**mevrouw** *Mrs*), **dhr.** (**de heer** *Mr*).

▶ Irregular verbs do not form their various forms in the perfect and imperfect tenses according to rules. It is therefore important to learn their formation by heart. Some of the most often used verbs are irregular, such as **zijn** *to be*, **hebben** *to have*, **doen** *to do*, **gaan** *to go*, **worden** *to become*.

20

Pointing the way

20.1 Where to start

If you are not using this book as a reference book, but want to study Dutch grammar from scratch, the following guide will help you.

A Guide

Below you will find a list of topics ordered progressively (from easy to difficult) to help you if you are studying on your own. This order is only a suggestion; feel free to change it.

B What you need to know first

The main part of learning grammar is how words are grouped together in a meaningful order. But in learning how to do this, you need to know what all the different elements in a sentence are, what they do, where they are supposed to be etc. In this guide, therefore, we suggest that you start with the basic word types first, and simple sentence structures in the present tense. From there, you will be taken through more complex word categories and structures, and the other tenses.

C A good start

Begin with Sections 1.1 and 1.2, followed by Section 19.2 (dictionaries) and Sections 1.4 and 1.5 (spelling), to give you a good basis for tackling any of the other sections.

D The basics

Study the following sections to get to grips with some basic concepts: Sections 1.3; 4.1; 2.1; 5.1 (NB some of the exercises in Section 5.1 are quite difficult); 5.2–5.3; 6.1–6.2; 3.1–3.4.

E Embellishing

After the basic elements, you can move on to add extra bits. This means being able to describe more and to make comparisons: Sections 2.3–2.5; 2.6–2.7; 2.2; 4.2; 11.1–11.2; 2.8.

F Bigger and better

Now you can learn how to formulate longer sentences with more than one verb and different types of sentences. You'll also have a look at some different word types and talking about the future: Sections 9.2; 6.3; 9.3; 14.1–14.4; 16.1–16.3; 8.1–8.2; 9.1.

G The past

By this stage you have come to grips with the basic sentence structure. You might want to move on to talking about the past: Sections 7.2–7.4; 7.6; 7.1; 7.5; 10.1–10.2; 10.3.

This might also be a good time to revisit some of the earlier sections to tackle any points which you had difficulties with the first time around.

H Er

This little word has various different meanings – some more difficult than others. You could study the easier uses earlier on, but to understand everything fully we thought that it might be best to leave it until now: Sections 13.1–13.3.

I More complex sentences and linking

At this stage you should learn about the differences between main and sub-clauses, and how to combine sentences and sentence parts: Sections 15.1–15.6; 17.1–17.3.

J Passive and style

Time for passive sentences and various stylistic issues. If you like, you can have a look at the sections on exclamations and interjections earlier as well: Sections 10.4–10.5; 18.1–18.7.

K Rounding things up

The remaining topics. Feel free to study these earlier as well, when the need arises: Sections 2.9; 2.10; 12.1; 19.1–19.5.

Insight

Studying grammar is most effectively done in practical situations. The exercises in this book are very useful for practising the grammatical explanations, but also study these points in more realistic and communicative contexts, such as texts on Dutch websites, newspaper articles, or spoken Dutch on Dutch or Flemish radio. That way you will be able to observe Dutch grammar at work in its natural surroundings.

20.2 Logging learning experiences

On this page you will find a form to record your learning progress. Make as many copies as you like and log your experiences regularly.

A What have I learned? (give a short description)

B Test yourself: write down some sentences using the points you have listed under A.

C Difficulties: which points do you feel you need to spend more time on to master fully?

D Carefully study again all the sections relating to the points listed under C, making a point of looking up all the references and checking the glossary. Try to do all the exercises.

Test yourself

1 Explain how to form the present tense of regular verbs.

2 What other structures can you use to talk about activities in the 'here and now'?

3a Which two auxiliaries can you use to form the present perfect tense? What other word do you need to form this tense?

3b Explain how to decide whether the last letter of past participles of regular verbs is a **t** or a **d**.

4 How do you form the singular and plural forms of the imperfect (regular verbs)?

5 What are the imperfect forms and past participles of the verbs **hebben, zijn, gaan, drinken, zien, lezen, vragen, zitten**?

6 When do you use the imperfect tense as opposed to the perfect tense, and vice versa?

7 Name the modal verbs and their various meanings.

8 Which verbs – other than modal verbs – can be combined with an infinitive? Which of these are used with **te** in front of the infinitive?

9 In front of nouns, adjectives get an extra e. What is the one exception to this rule?

10 What are the differences between main clauses and sub-clauses?

11 Name the five words (conjunctions) used to link main clauses.

12 Name as many conjunctions used to link main and sub-clauses as you can.

Can you do the following?

1 Describe a typical day in your life. Use short sentences in the present tense (eg.: **Ik sta om half 8 op**).

2 Make a list of activities you did during one of your (more active) holidays. Note that you'll have to use the present perfect.

3 Think of a particularly exciting event which you experienced in the past. Describe this event. Note that you'll have to use a mix of the present perfect and imperfect tenses.

4 Compare your life as a child with your life now. What did you have to, or were you (not) allowed to do in the past (**ik moest/ mocht/hoefde (niet)**), which you are (not) now? Also compare your abilities and desires from the past with your present situation (eg: **ik kon/kan, wilde/wil ...**).

5a Give a description of one of your favourite paintings or objects/artefacts. Use as many adjectives as possible.

5b Compare your chosen topic from 5a with one of your least favourite paintings or objects/artefacts.

6 Think of a number of your pet hates as far as other people are concerned. Indicate how you would like people to change their behaviour. Start with **ik vind dat ...**

7 Name the (many) reasons why you're studying Dutch. Start with: **ik leer Nederlands omdat ...**

8 Describe one of your favourite novels, films or plays, and indicate why you like it so much.

9 Describe your experiences or observations of Dutch and/ or Flemish culture. Indicate the differences from your own background/culture. Note that you will have to use a variety of structures and tenses.

Taking it further

As you become more confident using Dutch you may feel that
you'd like some more practice or that you'd like to have a look
at different kinds of texts and materials available in Dutch.
The internet is a wonderful tool for tapping into original Dutch
language in all sorts of different areas of everyday – and not so
everyday! – life. Below we've listed a number of Dutch (.nl) and
Flemish (.be) websites which you might find useful, helpful and/or
interesting.

Media

http://www.volkskrant.nl
http://www.nrc.nl
http://www.telegraaf.nl
http://www.destandaard.be
http://www.tijd.be/nieuws
http://www.rnw.nl
http://www.nu.nl

Tourism

http://www.anwb.nl
http://www.vvv.nl
http://www.vtb-vab.be
(see also the Amsterdam/Antwerp websites listed below)

National/local authorities

http://www.postbus51.nl
http://www.amsterdam.nl
http://www.vlaanderen.be
http://www.antwerpen.be

Reading in Dutch is a good way of building up your vocabulary. You can start with children's books, some of which come accompanied by cassettes or CDs, which give you added listening practice. Both in the Netherlands and in Flanders there are specialist children's bookshops in larger towns where you can get advice.

If you would like to find out more about Dutch society, history and culture, we can recommend:

William Shetter, *The Netherlands in Perspective: The Dutch Way of Organizing a Society and its Setting*. Utrecht: Nederlands Centrum Buitenlanders, 1997.

Key to exercises

SECTION 1

1A a 4 **b** 2 **c** 3 **d** 6 **e** 5 **f** 1

1B b Frederik / geeft / het cadeau aan zijn vriendin **c** Ik / lees /
de krant **d** De baby / eet / de banaan **e** Jackie / draagt / de koffer
f De popster / signeert / foto's

1C a namen **b** talen **c** benen **d** sigaretten **e** scholen **f** flessen **g** boten
h minuten **i** ogen **j** koren **k** bomen **l** muren

1D a wij maken **b** wij kennen **c** wij vertellen **d** wij drogen
e wij bezitten **f** wij wassen **g** wij roken **h** wij raken **i** wij keken
j wij praten

1E a hij/zij loopt **b** zij bevalt **c** hij/zij hoopt **d** hij/zij verdwaalt **e** hij/
zij kookt **f** hij/zij stapt over **g** hij/zij stuurt **h** hij/zij ervaart **i** hij/zij
overwint **j** hij/zij hoort **k** hij/zij slaapt **l** hij/zij telt

1F a ik kus **b** ik verhuis **c** ik voetbal **d** ik blaas **e** ik hak **f** ik bel
g ik tennis **h** ik geef **i** ik lik **j** ik streef

1G a flessen **b** vazen **c** neven **d** brieven **e** huizen **f** dieven **g** bussen

1H a wij kiezen **b** wij leven **c** wij wassen **d** wij beven **e** wij geven
f wij razen

SECTION 2

2A a Ik heb veel <u>werk</u>, dus ik werk van 's ochtends vroeg tot 's
avonds laat. Gelukkig heb ik een <u>computer</u>, dat is erg handig voor
de <u>administratie</u>. Ik heb een <u>collega</u>. Zij werkt ook hard. We gaan

vaak samen lunchen. We kopen meestal een <u>broodje</u> en een <u>kopje</u> <u>koffie</u>. Als het mooi <u>weer</u> is, eten en drinken we onze <u>lunch</u> in het <u>park</u>. Als ik geen <u>honger</u> heb, geef ik mijn <u>broodje</u> aan de <u>eendjes</u>. De <u>koffie</u> drink ik altijd zelf.

2B countable: potlood, telefoon, oog, droom, ding, jaar uncountable: water, zout, hoop, suiker, vuil, drop

2C a een **b** de **c** het **d** de **e** - **f** een **g** - **h** het **i** - **j** -

2D a de bushalte **b** de koffiefilter **c** de televisiegids **d** het studieboek **e** de discussieleider **f** het hoofdkantoor **g** het toiletpapier

2E a de rode of de witte? **b** de grote / de kleine **c** het drukke **d** het mooie **e** zwarte / bruine / kale

2F a de gewonde(n) **b** gevangene **c** genomineerden

2G a deze, die **b** die **c** dit/dat **d** dit/dat **e** die **f** dit/dat **g** deze/die **h** deze/die **i** deze/die **j** die/deze **k** dit/dat

2H a mooi, slank, rijk en sexy **b** aantrekkelijk, arm, verliefd en artistiek **c** groot, gevaarlijk en dodelijk

2I a De rode roos **b** De dikke bijbel **c** De boze vader **d** De vieze keuken

2J a enthousiaste, ervaren, snel, groeiende, bijzonder, hoog, erg, prettige

2K a de man **b** de schande **c** de rede **d** het (on)geluk **e** de zin

2L b het schrift, schrijven **c** het geloof, geloven **d** de hoop, hopen **e** het werk, werken **f** de brand, branden

2M a Ik wil een kleine auto, maar mijn man wil een grote. **b** Wilt u gele bloemen? Nee de rode graag. **c** Hans heeft een leuke docent, maar ik heb een saaie. **d** Wie heeft het gedaan? Die grote jongen of die kleine?

2N a zouts, zoets **b** moois **c** speciaals **d** actiefs

2O warmer, warmst; aardiger, aardigst; vervelender, vervelendst; harder, hardst; zachter, zachtst

2P zuurder, zuurst; creatiever, creatiefst; representatiever representatiefst; gemener, gemeenst; bozer, boost; dikker, dikst; idioter, idiootst

2Q Henry is zwaarder, gespierder, jonger, vrolijker. Erik is ouder en depressiever.

2R a Zijn fiets is duurder dan haar fiets. **b** Mijn hoofdgerecht is lekkerder dan mijn voorgerecht. **c** Deze foto's van mij zijn mooier dan die foto's van jou. **d** Mijn voetbalteam is beter dan jouw voetbalteam. **e** De carrière van Madonna is succesvoller dan de carrière van mijn tante Truus.

2S a Amsterdam en Brussel zijn niet zo groot als/minder groot dan Londen. **b** De verfilming van het boek is niet zo interessant als/ minder interessant dan het boek zelf. **c** In Nederland wonen minder mensen dan in de Verenigde Staten. **d** De meeste van mijn collega's zijn niet zo vriendelijk als/minder vriendelijk dan de mensen op jouw werk. **e** De rest van mijn familie is niet zo artistiek als/minder artistiek dan mijn zus en ik.

2T a Cricket is net zo interessant als American Football. **b** Honden zijn liever dan katten. **c** Een Mercedes is net zo'n comfortabele auto als een Rolls Royce. **d** Pagers zijn niet zo handig als mobieltjes. **e** New York is een minder dynamische stad dan Londen. **f** Een elektronische agenda is net zo praktisch als een filofax.

2U a rollen **b** auto's **c** kalenders **d** manchetten **e** brieven **f** kaarten **g** kranten **h** straten **i** ezels **j** multomappen **k** agenda's **l** kazen **m** medici **n** schoonheden

2V a kist **b** zonnevlek **c** rug **d** idioot **e** partij **f** Libanees **g** verlies **h** tralie **i** hek **j** muur **k** gevangenis **l** ei **m** verantwoordelijkheid **n** politicus

2W dieven; klanten; overvallers; bankbiljetten; munten; bankbediendes; boeven; pistolen; kogels; kinderen; baby's; bankrekeninghouders; lijfwachten; criminelen

2X a het computerbedrijf **b** de melkchocola **c** het babygehuil **d** de afvalbak **e** de asfaltweg **f** de tabakswinkel **g** de tariefsverhoging **h** de verkeersdeskundige **i** de presidentskandidaat **j** het konijnenhok

2Y a het broodje **b** het labeltje **c** het papiertje **d** het boekje **e** het wolkje **f** het snorretje **g** het telefoontje **h** het stroompje **i** het ringetje **j** het woninkje **k** het tafeltje **l** het ideetje **m** het tongetje **n** het bloempje

2Z a lieverdje (d) **b** artikeltje (a + b) **c** studentjes (e) **d** wijntje (c) **e** vogeltjes (a + c) **f** brilletje (c)

SECTION 3

3A a twee plus zes is acht **b** zesenveertig min dertien is drieëndertig **c** negenennegentig plus drieëntwintig is honderdtweeëntwintig **d** zeven keer acht is zesenvijftig **e** tweeënveertig gedeeld door zeven is zes **f** tweeënzeventig gedeeld door acht is negen **g** twaalf keer vijf is zestig **h** achtentachtig min twaalf is zesenzeventig

3B a honderdeen **b** vijfenzeventig **c** tweeëntachtig **d** zesennegentig **e** driehonderdvijfenzestig **f** tweehonderdachtendertig **g** vierhonderdachttien

3C Amsterdam = vijfhonderdduizend euro; Alkmaar = vierhonderdzevenenvijftigduizend euro; Groningen = driehonderdtweeënvijftigduizend euro; Drente = tweehonderddrieëntwintigduizend euro

3D a 300.000 **b** 8.000.000.000 **c** 56.000.000 **d** 9.868 **e** 2725

3E a tweede **b** vijfde **c** twaalfde **d** dertiende
e tweehonderdnegentiende **f** negenentachtigste **g** drieënvijftigste

3F a eerste **b** derde **c** achtste **d** miljoenste **e** honderdtweeënvijftigste
f tweeëntwintigste **g** drieënvijftigste

3G a vijftiende **b** drieëntwintigste **c** zeventiende **d** eenendertigste

3H a elf **b** veertiende **c** vijftien **d** eenendertig **e** dertig **f** zesde

3I a nul komma dertien **b** zes komma tweeëntwintig **c** tweeëndertig
komma nul vijf **d** nul komma nul **e** drie vierde, drie kwart **f** vijf
zesde **g** twee derde

3J a 1.900 **b** 200.000 **c** 3825 **d** 2.670.000 **e** 0,4 **f** 1,13 **g** 8,17

3K Het is vijf graden (boven nul) in Amsterdam. In Londen is
het 9 graden. In Athene is het 19 graden. Het is een graad
boven nul in Bonn. En in Moskou is het acht graden onder
nul/min acht.

3L a Twintig procent van de Nederlanders ging naar Spanje en
13 procent naar Engeland. Achttien procent van de Nederlanders
ging naar Italië, en vijf procent ging naar de VS en Canada. Zes
procent van de Nederlanders ging elders op vakantie.

3M a De bananen wegen driehonderd gram/drie ons. **b** De kaneel
weegt vijfendertig gram. **c** De drop weegt een ons/honderd gram.
d Het stuk kaas weegt anderhalf pond/zevenhonderdvijftig gram.

3N a Tweehonderd gram/twee ons ham. **b** Vijfhonderd gram/een
pond suiker. **c** Anderhalve kilo kaas. **d** Tweehonderdvijftig gram/
tweeëneenhalf ons/een half pond koekjes. **e** Drie liter melk.

3O a Over een minuut of vijf. **b** Over ongeveer twee uur. **c** Over
een week of drie. **d** Over ongeveer twee maanden. **e** Zij loopt tegen
de veertig. **f** Hij is rond de 35 euro.

3P a een meter **b** een vierkante meter **c** vijftig kilometer **d** een liter
e zeven centimeter

SECTION 4

4A a Ik; Jij **b** Wij **c** Jullie **d** Hij **e** Zij **f** Zij **g** u **h** Het

4B a u **b** we **c** jullie **d** jij; Ik **e** Ze **f** Ze **g** Je

4C a ons **b** ze; hen/hun **c** hem **d** me **e** u **f** hem; haar **g** me **h** jullie **i** je

4D a je **b** u **c** je **d** u **e** u

4E a Ze **b** hij **c** Ze **d** Hij **e** hij **f** het **g** ze **h** hem

4F a die **b** die **c** het **d** die **e** die/hij **f** het **g** die

4G a jouw/uw **b** zijn **c** ons **d** haar **e** jullie **f** hun **g** mijn **h** onze **i** zijn

4H a Is dit de agenda van David?/Is deze agenda van David?
b Het is de agenda van Erwin/Die/Deze agenda is van Erwin.
c Gaan we in de auto van Esther? **d** Ja, we gaan in die van haar/
in de auto van Esther. **e** Ik rijd in de auto van mijn ouders. **f** De
computer van mijn broer heeft 1500 euro gekost. **g** Komt de vader
van Josje ook? **h** Alleen de moeder van Josje komt.

4I a die van jou? **b** met die van mij? **c** die van hen/hun **d** die van
haar **e** die van hem of die van mij?

SECTION 5

5A 1 wonen, heeft, hoorden, was, gevormd, scheidde ... af [a
separable verb], werd, gevormd, woont, spreekt **2** kan, hebben,
leidde, werden, gedoemd, was, uit ... sterven [a separable verb],
had, speelden, is, verandert

5B 1 subject = 15 miljoen mensen (wonen) – plural; subject =
België (heeft) – singular; subject = zowel het noorden als het zuiden
(hoorden) – plural; subject = het Koninkrijk der Nederlanden

(was gevormd) – singular; subject = het zuiden (scheidde [zich] af) – singular; subject = de staat België (werd gevormd) – singular; subject = iets meer dan de helft van alle Belgen (woont) – singular; subject = men (spreekt) – singular

2 subject = klimaatverandering (kan [gevolgen] hebben) – singular; subject = een daling van de temperatuur met enkele graden tijdens de ijstijden (leidde) – singular; subject = grote gebieden (werden) – plural; subject = de mammoet (was gedoemd) – singular; subject = de klimaatsverandering tijdens de ijstijden (had) – singular; subject = veranderingen in de baan van de aarde rond de zon (speelden) – plural; subject = het (is) – singular; subject = de mens (verandert) – singular

5C a ben **b** mogen **c** viert **d** weet, heet **e** had, zou **f** moet **g** is **h** zul **i** heb, hebt **j** moeten

5D a second (4) **b** final (1) **c** final (3) **d** zijn = second (4); geweest = final (1) **e** final (2) **f** krijg = final (3); ga = second (4) **g** 'zullen' is a finite verb at the beginning of a question **h** second (4)

5E a help **b** wandel **c** fiets **d** schilder **e** tuinier **f** ontbijt **g** vergader **h** roddel

5F a neem **b** loop **c** kook **d** maak **e** studeer **f** slaap **g** zwem **h** stap **i** lees **j** reis **k** geloof **l** blijf

5G a slaap **b** woont **c** blijft **d** stopt **e** vriest **f** komen **g** ontbijt

5H a help **b** verdien **c** neem **d** maakt **e** spreek **f** leest **g** blijf **h** gelooft

5I a heeft **b** heeft **c** heb **d** heb **e** hebben **f** hebben **g** hebt

5J a is **b** bent **c** zijn **d** is **e** ben **f** zijn **g** ben

5K a doet **b** gaat **c** doe **d** komt/gaat **e** komen/gaan **f** doen **g** kom/ga **h** gaan **i** ga

5L **a** (a) or (c) **b** (b) **c** (d) **d** (d) **e** (b)

5M **a** Ik werk hier al drie jaar. **b** Ik woon hier sinds zes maanden. **c** Ik studeer hier pas een jaar. **d** Ik ben pas een half jaar getrouwd. **e** Ik heb die hoofpijn al twee weken.

5N **a** Ik woon hier pas vijf maanden. **b** Harry woont hier al tien jaar. **c** Ik studeer hier pas een jaar. **d** Harry studeert hier al zes jaar. **e** Harry rookt al acht jaar. **f** Ik rook pas sinds vorige week.

5O **a** Maaike is een jurk aan het naaien/zit een jurk te naaien. **b** Connie is druk aan het praten/staat/zit druk te praten. **c** Richard is in de schuur aan het werken/staat/zit in de schuur te werken. **d** Harm is een boek aan het lezen/ligt/zit een boek te lezen.

SECTION 6

6A **a** kan **b** moeten **c** zal **d** willen **e** mag **f** hoeft **g** moet **h** kan/kun **i** willen **j** zal **k** hoeft **l** mag

6B b, c, d, f

6C **a** Hij heeft een grote geldboete moeten betalen. **b** Ze hebben dat huis goedkoop kunnen kopen. **c** Ze hebben het zelf gewild. **d** Karin heeft het natuurlijk niet hoeven te doen.

6D **a** kan **b** wil **c** moet **d** Kan/Kun **e** mogen **f** willen **g** zullen/kunnen **h** moeten/mogen **i** kan/kunt **j** kan **k** Zullen **l** Wilt

6E **a** moest **b** wilde **c** Mag/Kan **d** mochten **e** kon **f** wilde **g** moeten/kunnen **h** zal

6F **a** Zullen we een video huren? **b** Zullen we squashen? **c** Zullen we in het nieuwe winkelcentrum winkelen? **d** Zullen we naar de bioscoop gaan? **e** Zullen we in de stad koffie drinken?

6G a Ik wil eigenlijk televisie kijken, maar ik moet de woonkamer stofzuigen. **b** Ik wil eigenlijk naar het strand (gaan), maar ik moet de afwas doen. **c** Ik wil eigenlijk iets met vrienden drinken, maar ik moet bij mijn ouders op visite (gaan). **d** Ik wil eigenlijk op mijn nieuwe computer internetten, maar ik moet de wc schilderen. **e** Ik wil eigenlijk naar muziek luisteren, maar ik moet mijn huiswerk doen.

6H a Kan hij goed brieven schrijven? **b** Kun/kan je goed luisteren? **c** Kunnen ze goed zwemmen en snorkelen? **d** Kunt/kan u goed Engels praten? **e** Kan ze goed professionele presentaties geven?

6I a Op maandag vergader ik over het project. **b** Op dinsdag lunch ik met Willem. **c** Op donderdag drink ik koffie met Amy. **d** Op vrijdag doe ik boodschappen. **e** Op zaterdag eet ik bij Jolanda. **f** Op zondag bezoek ik opa en oma.

6J a We willen/gaan eerst een paar dagen ontspannen op het strand. **b** Daarna willen/gaan we een paar dagen de Provence bekijken. **c** De tweede week willen/gaan we naar de Pyreneeën. **d** We willen/gaan wandelen in de bergen.

6K a Ik zal het niet vergeten. **b** Ik zal het doen. **c** Ik zal er op tijd zijn. **d** Ik zal mijn best doen.

SECTION 7

7A Ik heb gisteren iets raars gezien.; reden; we hielden een vrachtauto aan; reed; bleek; kookte; moest; We hebben hem een boete van 240 euro gegeven.

7B Een woordvoerder heeft gisteren bekendgemaakt dat het veilinghuis Christie's in Londen de oorlogscollectie van de familie Rothschild heeft geveild.; bestond; In 1938 namen de nazi's de collectie in beslag; dwong; vertelde; Deskundigen hebben de opbrengst van de veiling op 63 miljoen geschat.

7C besloot; arriveerde; aankwam; waren; deed; De reizigers boden elkaar pepermuntjes aan.; zag; lagen; stapte; zat

7D a geklaagd **b** gehoord **c** volgeboekt **d** gegroeid

7E a Ik heb 's ochtends mijn huis schoongemaakt. **b** Ik heb met een vriend aan de telefoon gepraat. **c** Ik heb het avondeten gekookt. **d** Ik heb een brief verstuurd. **e** Ik heb naar mijn favoriete CD geluisterd. **f** Ik heb mijn moeder gebeld. **g** Ik ben met roken gestopt. **h** Ik heb de videorecorder geprogrammeerd.

7F a Jeff heeft zelf zijn nieuwe computer geïnstalleerd. **b** We zijn naar een andere stad verhuisd. **c** Hebben jullie tegen het buitenlandse beleid van de regering geprotesteerd? **d** Wie heeft dat project afgemaakt? **e** Maartje heeft haar bankzaken erg goed geregeld. **f** Ik heb het hem nooit verteld. **g** De minister heeft het tijdens haar reis door China gezegd. **h** Leonardo di Caprio is met zijn moeder naar Venetië gereisd.

7G a heeft **b** zijn **c** hebben **d** heeft **e** zijn **f** zijn **g** heeft **h** is

7H a ben **b** hebben **c** hebben **d** zijn **e** zijn **f** hebben **g** zijn; hebben

7I a Ik ben uit ... naar Nederland gekomen. **b** Ik ben om kwart over acht van huis gegaan. **c** Ik ben van ... naar Schiphol gevlogen. **d** Ik heb mijn vlucht via het internet geboekt. **e** De vlucht heeft tweeëneenhalf uur geduurd. **f** Ja ik heb een hotelkamer voor vijf nachten gereserveerd.

7J a Dinsdagmiddag heb ik schoenen gekocht. **b** Woensdag heb ik om half elf thee gedronken bij Karin. **c** Donderdag heb ik om half negen gezwommen. **d** Vrijdag heb ik om acht uur het rapport aan mijn baas gegeven, en ik ben om zeven uur 's avonds met Jan uitgegaan. **e** Zaterdagochtend heb ik boodschappen gedaan. **f** Zondag heb ik om acht uur bij mam en pap gegeten.

7K a Nee, ik had vroeger moeten beginnen. **b** Nee, ik had zuiniger moeten zijn. **c** Ja, ik had minder moeten kopen. **d** Nee, ik had beter moeten luisteren.

7L a Ja, ik heb mijn computer laten repareren. **b** Ja, ik heb mijn haar laten knippen. **c** Ja, ik heb mijn videorecorder laten maken. **d** Ja, ik heb mijn flat laten schoonmaken.

7M a Andy had net afgesproken bij Arjen te gaan eten toen Gwen Andy te eten vroeg. **b** Ik had net afgewassen toen Mariëlle aanbood te helpen. **c** Jane had net haar huis verkocht toen de huizenmarkt instortte. **d** Ik had de film nog niet gezien toen Mick me het einde vertelde. **e** Het feest was net geëindigd toen ik eindelijk arriveerde. **f** Ik had mijn bestanden nog niet gesaved toen mijn computer crashte.

7N a Als ik harder had gewerkt, dan had ik nu promotie gekregen. **b** Als ik minder had gesport, dan was ik nu niet zo fit geweest. **c** Als ik de hele tijd thuis was gebleven, dan had ik nu niet zoveel goede films gezien. **d** Als ik een piercing had genomen, dan had ik nu een zilveren ring kunnen kopen. **e** Als ik beter naar mijn moeder had geluisterd, dan was ik nu gelukkiger geweest. **f** Als ik een miljoen had gewonnen, dan was ik nu niet hier geweest.

7O d, b, a, e, c

7P a Mijn televisie werkte niet. **b** Ik ontdekte het 's ochtends vroeg. **c** Ik belde een vriend, hij beloofde 's middags langs te komen. **d** Ik wachtte de hele middag, en om half 6 belde hij op. **e** Hij vertelde dat zijn auto niet goed startte. **f** Ik protesteerde natuurlijk. **g** Woedend gooide ik de telefoon op de haak, en belde een professionele monteur.

7R a voelde; belde; wenste; beloofde **b** ontmoette; reisden; wilden; probeerden

7S a Donald kwam om half acht op het kantoor. **b** Hij keek vrolijker dan normaal. Hij lachtte opgewekt. **c** Hij vroeg zijn secretaresse

niet om koffie. Hij maakte het zelf. **d** Hij riep om negen uur
iedereen bij elkaar. **e** Hij zei dat hij iets belangrijks moest zeggen.
f Hij vertelde iedereen dat het goed ging. Hij gaf iedereen een extra
bonus.

SECTION 8

8A a Wil je uit eten of blijf je liever thuis? **b** Ik had geen idee dat ik
elke maand zoveel geld uitgaf. **c** Moet ik mijn moeder opbellen of
doe jij het? **d** Hoe laat komt de trein op het station aan? **e** Als je het
goed vindt, neem ik vanavond een vriend mee. **f** Wat doe jij naar
het feest aan? **g** Papa wil dat je alles opeet!

8B a Ik vind dat jij te veel geld uitgeeft. **b** Ik vind dat zij altijd zulke
rare kleren aandoet. **c** Ik vind dat jullie je werk te laat afmaken.
d Ik vind dat hij zijn vriendin niet vaak opbelt. **e** Ik vind dat het
eten in dit restaurant erg tegenvalt.

8C a Hij ademt diep in. **b** Ik studeer volgend jaar af. **c** Hij maakt
zijn werk af. **d** Jet komt om 9 uur aan. **e** Hij loopt het journaal op
TV niet mis. **f** Wanneer geef je mijn CD terug?

8D a Ik woon de presentatie bij. **b** Ik onderhandel. **c** We leggen het
werk neer. **d** Ik ondersteun het plan. **e** Ik rust eerst uit. **f** We bieden
hem die baan aan. **g** We bespreken het probleem.

8E a Marijke neemt een paar dagen vrij om het huis schoon
te maken. **b** ... om de garage op te ruimen. **c** ... om haar
belastingformulier in te vullen. **d** ... om haar cursus astrologie voor
te bereiden. **e** ... om lekker uit te rusten.

8F a ... of ze het werk neer zullen leggen. **b** ... of ze het cadeau
dit jaar niet op kan sturen. **c** ... waar je die informatie op kan
zoeken. **d** ... dat we u deze baan aan mogen bieden. **e** ... of we die
vergadering vanmiddag bij moeten wonen?

8G a beloofd **b** herhaald **c** erkend **d** gedoogd **e** verteld

8H **a** herschrijven **b** herverdelen **c** hergebruiken **d** laten herscholen **e** herstructureren

8I **a** kijken **b** bekijken **c** antwoorden **d** beantwoorden **e** luister **f** beluisteren

8J **a** Het plan verandert steeds. **b** ... om haar borsten te laten verkleinen. **c** verbeteren **d** De regisseur gaat haar boek verfilmen. **e** Ze verblinden me.

SECTION 9

9A **a** ons **b** me **c** je **d** zich **e** zich **f** je

9B **a** Ja, mijn beste vriendin maakt zich zorgen over de toekomst / Nee, mijn beste vriend(in) maakt zich geen zorgen over de toekomst. **b** Ja, mijn buren ergeren zich aan lawaai. / Nee, mijn buren ergeren zich niet aan lawaai. **c** Ja, ik trek me iets aan van kritiek. / Nee, ik trek me niets aan van kritiek. **d** Ja, mijn vader interesseert zich voor moderne kunst. / Nee, mijn moeder interesseert zich niet voor moderne kunst. **e** Ja, ik kan me goed concentreren. / Nee, ik kan me niet goed concentreren. **f** Ja, mijn baas kan zich goed uitdrukken in het Nederlands. / Nee, mijn baas kan zich niet goed uitdrukken in het Nederlands. **g** Ik interesseer me voor ...

9C **a** Spannen jullie je in, ... **b** Bedrinken jullie je, ... **c** Schrikken jullie je dood, ...

9D **a** reflexive: Herinner jij je ... **b** not reflexive **c** not reflexive **d** reflexive: Onze hond verdedigde zich goed ... **e** not reflexive **f** not reflexive **g** reflexive: ... dus ik verveel me de hele week al vreselijk. **h** not reflexive

9E **a** ... maar voel je je ook beter? **b** ... dat je je vergist in mijn naam. **c** Irene zou zich wat minder ... **d** Hebben de kinderen zich goed gedragen ... **e** Ik hoop dat iedereen zich heeft ... **f** Hij verbaasde zich ... **g** ... schrok ik me dood!

9F a vergeet **b** hou ... op **c** vul ... in **d** snijd **e** lees; maak

9G a bescherm **b** geniet **c** bel **d** vrij; vrij **e** kies **f** bekijk

9H b betalen **c** ontsteken **d** rijden **e** parkeren **f** kloppen

9I a Doe vier schepjes koffie in het koffiefilter. **b** Doe het deksel op de koffiepot. **c** Plaats de koffiepot onder het filter. **d** Druk op het aan/uit knopje.

9J a de krant te lezen. **b** naar muziek te luisteren. **c** met de buurvrouw te praten. **d** je erg aardig te vinden. **e** je altijd trouw te zijn. **f** van een hoge brug te springen.

9K a Ik heb zitten (te) lezen. **b** Ik heb vroeger niet vaak hoeven af (te) wassen. **c** Ik heb nooit op het dak durven (te) klimmen **d** Ik heb hem beloofd de boodschappen te doen. **e** Ik ben vergeten mijn moeder te bellen. **f** Ik ben begonnen Nederlands te studeren. **g** Ik heb geprobeerd de Matterhorn te beklimmen.

9L a eten? **b** een eind fietsen. **c** zijn huis verbouwen. **d** huilen? **e** lekker voetballen?

9M a Ja, ik heb hem voorbij zien fietsen. **b** Ja, ik heb ze horen zingen. **c** Nee, ik heb ze laten maken. **d** Nee, ik ben gaan fietsen.

9N a proberen te werken. **b** laten zien. **c** blijven wonen. **d** zien optreden. **e** gaan dansen. **f** komen ophalen. **g** laten repareren?

9O a Ik gebruik papier om er een boodschappenlijstje op te schrijven. **b** Ik gebruik een schaar om er mijn nagels mee te knippen. **c** Ik gebruik een punaise om er een foto mee aan de muur te prikken. **d** Ik gebruik een doos met een roze lintje om er mijn liefdesbrieven in te doen.

9P a Ik ga naar de kerk om naar het orgel te luisteren. **b** Ik ga naar het strand om te zonnebaden. **c** Ik ga naar het sportveld om mijn vriendje te zien. **d** Ik ga naar de bibliotheek om te slapen.

9Q Ik probeer om een vliegende auto te ontwerpen. **d** Hij weigert gewoon om te komen. **f** Niet vergeten om de vuilnisbak buiten te zetten!

SECTION 10

10A a Als ik terug in de tijd kon, zou ik Cleopatra willen opzoeken. **b** ... zou ik naar een concert van Mozart willen gaan. **c** ... zou ik Versailles in de tijd van Louis XIV willen bezoeken. **d** ... zou ik met Marilyn Monroe/James Dean willen trouwen. **e** ... zou ik bij Freud in behandeling willen gaan. **f** zou ik een goedkoop schilderij van Rembrandt willen kopen. **g** ... zou ik Jeanne d'Arc willen redden. **h** ... zou ik dinosauriërs willen zien.

10B a 4 **b** 3 **c** 2 **d** 5 **e** 1

10C a Als ik de Minister-President was, zou ik het onderwijs verbeteren. **b** Als ik perfect nederlands sprak, zou ik in Nederland gaan wonen. **c** Als ik meer vrije tijd had, zou ik meer naar muziek luisteren.

10D a Zou je/me even willen helpen met deze brief? **b** Zou jij die boodschap voor me kunnen aannemen? **c** Zou je dit werk even voor me willen nakijken? **d** Zou je deze brief vanmiddag voor me op de post kunnen doen? **e** Zou je me dat boek even kunnen geven? **f** Zou je me over een uurtje kunnen terugbellen?

10E a Ik zou vroeger naar bed gaan, als ik jou was. **b** Ik zou gezonder eten, als ik jou was. **c** Ik zou een nieuwe baan zoeken, als ik jou was. **d** Ik zou alles met hem/haar bespreken, als ik jou was. **e** Ik zou minder vaak naar het buitenland bellen, als ik jou was. **f** Ik zou naar de radio luisteren, als ik jou was.

10F a Je zou op die cursus hard moeten werken. **b** Er zou een coup hebben plaatsgevonden. **c** Er zou een bom zijn ontploft in een winkelcentrum. **d** Alle kaartjes zouden zijn uitverkocht. **e** Er zou in Amerika een UFO zijn geland. **f** Er zou een vliegtuig zijn neergestort.

10G a no inversion **b** inversion: zou/je **c** no inversion **d** inversion: heeft/ze **e** inversion: haat/jij **f** inversion: is/Frankrijk **g** no inversion **h** inversion: zijn/alle foto's van mijn vakantie

10H a Meestal houdt Henk niet van Westerns. **b** Sinds kort ben ik lid van een filmclub in de stad. **c** Gisteren is mijn baas op vakantie gegaan. **d** Wanneer heb jij Carolien gezien? **e** Over het algemeen vind ik mijn elektronische agenda erg handig. **f** Misschien is ze te laat omdat er een probleem was met de auto. **g** Hopelijk hebben Jan-Peter en zijn vriendin de kaartjes gereserveerd. **h** Op kantoor hebben we net allemaal nieuwe computers.

10I a David gaat naar huis omdat hij veel te veel gedronken heeft. **b** Mijn moeder vraagt of wij morgenavond willen komen eten. **c** Heb je die bank gekocht die je zo graag wilde hebben? **d** Ik zei dat ik tot voor kort nog nooit in Afrika was geweest. **e** Ik heb die nieuwe film gezien die zoveel geld heeft gekost. **f** Klaas zegt dat hij geen zin heeft om naar Peru op vakantie te gaan.

10J a heeft **b** hebben **c** zal **d** kan **e** hadden **f** heeft

10K a ze **b** we **c** hij **d** Sandra **e** jullie **f** je

10L a Ford auto's worden in Engeland geproduceerd. **b** Camembert wordt in Frankrijk gemaakt. **c** Tomaten worden in het Westland gekweekt. **d** Philips radio's worden over de hele wereld verkocht. **e** Aandelen worden op de beurs verhandeld.

10M a Himalayan Treks organiseert de reis. **b** Het Rode Kruis vangt de vluchtelingen op. **c** Een paar mannen trokken de boot op het strand. **d** Mijn kinderen maken vanavond het eten klaar. **e** De studenten brengen de boeken vaak te laat terug.

10N **a** De Telegraaf wordt door veel Nederlanders gelezen.
b De P.C. Hooftprijs werd vorig jaar door Judith Herzberg
gewonnen. **c** Bernadette wordt door haar moeder met haar
huiswerk geholpen. **d** Het startsignaal voor de marathon werd door
de burgemeester gegeven. **e** De beslissing van de regering wordt
door weinig mensen gesteund.

10O **a** De British Library is van baksteen gemaakt. **b** Een kas is
van glas gemaakt. **c** Het Parthenon is van marmer gemaakt. **d** Veel
moderne gebouwen zijn van beton gemaakt. **e** Het Vikingschip is
van hout gemaakt.

10P **a** De tafel was bekrast. **b** De meeste glazen waren gebroken.
c De vloer was met een laag viezigheid bedekt. **d** De muur was met
graffiti beschilderd. **e** De hi-fi was hard aangezet.

10Q **a** De uitnodigingen moeten worden verstuurd. **b** De
burgemeester moet worden uitgenodigd. **c** De caterer moet worden
besteld. **d** Er moet een band worden geregeld. **e** Er moet een zaal
worden gehuurd.

10R **a** De uitnodigingen zouden verstuurd worden. **b** De
burgemeester zou worden uitgenodigd. **c** De caterer zou besteld
worden. **d** Er zou een band worden geregeld. **e** Er zou een zaal
gehuurd worden.

10S **a** De beste rockband zou uitgenodigd moeten worden. **b** De
wijn zou van tevoren ontkurkt moeten worden. **c** De zaal zou
mooier versierd moeten worden.

10T **a** P **b** P **c** P

10U **a** Na ontvangst van betaling sturen wij het boek naar u op.
b Ik verwacht nu elk moment een beslissing. **c** Wij onderzoeken
uw klacht. **d** Sommige mensen signaleren problemen met het
nieuwe computerprogramma. **e** Wij kunnen dit op twee manieren
interpreteren.

10V **a** 2 **b** 2 **c** 1

SECTION 11

11A a before preposition **b** at the end of the sentence, but before the past participle in final position **c** before an adverb 'mooi' **d** at the end of the sentence **e** before the adjective 'serieus'

11B a Nee, ik werk vanavond niet. **b** Nee, ik lees de krant niet. **c** Nee, ik begrijp de vraag niet. **d** Nee, ik vertrouw hem niet. **e** Nee, ik heb uw brief niet ontvangen. **f** Nee, ik heb dat programma niet gezien. **g** Nee, ik ben mijn cheques niet vergeten. **h** Nee, ik ga niet zwemmen. **i** Nee, ik wil de auto niet wassen. **j** Nee, ik kan je niet helpen. **k** Nee, ik ga straks niet naar de stad. **l** Nee, ik werk niet in dat nieuwe gebouw. **m** Nee, ik ben niet naar het theater geweest. **n** Nee, ik vind de voorstelling niet mooi. **o** Nee, ik hou niet van Country 'n Western. **p** Nee, ik kom morgen niet op de koffie. **q** Nee, ik ben niet naar de kapper geweest. **r** Nee, ik heb het niet koud. **s** Nee, ik ben niet ziek. **t** Nee, ik heb niet hard gewerkt.

11C a Nee, ik heb geen nieuwe auto. **b** Nee, ik heb geen dorst. **c** Nee, ik heb geen hoofdpijn. **d** Nee, ik heb geen koffie. **e** Nee, ik heb geen suiker in mijn koffie. **f** Nee, ik heb geen pijn. **g** Nee, ik heb geen geld bij me. **h** Nee, ik drink geen wijn.

11D a Petra wil niet stoppen met werken. **b** Er zit geen zand tussen mijn tenen. **c** Het was geen droom. **d** Wij zijn niet verdwaald. **e** Ik vind hem niet aardig. **f** Jan gelooft mij niet. **g** Ik heb geen grijs haar. **h** De minister heeft geen besluit genomen.

11E a Nee, ik heb mijn huiswerk nog niet gedaan. **b** Nee, mijn vader is nog niet met pensioen. **c** Nee, ik heb nog geen cadeautje gekocht. **d** Nee, ik ben nog niet klaar met mijn studie. **e** Nee, het eten is nog niet klaar. **f** Nee, ik heb nog geen antwoord gekregen op mijn brief.

11F a Nee, hij gelooft niet meer in Sinterklaas. **b** Nee, ik werk niet meer bij het ziekenhuis. **c** Nee, ik heb geen zin meer in koffie. **d** Nee, ik woon niet meer bij mijn ouders. **e** Nee, ik ben niet misselijk meer. **f** Nee, ik heb geen tijd meer.

11G a Ik heb maar vijf kinderen. **b** De bus gaat pas om drie uur.
c Mijn dochtertje is pas twee jaar (oud). **d** Ik hoef nog maar vijftien
kaarten te schrijven.

11H a Niemand heeft me met mijn werk geholpen. **b** Ik ben nog
nooit in Bejing geweest. **c** Ik kan de schaar nergens vinden. **d** Ik heb
niets gemerkt.

SECTION 12

12A a onbeschadigd; onvriendelijk **b** wanorde; wanbegrip
c ontbossen; ontvouwen **d** onderarm, ondertitel **e** impopulair;
immigratie

12B a wanhopen, wanhoop, wanhopig **b** (aan)kopen, (aan)koop,
verkoopbaar **c** (zich) verantwoorden, verantwoordelijkheid,
verantwoordelijk **d** geloven, geloof, gelovig/ongelofelijk/
ongelooflijk **e** zien, zicht, zichtbaar **f** mogen, mogelijkheid, mogelijk
g (zich) interesseren, interesse, interessant **h** praktizeren, praktijk,
praktisch

12C a vergelijkbaar **b** onmogelijkheid **c** onafhankelijkheid
d krachtige **e** geurige

SECTION 13

13A a Er is een man in de tuin aan het werken. **b** Er vertrekt een
trein om 8 uur. **c** Er ligt een boek op de tafel. **d** Er is een café op de
hoek van de straat. **e** Er hangen natte kleren aan de lijn.

13B a Zit er nog een beetje wijn in de fles? **b** Wat is er gebeurd?
c Op koninginnedag zijn er veel mensen op straat. **d** Morgen komt
er iemand op bezoek. **e** Is er een dokter in de zaal?

13C a Er is veel water. **b** Er zijn veel kerken. **c** Er zijn veel
fietspaden.

13D a Er worden veel drugs gebruikt. **b** Er wordt veel koffie gedronken. **c** Er wordt veel gefietst. **d** Er worden veel verjaarsfeestjes gevierd.

13E a Sommige mensen gebruiken veel drugs. **b** Sommige mensen drinken veel koffie. **c** Sommige mensen fietsen veel. **d** Sommige mensen vieren veel verjaarsfeestjes.

13F a Ik kom er regelmatig. **b** Ik woon er nu drie jaar. **c** Ik zit er bijna elke dag te weken. **d** Ik ben er gisteren geweest. **e** Ik ben er gisteren niet geweest.

13G a Ik heb er één. **b** Eef heeft er vier. **c** Ik heb er twee. **d** Ik heb er zelfs drie. **e** Ik heb er geen een.

13H a Ja, ik hou(d) ervan. / Nee, ik hou(d) er niet van. **b** Ja, ik heb er een hekel aan. / Nee, ik heb er geen hekel aan. **c** Ja, ik ben er bang van. / Nee, ik ben er niet bang van. **d** Ja, ik ben er tevreden over. / Nee, ik ben er niet tevreden over. **e** Ja, ik ben er goed in. / Nee, ik ben er niet goed in. **f** Ja, ik heb er goede herinneringen aan. / Nee, ik heb er geen goede herinneringen aan. **g** Ja, ik verlang ernaar. / Nee, ik verlang er niet naar.

13I a Er zijn te veel auto's op de weg. **b** Er ligt veel hondepoep op straat. **c** gisteren was er een feest bij de buren. **d** Er waren veel mensen. **e** Er werd veel gelachen en gedronken. **f** Waarschijnlijk komt er een nieuw hoofd op school.

13J a Ik kijk er niet naar. Daar kijk ik niet naar. **b** Ik bel Hans er (niet) over. / Daar bel ik Hans (niet) over. **c** Leontien is er (niet) blij mee. / Daar is Leontien (niet) blij mee. **d** Ik kom er (niet) uit. Daar kom ik (niet) uit. **e** Ik wacht er (niet) op. / Daar wacht ik (niet) op. **f** Ik ben er (niet) naartoe geweest. / Daar ben ik (niet) naartoe geweest.

13K a Op kantoor heb ik er twee. **b** Carrie is er ontevreden over. **c** Pam gaat er drie middagen per week naartoe. **d** Nico geeft Ineke er twee. **e** Tineke schaamt zich ervoor. **f** U komt er zeker net vandaan? **g** Ik geloof niet dat hij ervan houdt. **h** Joop zegt dat hij zich er geen zorgen over maakt.

13L a We wachten op haar. **b** Ik ben bang van hem. **c** Herman is er bang van. **d** Niemand gelooft er meer in. **e** We hopen erop. **f** We drinken erop. **g** Hannes luistert nooit naar haar. **h** Onze club speelt tegen ze/hen.

13M a tot **b** toe **c** met **d** mee **e** met **f** mee

13N a er ... vandaan **b** er ... naartoe **c** er ... naartoe **d** er ... naartoe

SECTION 14

14A aan; in; aan; met; van; naar; om; in; aan; op [part of the separable verb]

14B a met z'n allen **b** op tijd **c** uit het zuiden **d** met echte bloemen erop **e** met z'n tweeën **f** onder de douche

14C a in een vol glas water **b** over een stoel **c** in de kamer **d** een donkere gang in **e** de hoek om **f** op het balkon **g** mijn gevoel voor richting **h** van de kou

14D a met **b** tot **c** mee **d** tot **e** toe

14E a literal **b** literal **c** figurative **d** literal **e** literal **f** figurative **g** literal **h** figurative **i** figurative **j** literal

14F a kruip door de tunnel **b** spring in het water **c** klim in de boom, voor het huis **d** klim op het rek **e** ren tussen de palen door **f** zwem onder de brug door **g** plaats de vlag naast/voor de muur **h** ga er naast zitten

14G 1 g 2 b 3 a 4 a 5 d 6 a 7 a 8 c 9 e 10 c 11 a, a

14H a Loop de trap af en ga de deur door/uit. Ga naar rechts. Loop langs het hek. Steek de weg over. Loop tot de boom en pak de envelop. Haal de brief uit de envelop. Ga naar het adres dat wordt genoemd.

14I a van b op c met d van e aan f van g over h voor

14J a met b mee c met d met e ermee f met g ermee h met

14K a op b in c in d in e van f aan

14N a voor/van b naar c over/met d naar e over f naar

SECTION 15

15A a main clause 1 = het blijft de komende dagen zacht; main clause 2 = maar de zon blijft weg b one main clause c main clause = de kans op regen zal na het weekeinde toenemen; subclause = omdat er een lagedrukgebied boven Nederland ligt d main clause 1 = de temperatuur zal overdag rond de 9 graden liggen; main clause 2 = 's nachts zal deze dalen tot 4 graden boven nul e main clause 1 = verder in Europa is het weer wisselvallig; main clause 2 = in de Alpen is het zonnig op de skipistes f main clause = volgende week zal het zacht blijven in Nederland; subclause = terwijl het in de Alpen goed skiweer blijft

15B a De benzineprijzen zullen volgende maand dalen. b Nieuwe auto's zijn schoner. c Sieme heeft echt een auto nodig. d Hij reist soms ook met de trein. e Reint reist altijd met het openbaar vervoer. f Reint is erg milieubewust.

15C a Jari vindt dat hij geluk gehad heeft. b Je weet toch dat Bernlef veel prijzen gewonnen heeft? c Remi zegt dat hij geen tv gekeken heeft. d Maar Chris zegt dat hij dat wel gedaan heeft. e Ik ben bang dat ik me verslapen heb. f Ik heb gehoord dat Kim een nieuwe band opgericht heeft.

15D a maar ik vind het wel leuk een kerstdiner klaar te maken. b en ik heb een hekel aan schoonmaken. c dus ik haal altijd kant-en-klaar maaltijden. d want ik laat altijd alles aanbranden.

15E a maar **b** dus **c** of

15F a Van Goghs schilderijen waren iets nieuws want hij schilderde op een expressieve manier. **b** Hij voelde zich mislukt in zijn werk en hij voelde zich mislukt in zijn persoonlijke leven. **c** In het begin gebruikte hij vooral donkere en bruine kleuren maar later schilderde hij met felle en intense kleuren. **d** Zijn schilderijen zijn nu wereldberoemd dus ze zijn veel geld waard. **e** Is van Gogh beroemd omdat zijn werk zo vernieuwend was of is hij beroemd omdat hij zijn oor heeft afgesneden.

15G a Ik zou weleens willen weten waarom een giraf een lange nek heeft. **b** ... wat de zin van het leven is. **c** ... waarom ik nooit genoeg geld heb. **d** ... hoe kinderen hun moedertaal leren. **e** ... waar sterren vandaan komen. **f** ... wie de eerste popster was. **g** ... welke oceaan het diepste is.

15H a Denkt u dat er leven op andere planeten bestaat? **b** ... studenten collegegeld moeten betalen? **c** ... supermarkten 24 uur open moeten zijn? **d** ... de werkweek uit 4 dagen moet bestaan? **e** ... mensen met veel geld meer belasting moeten betalen? **f** ... alle kinderen thuis een computer moeten hebben?

15I a Thea heeft gevraagd of we alle gegevens verzameld hebben. **b** ... we het rapport hebben geschreven. **c** ... we de conferentie georganiseerd hebben. **d** ... we de sprekers hebben uitgenodigd. **e** ... we het werk nog steeds leuk vinden.

15J a Terwijl jij niks zit te doen, zit ik hard te werken. **b** Nu ze kinderen heeft, zie ik Chantal nooit meer. **c** Voordat je weg gaat, zet ik nog even koffie. **d** Zolang je hem niet aanraakt, zal de hond niet bijten. **e** Toen ik klein was, logeerde ik vaak bij mijn opa en oma op de boerderij.

15K a Ik heb zoveel tijd voor mezelf nu mijn jongste kind op school zit. **b** Vera komt zodra ze beter is. **c** Je zult weinig leren zolang je je best niet doet. **d** Ik heb hoofdpijn sinds de televisie

aanstaat. e Wil je een fles wijn voor me meebrengen wanneer je
naar de supermarkt gaat. f Voeten vegen voordat je binnenkomt.

15L a Nu mijn jongste kind op school zit, heb ik zoveel tijd voor
mezelf. **b** Zodra ze beter is, komt Vera. **c** Zolang je je best niet
doet, zul je weinig leren. **d** Sinds de televisie aanstaat, heb ik
hoofdpijn. **e** Wanneer je naar de supermarkt gaat, wil je een
fles wijn voor me meebrengen? **f** Voordat je binnenkomt, voeten
vegen.

15M a Ik kan het niet zoals hij het doet. **b** Hij kan het niet
uitleggen hoewel hij het goed begrijpt. **c** Wij vertrekken als het
weer opklaart. **d** Ik blijf morgen een dagje thuis omdat ik me niet
lekker voel. **e** Ik ga je niet helpen tenzij je me meer betaalt.

15N a 2 **b** 3 **c** 4 **d** 1

15O a als **b** zoals **c** tenzij **d** terwijl **e** doordat **f** alsof

15P a Die psychopaat lijkt zo normaal, daarom is het juist zo'n
enge man. **b** De brug was open, daardoor kwamen we te laat op
school. **c** Maandag kan ik niet komen, dan komen mijn ouders
op bezoek. **d** Eerst gingen we ergens wat drinken, toen gingen we
naar de voorstelling en daarna bracht ik hem weer terug naar het
station. **e** We hebben lang genoeg gewacht, nu gaan we.

15Q a Jan is helemaal niet moe. Integendeel, hij barst van de
energie. **b** Het gaat heel goed met haar. Althans/tenminste, ze
heeft een nieuw vriendje. **c** Nederlanders zijn erg gelukkig.
Tenminste/althans, dat stond in een artikel in de krant. **d** Ik heb
geen zin om naar de bioscoop te gaan. Trouwens, ik heb er ook
geen geld voor.

15R a Wij bieden kwalitatief hoog onderwijs in de Nederlandse
taal. Daarnaast bieden wij een interessant cultureel programma.
b Heeft u nog niet on line uw boodschappen gedaan, dan moet
u snel onze gids voor 'on line shopping' aanvragen. **c** Wij zoeken

een vlotte verkoopassistent. Ook mensen zonder ervaring kunnen solliciteren. **d** Onze stichting wil jonge mensen met drugsproblemen helpen. Daartoe hebben wij praatgroepen voor drugsverslaafden.

15S a Na een inbraak weten mensen vaak niet precies wat er is gestolen. Daarom is het belangrijk dat u uw eigendommen registreert. Dan weet u precies wat u mist na een inbraak. Dus, vul nu de bon in, anders bent u uw gestolen eigendommen voor altijd kwijt. In deze folder zit een formulier. Daarop kunt u al uw gegevens invullen.

15T a Ook hebben we het gehad over het aantal leerlingen dat ziek is. **b** Tevens hebben we gediscussieerd over de grote hoeveelheid huiswerk die leerlingen krijgen. **c** Verder is de organisatie van het grote schoolfeest besproken.

15U a antecedent = een bedrijf (a 'het'-word); relative clause = dat u kunt vertrouwen **b** antecedent = de fietsen (a 'de'-word); relative clause = die ze daar verhuren **c** antecedent = die oranje verf (a 'de'-word); relative clause = die ik voor die muur heb gebruikt **d** antecedent = niemand (refers to people); relative clause = die zoveel voor onze school heeft gedaan **e** antecedent = het computerspelletje (a 'het'-word); relative clause = dat mijn kinderen willen hebben **f** antecedent = weinig Nederlanders (refers to people); relative clause = die geen vreemde talen spreken **g** antecedent = een jasje (a 'het'-word); relative clause = dat van Diana was geweest

15V a dat **b** die **c** die **d** die **e** dat **f** dat

15W a De auto die ik gekocht heb, is rood. **b** De appels die ik gekocht heb, zijn niet lekker. **c** De kaas die ik gekocht heb, is erg pittig. **d** Het kastje dat ik gekocht heb, is bijna 100 jaar oud. **e** Het vloerkleed dat ik gekocht heb, is fel gekleurd. **f** De sjaal die ik gekocht heb, is van goede kwaliteit.

15X a wat **b** wat **c** wat **d** wie **e** wat **f** wat **g** wie

15Y a Het vak waar ik de grootste hekel heb, is wiskunde. / Het vak waaraan ik de grootste hekel heb, is wiskunde. **b** De muziek waar ik het meest van hou, is jazz. / De muziek waarvan ik het meest hou, is jazz. **c** De sport waar ik de grootste hekel aan heb, is voetbal. / De sport waaraan ik de grootste hekel heb, is voetbal. **d** Het eten waar ik het meest van hou, is lasagne. / Het eten waarvan ik het meest hou, is lasagne. **e** De drank waar ik de grootste hekel aan heb, is melk. / De drank waaraan ik de grootste hekel heb, is melk.

15Z [NB the following are only suggestions] **a** De Europese politiek is iets waar ik in geïnteresseerd ben. **b** Computers zijn dingen waaraan ik een hekel heb. **c** De koningin van Engeland is iemand voor wie ik bewondering heb. **d** Mijn buurman is iemand met wie ik medelijden heb. **e** Voetbal is iets waar ik geen aandacht aan besteed. **f** Astrologie is iets waar ik niet in geïnteresseerd ben. **g** Mijn manager is iemand op wie ik jaloers ben.

SECTION 16

16A a vroeg **b** gauw **c** vlug; naar het station **d** met de trein; naar de stad **e** in de stad; altijd **f** op haar werk; vrolijk **g** eerst **h** dan **i** meestal

16B a degree **b** sentence **c** place **d** frequency **e** time **f** degree **g** manner **h** degree; frequency **i** degree; time; manner

16C a Je moet nu snel naar huis, anders kom je te laat. **b** We gaan over twee weken naar Frankrijk op vakantie. **c** Dat heb je niet goed gedaan. **d** Ik ga altijd graag naar Antwerpen. **e** Ajax heeft verleden week slecht gespeeld.

16D a We gaan volgend jaar met de buren naar Oostenrijk op vakantie. **b** Marloes heeft het werk gisteren snel afgemaakt. **c** Lees jij 's ochtends ook graag de krant? **d** Ik eet altijd langzaam maar mijn vrouw eet meestal snel. **e** Die man staat altijd al vroeg in de tuin te werken. **f** Kees heeft de laatste paar weken heel hard gewerkt.

16E a Remco speelt zaterdag met zijn elftal in Volendam voetbal. **b** Ik ga in juni lekker naar Australië op vakantie. **c** Kom je morgen met je vriend bij mij eten? **d** Gré heeft gisteren heerlijk gekookt. **e** Han schildert 's zomers vaak in de tuin als hij tijd heeft. **f** Het was vanochtend bij ons mooi weer. **g** Waarom ga je vanavond niet met Sofie in de stad eten?

16F a frequency **b** degree **c** sentence **d** sentence **e** degree **f** frequency

16H b, c, a/d

16I a naar je werk **b** met jou **c** met de auto of met de trein **d** met zijn vriendin **e** in hun nieuwe huis **f** met mijn broer

16J a Heel goed is dat krantenartikel geschreven. **b** Zelden zie je beroemde Hollywood-acteurs op straat lopen in Amsterdam. **c** Eén keer heb ik Harry Mulisch, de Nederlandse schrijver, in de tram zien zitten. **d** Al meer dan tien keer heb ik je nu verdorie geroepen. Kom uit je bed! **e** Altijd is die stomme printer kapot en die computer doet het ook nooit! **f** Fantastisch zijn die films van Hitchcock, vind je ook niet?

16K a Kan jij misschien even boodschappen voor me doen? **b** We gaan waarschijnlijk in juni twee weken op vakantie. **c** Karin heeft ongetwijfeld alles voor ons geregeld. **d** De medicijnen hebben blijkbaar niet erg goed geholpen.

SECTION 17

17A 1 a Frieda **b** ze **c** Janneke **d** vier mensen **e** ik **f** ik **g** dat **2 a** a **b** b **c** c **d** d **e** e **f** f **g** -

17B

	First position	Verb	Subject (if not first)	Middle part	Last verb place	Final position
a		Hebben	jullie	de trein alweer	gemist?	
b	Jacob	werkt		op zaterdag bij Albert Heijn.		
c	Hij	wil		veel geld	sparen.	
d		Zet		je fiets wel op slot.		
e		Gaan	jullie	een nieuw huis	kopen?	
f	Hoeveel doelpunten	heeft	Ajax		gescoord?	
g	De verkoop	is		(door onze actie) behoorlijk	gestegen	(door onze actie.)
h	Ik	word		soms (met een gevoel van angst) wakker		(met een gevoel van angst)

17C Daarom hoef je het niet te doen.; Over enkele ogenblikken zullen wij op schiphol landen.; Wat moet je doen om het probleem op te lossen?

17D

	First position	Verb	Subject (if not first)	Middle part	Last verb place	Final position
a	Als we gaan verhuizen	wil	ik	de grootste slaapkamer	hebben.	
b	Jij	mag		dan de slaapkamer met balkon	nemen.	
c	Een dagje naar Disneyland	is		ontzettend duur.		
d	Dan	kan	je	maar beter een dagje naar de Efteling	gaan.	

	First position	Verb	Subject (if not first)	Middle part	Last verb place	Final position
e	De trein waarmee ik elke dag naar mijn werk reis	rijdt		vanochtend niet.		
f	Je	moet		je wel	verzekeren	als je op reis gaat.

17E a Ben jij naar Mirjams feestje geweest? **b** Heb je je er vermaakt? **c** Geef mijn fiets terug. **d** Steek jij de kaarsjes aan? **e** Wat heb jij die kip lekker klaargemaakt! **f** Ik heb er de hele dag naar gekeken.

17F

	1	2	3	4	5	
a	Roland kan niet komen	omdat	hij	een opdracht van een klant	moet afmaken	
b		Hoewel	ze	veel geld	hebben	leven ze heel zuinig.
c		Als	hij	niet zo jong	was gestorven	zou hij veel meer boeken hebben geschreven.
d	Irma woont nog steeds bij haar ouders	zodat	zij	voor haar moeder die ziek is	kan zorgen.	
e	Lieve heeft haar huis laten verbouwen	toen	ze	in verwachting	was	van haar jongste.

17G a Maar ik wist niet dat haar man haar sloeg. **b** Zij durft niet te lachten omdat ze zo'n slecht gebit heeft. **c** Terwijl hun moeder doodziek op bed lag, waren haar kinderen de erfenis aan het verdelen. **d** Ik voel me heel blij omdat ik een mooie diamanten ring voor de kerst heb gekregen. **e** Ze wilde haar dochter geven wat ze zelf had gemist.

17H a Edith heeft het met Nellie besproken. **b** Tja, dat hangt van jou af. **c** Ik ben nog nooit zo kwaad op iemand geweest. **d** Ik heb al zo lang niets gehoord van Janna. **e** We hebben allemaal hard aan het project gewerkt. **f** Ze heeft een uur op je zitten wachten.

17I a Ik heb altijd alleen gewerkt om geld te verdienen. **b** Saskia zegt dat ze wijn moet drinken om te ontspannen. **c** Dirk heeft bij ons gewerkt om ervaring op te doen. **d** Zij heeft nog nooit zo goed geacteerd als nu. **e** Arjen is nog even bij ons langsgeweest om dat boek te lenen. **f** Mijn moeder is gisteren langsgekomen om het nieuws te vertellen. **g** Ik had geen zin om met de trein te komen.

SECTION 18

18A a informal: use of 'jij' **b** informal: use of 'je' **c** informal: use of informal vocabulary 'stappen' and 'kroeg' **d** formal: use of last names only, plus more formal vocabulary 'eensgelijks' and structure 'prettig kennis te maken'. **e** formal: use of passive structure 'kan contact worden opgenomen' **f** informal: informal vocabulary 'de mazzel'

18B a maakt u **b** Vind je/Vinden jullie **c** weet u **d** heeft u **e** wil je **f** mag je; je moet **g** heeft u

18C a coacht **b** trainen **c** getapet **d** gefaxt **e** bridget **f** jog

18D rood, blauw, armstoel, principes, stijl, goed, zien, constructie, horizontale, verticale, lijnen, zitting, primaire, constructieve, radicale, breuk, traditie, stimulans, nieuwe, experimentele, ideeën, inspiratie, design, grafisch

18E a delight **b** surprise **c** relief **d** admiration **e** disappointment **f** resignation

18F a bah **b** brr **c** hé **d** hè **e** nou ja **f** nou ja

18G [possibilities:] **a** Wat een vreemd mens! / Wat een vreemde man! **b** Wat een arrogante kwal! / Wat een sexy meid! **c** Wat een lief mens! / Wat een eigenwijze vrouw! **d** Wat een boeiend schilderij! / Wat een raar schilderij!

18H a Zo'n vreemd mens/vreemde man is dat! **b** Zo'n arrogante kwal/sexy meid is dat! **c** Zo'n lief mens/eigenwijze vrouw is dat! **d** Zo'n boeiend/raar schilderij is dat!

18I a Zeg, jij hebt toch ook dat boek over Hannibal Lecter gelezen? **b** Wat een troep hier, zeg! **c** Zeg, ga jij wel eens naar de kerk? **d** Dat is verschrikkelijk, zeg!

18J a Ja, hoor! **b** Nee, hoor! **c** Nee, hoor! **d** Ja, hoor!

18K a showing concern **b** checking information **c** showing irritation **d** contrast **e** checking information

18L a Het is toch half 11? **b** Eet toch je bord leeg. **c** Ga toch slapen. **d** Je hebt toch melk in je koffie?

18M a softening an order **b** advice **c** softening a question/politeness **d** softening a question **e** expresses an irritation **f** speaker feels he/ she is right **g** it simply happened **h** negative attitude **i** softening a negative attitude **j** change of plan **k** assumption

18N a Doe het raam maar open. **b** Ik ben gewoon beter in communiceren dan jij! **c** Je komt vanavond zeker weer laat huis, hè? **d** Stop eens met schrijven! **e** Ik heb eigenlijk geen zin om vanavond te koken.

18O a The second sentence is more openly negative. **b** Sentence one states this as truth. Second gives an assumption. **c** The first sentence shows irritation; the second is a kind advice **d** The first sentence is more direct, and the second is more apologetic.

18P a verdomme **b** zak **c** lul **d** shit **e** zootje **f** flink op je bek (gaan) **g** donder op

18Q a topic = de reorganisatie op zijn werk; comment = veroorzaakt veel stress **b** topic = het konijntje dat jullie me hebben gegeven; comment = is gisteren doodgegaan **c** topic = die manager van jou; comment = is een verschrikkelijk mens, hè? **d** topic = Arie; comment = komt morgen om mijn wasmachine te maken **e** topic = die tentoonstelling van Pollock die vorig jaar in Londen was; comment = heb ik in Amsterdam gezien **f** topic = we; comment = zijn gisteren een dagje naar Brussel geweest **g** topic = die vacature waar je het gisteren over had; comment = ik heb ... uit de krant geknipt **h** dat huis dat Lisette en Hans hebben gekocht; comment = is nu een kapitaal waard

18R a 'het gezin' refers to 'Anne Frank met haar ouders en haar zus'; 'het Achterhuis' refers to 'onderduiken' **b** 'tijdens deze periode' refers to 'tot 1944' **c** 'hierin' refers to 'een dagboek' **d** 'haar laatste notitie' refers to 'beschreef zij haar leven en emoties' **e** 'drie dagen later' refers to '1 augustus 1944' **f** 'na de oorlog' refers to the whole previous paragraph **g** 'het boek' refers to 'haar dagboek te publiceren'

18S Kinderen zijn tegenwoordig geen kinderen meer. Dat zei psycholoog professor Kuip. Vroeger gingen kinderen naar school om te leren lezen en schrijven. Op die manier kregen ze toegang tot de wereld van volwassenen. Die toegang krijgen kinderen nu via computer, televisie en internet.

18T a café **b** een reactie geven op **c** mijn ervaring is dat dit goed werkt **d** invitatie **e** er zal worden gestreefd naar een oplossing **f** in de nabije toekomst **g** een beslissing geven **h** steun verlenen aan **i** ik heb een verkoudheid **j** ik heb bewondering voor die vrouw

18U a Op dat moment hoorde ik een geweldige knal en zag ik een felle lichtflits in de donkere straat. This sentence is made more dramatic by the use of descriptive adjectives. **b** Mijn moeder kwam uit een religieus gezin. Zij was een strenge en zwijgzame vrouw voor wie het personeel een beetje bang was. In gedachten zie ik mijn ouders altijd door iets gescheiden, een gepolijste tafel, een

zwarte vleugel, en de glimmende parketvloeren, waar iedereen
op vilten pantoffels liep. The unloving and cold character of the
mother/parents is emphasized by describing the parental home with
hard, cold, dark, silent adjectives.

18V The first text is more informal than the second ('je'/'jij' in
the first, and 'u' in the second text). The first text uses mainly
simple, short, active sentences. In this text you, as the reader, are
being spoken to directly ('als jij ziek zou worden...') you feel more
directly involved, and the message of the text is driven home
in a direct, straightforward way. The second text uses mainly
long, complicated, passive structures. This creates distance between
the text and the reader. You feel less involved and you get the
sense of being informed in an impersonal manner by an
anonymous body.

SECTION 19

19A a Vliegtuigen die meer dan twintig jaar oud zijn, moeten goed
worden gecontroleerd. **b** We gaan morgen met mijn ouders in de
stad eten. **c** Kangoeroes, die alleen in Australië voorkomen, vind
ik zulke grappige beesten. **d** Mijn hond, zei de jongen, is twee jaar
oud. **e** Als je morgen tijd hebt, kom ik even langs om over dat werk
te praten. **f** Ze hebben hun huis pas verbouwd, dacht ik. **g** Heb
jij enig idee waar ze naartoe zijn verhuisd? **h** Hoewel het vreselijk
slecht weer was, zijn we toch gegaan. **i** Als jullie willen, kan ik
een tafel voor ons reserveren. **j** Mijn vrouw vindt dit soort films
vulgair, dom en infantiel.

19B a In the first sentence, the gardener is called Ton. In the
second, Ton and the gardener are two different people. **b** In the
first sentence, his boss once more asked him to consider the offer.
In the second, he was asked by his boss to consider the offer again.
c In the first sentence she says, 'I don't want to marry him.'
In the second, she doesn't say: 'I want to marry him.' **d** In the
first sentence, it isn't clear whether both the book and the CD are

to do with Barbra Streisand, whereas, in the second sentence,
the book definitely has nothing to do with Miss Streisand.

19C a noun b noun c adjective d noun e verb f adjective g adjective
h noun i noun j verb k adjective l noun m adjective n adjective
o noun p noun

19D a de b het c de d het e de f het g de h de i de j het k de l het
m de n de o het p de

19E a to hunt, to pursue, to race b to work out, to imagine,
to check c image, statue, picture d pattern, patron, cartridge e to
perform, to appear, to act, (a) performance, (an) appearance
f measure, size, bar (in musical notation) g bus, box, tin

19F a vinden b wonen c opbellen d tafeltennissen e schilderen
f faxen g doorkijken h vertalen i sturen j bediscussiëren k opleveren
l schilderen m verhuizen n geven

19G a zijn b kopen c gaan d kunnen e moeten

19H a huis (house) b bril (spectacles) c horloge (watch) d vraag
(question) e kind (child) f politicus (politician) g glas (glass) h uur
(hour) i boekensteun (bookend) j boom (tree)

19I a platlopen b grond c hoogte d hand e hand f bel g donder
h kater i teen j geknipt

19K a a.u.b. b o.l.v. c z.s.m. d d.m.v. e m.i.v.; a.s.; p.m. f t.a.v.

19L a jongstleden b s'il vous plaît c in verband met; met andere
woorden d door middel van; zo spoedig mogelijk e maximaal;
persoon; per maand; inclusief

19M a drs. M. Harskamp b mr. J. Aleman c prof. L. Krosse
d Dhr. Vanderbilt e Mvr. Hetjes

19N Text 1 VVV = the Dutch tourist board (Vereniging voor Vreemdelingen Verkeer); ANWB = the Dutch automobile organization (Algemene Nederlandse Wielrijdersbond); NBT = Dutch tourist organization (het Nederlands Bureau voor Toerisme); Text 2 FNV = the largest Dutch trade union (Federatie van Nederlandse Vakverenigingen) Text 3 HSL = Hogesnelheidslijn; Text 4 m.i.v. = met ingang van (word/expression); a.s. = aanstaande (word/expression); m/v = man/vrouw (word/expression); min. = minimaal; MBO = Middelbaar Beroeps Onderwijs (a type of school); HBO = Hoger Beroeps Onderwijs (a type of school); CAO = Centrale Arbeidsovereenkomst (a Dutch law regarding labour agreements); c.v. = curriculum vitae; BSO = Buitenschoolse Opvang (a name of an organization for after-school care); t.a.v. = ter attentie van (word/expression); mevr. = mevrouw

Glossary

active Most sentences are in the active form. It means that the subject carries out the action of the verb, e.g. in the sentence **Heleen kust Arie** (*Heleen is kissing Arie*), Heleen is the subject and she is doing the kissing. Active is the opposite of **passive**.

adjective A word which describes a noun, e.g.: Amsterdam is geweldig. Het is een **fantastische** stad. (*Amsterdam is fabulous. It is a fantastic city.*) Adjectives can also be **comparatives** and **superlatives**.

adverb Adverbs tell you when, how or where the main action of the sentence takes place. Often an adverb adds detail to a verb, but it can also describe an adjective or another adverb, e.g.: Hij zingt mooi. (*He is singing beautifully.*) Hij zingt **erg mooi**. (*He is singing very beautifully.*)

agent The person(s) or thing(s) which carry out the action of the verb. In an active sentence the agent is the subject. In a **passive** sentence, the agent is not the subject and might not even be mentioned.

antecedent *Ante* means *before*. The antecedent is the word to which a relative pronoun refers, and normally comes immediately before the **relative pronoun**, e.g. **Het liedje** dat hij zingt, komt uit Phantom of the Opera. (*The song he is singing comes from Phantom of the Opera.*)

article The definite **articles** in Dutch are **de** and **het** (*the* in English). The indefinite **article** in Dutch is **een** (*a, an* in English).

auxiliary verb A verb which does not carry meaning in itself, but is used to support another verb. The main auxiliaries are **hebben** and **zijn** when they are used in combination with another verb in the **perfect** or **past perfect tense**, e.g.: ik **heb** gewerkt.

clause A sentence or part of a sentence which normally contains at least one verb and often a subject. There are **main**, **relative** and **subordinating clauses**.

comment This is part of the **information structure** of a sentence. The comment is the part of the sentence which gives new information. It often comments on information stated at the beginning of the sentence.

comparative An adjective used to compare things, ideas or people: Petra is nu **zwaarder** dan vroeger. (*Petra is heavier now than she used to be.*)

compound word A word which consists of two separate words (one of which is normally a **noun**) written as one.

conditional A sentence including a particular condition which has to be met before something can happen. Often a form of the verb **zouden** is used.

conjunction A word which links two words, sentences or parts of sentences. There are **co-ordinating** and **subordinating conjunctions** and **conjunctive adverbs**.

conjunctive adverb An adverb which can be used to link two sentences or two main clauses. After this adverb there is **inversion**.

consonant All letters of the alphabet, except a, e, i, o, u (which are vowels).

co-ordinating conjunction A word (**maar, en, want, of, dus**) which links two main clauses (or two sub-clauses). The word order in the main clauses does not change.

diminutive A noun which has **je, tje, etje, pje** or **kje** at the end to indicate something is small, cute or insignificant. (As in the English -*let*: *piglet*.)

exclamation A word, short sentence or expression spoken or written with extra force. It often indicates an emotion or attitude.

finite verb This is the verb in a sentence (sometimes called the main verb) which changes its form depending on the **subject** of the sentence, e.g.: Rita **moet** haar huiswerk maken. (*Rita has got to do her homework.*)

imperative The imperative normally takes the form of the stem of the verb. It is used to give orders or instructions, e.g.: **Kom** hier. (*Come here.*)

imperfect tense A past tense which is formed by adding (in regular verbs) **te(n)** or **de(n)** to the verb. It is used to describe habits and regular occurrences in the past and to describe a series of events.

infinitive The full form of the verb as it is listed in the dictionary. In Dutch the infinitive normally ends in **-en**: **werken, leven**.

information structure The way in which information is organized in a sentence. The convention is to start the sentence by stating what it is about (the **topic**), and then to give more information (the **comment**).

inseparable verbs Verbs which have a **prefix** which cannot be separated from the verb part, e.g.: **stofzuigen** (*to hoover*), **vergroten** (*to make bigger*), **ontnemen** (*to take away*).

interjections Little words whose meaning often depends on the context. They are used to make communication flow better, or to express a feeling or attitude.

inversion This is the term used when the subject in the sentence comes after the finite verb, rather than before.

irregular verbs Verbs that do *not* change their present and past tense forms according to a regular pattern.

main clause A sentence or part of a sentence which can stand on its own. It normally has at least one **verb** and a **subject**.

modal verbs Verbs which express whether something can, must, or may etc. be done. (e.g. **kunnen, mogen, moeten, willen** etc.).

negative A word or (part of) a sentence which denies or contrasts something (e.g. **niet** *no/not*, **geen** *not any*, **nooit** *never*, etc.).

noun A word used to name a person, an object or an abstract quality, e.g.: **het huis**, *house*, **het kind** *child*, **de liefde**, *love*.

object The person, thing or idea which is at the receiving end of the action in the sentence. A *direct object* undergoes the action directly, e.g.: hij feliciteerde **haar** (*he congratulated her*). An *indirect object* 'receives' the direct object, e.g.: Hij geeft het boek aan **zijn zoontje**. (*He gives the book to his little son.*)

passive This is the opposite of the active form. The **subject** of the sentence is not carrying out the action, but is undergoing it. e.g. **Arie** wordt (door Heleen) gekust. *Arie is being kissed (by Heleen).* In this sentence Arie is the subject, but he is not doing the kissing.

past participle The form of the verb used in the **perfect** and **past perfect** tenses. The formula for forming this in regular verbs is: **ge** + stem of the verb + **t** or **d**, e.g.: **gewerkt**, *worked*, **geleerd**, *learnt*.

. . . .

past perfect tense A past tense which is formed by using the imperfect form of **hebben** or **zijn** and a **past participle**. It is used to refer to past events that took place before something else.

. . . .

perfect tense A past tense which is formed with a form of the verbs hebben or zijn and a past participle. It is used to refer to events in the past which have now finished.

. . . .

preposition A preposition is a word like *up, for, in* etc. It often indicates where something is, but prepositions are also used figuratively. Many verbs have fixed prepositions, e.g.: **denken aan**, *to think of/about*, **geloven in**, *to believe in*.

. . . .

prepositional phrase A group of words which start with a preposition, e.g.: **in de keuken**, *in the kitchen*, **op mijn werk**, *at (my) work*.

. . . .

plural The form of a noun or verb which indicates there is more than one, e.g.: De **kinderen** spelen buiten. *(The children play outside.)* See also **singular**.

. . . .

pronoun A word which can replace a noun to avoid repetition. There are various kinds of pronouns: personal pronouns can be divided into subject pronouns (**ik** *I*, **jij** *you*, **hij** *he*, **wij** *we* etc.) and object pronouns (**mij** *me*, **jou** *you*, **hem** *him*, **ons** *us* etc.) Other pronouns are possessive pronouns which indicate ownership (**mijn** *my*, **jouw** *your*, **zijn** *his*, **haar** *her* etc.), and reflexive pronouns which are used in combination with a reflexive verb (**mij(zelf)** *myself*, **jou(zelf)** *yourself*, **zich(zelf)** *him/herself* etc.).

reflexive verbs A verb whose subject and object refer to the same person, animal or idea. An example: Het meisje **wast zichzelf.** (*The girl is washing herself.*)

....

regular verbs Verbs which change their present and past tense forms according to a regular pattern.

....

relative clause Part of a sentence which gives added information about a person, thing or idea: the **antecedent.** A relative clause starts with a relative pronoun.

....

relative pronoun A pronoun (such as **die** and **dat**) which refers to and gives more information about the **antecedent.**

....

separable verb A verb which is made up of two parts: a prefix and a main verb. The prefix can be split up from the main verb part according to certain rules.

....

singular The form of a **noun** or a **verb** which indicates there is only one, e.g.: Het **kind speelt** buiten. (*The child is playing outside.*)

....

stem The form of the verb which goes with **ik**, e.g.: **werk, woon, fiets.** (Often this is the **infinitive** without **-en.**)

....

style A particular way of writing or speaking which you adapt according to the circumstances of whom you are addressing, in which situation and why.

....

sub-clause (Also called **subordinating clause.**) It is a part of a sentence which cannot stand on its own and it needs to be linked to a main clause. Its two characteristics are that it starts with a subordinating conjunction and that the verb goes to the end.

subject The subject of a sentence is the person, thing or idea that usually carries out the action of the verb. It is the person, thing or idea that the sentence is about.

subordinating conjunction A word which links a main clause and a sub-clause. Examples are: **terwijl** *while*, **omdat** *because*, **sinds** *since*

suffix A part of a word which is attached at the end. Often it changes the word into a different grammatical category.

superlative This indicates that something surpasses everything else, e.g.: **grootste**, *biggest*, **duurste**, *most expensive*.

syllable The different parts into which a word can be broken up when you pronounce it, e.g.: **com-pu-ter**.

tense Tense indicates whether you talk about the present, the past or the future.

topic The known information in a text. It normally goes at the beginning of a sentence and states what this sentence is about.

verb Verbs are the words in a sentence which describe an action or activity, e.g. **denken** *to think*, **eten** *to eat*, **vrijen** *to make love*. Some verbs might serve different purposes if they are combined with other verbs, e.g. **modal verbs** and **auxiliary verbs**.

vowel The letters a, e, i, o, u.

Index

The numbers in the index are section numbers.